T0061867

TWO
BILLION
CALIPHS

TWO BILLION CALIPHS

A VISION OF
A MUSLIM FUTURE

HAROON MOGHUL

BEACON PRESS · BOSTON

Beacon Press
Boston, Massachusetts
www.beacon.org

Beacon Press books
are published under the auspices of
the Unitarian Universalist Association of Congregations.

25 24 23 22   8 7 6 5 4 3 2 1

This book is printed on acid-free paper that meets the uncoated paper
ANSI/NISO specifications for permanence as revised in 1992.

Text design and composition by Kim Arney

Library of Congress Cataloging-in-Publication Data

Name: Moghul, Haroon, author.
Title: Two billion caliphs : a vision of a Muslim future / Haroon Moghul.
Description: Boston : Beacon Press, 2022. | Summary: "With autobiography,
theology, and a little comedy, Two Billion Caliphs describes what Islam
is, where it comes from, and what it could be"—Provided by publisher.
Identifiers: LCCN 2021047020 | ISBN 9780807024652 (hardcover) |
ISBN 9780807024669 (ebook)
Subjects: LCSH: Moghul, Haroon. | Muslims—United
States—Biography. | Islam—Essence, genius, nature.
Classification: LCC BP80.M6155 A3 2022 | DDC 297.092 [B]—dc23
LC record available at https://lccn.loc.gov/2021047020

For my mother. My first and best teacher.
Then my mother.
Then my mother.

CONTENTS

A NOTE FOR THE READER

I GENERALLY REFER to the Creator as "God," not "Allah," since the meaning of both is the same—and the former is more familiar for English speakers.

For major figures (also) sacred to the Islamic tradition, I have elected to use English names when they are well known. Hence, for example, I refer to 'Isa and Maryam as Jesus and Mary, may God's peace and blessings be upon them both.

In the Islamic tradition, after each mention of particularly revered persons and beings, such as Prophets, saints—incidentally, a minority of Muslims consider the Virgin Mary a Prophet, too—as well as the Archangel Gabriel, one adds a prayerful invocation.

As a case in point, after each mention of the Prophet Muhammad, Muslims will and must say "may God's peace and blessings be upon him," or some variation thereof, sometimes in Arabic (or in other languages if Arabic is not their own).

While I do not write out such invocations in every applicable instance, this note is a reminder to myself and other Muslims to make such a prayer where it is respectful and required—and it should indicate to readers of other beliefs the reverence we hold for these individuals.

For the names of family and companions of the Prophet Muhammad, I have tried to strike a balance between ease of reading and pronunciation alongside adherence to established styles of transliteration from the original Arabic to my native English.

This means that while I choose to spell the name of the Prophet Muhammad's younger grandson as Husayn—may God elevate him—his name may be more familiar to American readers as "Hussain" or "Hussein." These are the same name, just spelled differently. To stay closer to transliteration while maintaining accurate pronunciation, however, I have chosen what might be the less familiar spelling (especially for readers outside the Islamic tradition).

Similarly, for the Prophet Muhammad's Coptic wife, may God elevate her, I have chosen to transliterate her name as "Marya," since that balances the Arabic spelling of her name with its obvious Christian origins.

God willing, these decisions make the book more accessible to a broader audience.

PROLOGUE

In the name of God,
Loving to All and Merciful to Each

*Most books are stories. They have beginnings, middles, ends.
Most religions have texts. They have geneses, interregnums,
apocalypses. But not the Muslim scripture. The Qur'an isn't
organized chronologically. It doesn't furnish us a history. It is not
the rise or fall of a people. It is not the arc of a merciful Prophet's
life, bending, as his did, toward love. It is a book about that Being
Who is the source of all being, the only Existence that must exist,
and because God did not begin and cannot end—He triumphs
where language falters—so must His book challenge us. Even when
the Qur'an initiates an anecdote, it frequently forfeits the thread
midway and will not return till you have been redirected through
several other themes, sundry reflections, and sometimes even some
chapters, themselves dissolving and reforming, coming together
and splitting apart, like the behavior of space and time at that
infinitesimal point where they become an uncategorizable unity.*

*For a recitation revealed to a descendant of Ishmael, the Qur'an
lavishes much of its attention on Moses, a descendant of Isaac.
For a work purporting to preach to the religious indigenes of
Arabia, it considers Jews, Christians, and Zoroastrians its major
audiences. It endlessly surprises and even confounds readers,
at least those readers who expect God's word to translate
anthropocentrically. But man is not God, and God is not*

man—and Who God is, and who we are, and most critically, the relationship between these two, is foundational and conclusive in Islam, but missing from too much of contemporary Muslim life, consumed as it is by identity politics, the transformation of a religion mostly of the Global South into a vehicle for resistance or obstinacy, and the subordination of faith, by an angry minority, into an agenda of conquest or control. The evaporation of monotheism into a vapid cloud of obscure Muslimness.

Islam is above all else a path toward the One Who neither inhabits space nor suffers time, Who should be praised for His awesomeness, His majesty, and His generosity, for He gave us life, and we are a good thing, so good that though we, being contingent, begin, we do not and never will end.

And so, I begin with God and never end, I hope, with God.

TWO
BILLION
CALIPHS

INTRODUCTION

An Embarrassment of Riches

IT WAS A LITTLE MORE THAN TEN YEARS AGO, though I might as well have been another person. My goal was teaching, researching, and writing about Islam and the Muslim world. Fortunate, then, that I was a doctoral candidate at Columbia University, enrolled in the Department of Middle Eastern and Asian Languages and Cultures. I wanted to be part of conversations beyond the ivory towers, too; in this spirit, I applied for a fellowship in the National Security Studies Program at the New America Foundation—whose president was one of my favorite journalists, Steve Coll.

I got it.

In my job at New America, I trained imams to use social media to bring about positive social change. I had deep concerns about government-led counter-extremism efforts, less concerned with morality and more with the convergence of an actor's politics with the sovereign's; viz., killing civilians is wrong in all cases, unless it advances our foreign policy.* In this case, though, we weren't

---

* To adequately elaborate on why I was (and am) so uncomfortable with governmental counter-extremism efforts would be impossible in so limited a space; suffice it to say that, first, the idea of a secular government picking and choosing between theologies is worrisome and, second, the potential for abuse in light of gross disparities of power is massive. Beyond Mahmood Mamdani's excellent work, *Good Muslim, Bad Muslim: America, The Cold War, and the Roots of Terror*, there are a number of other helpful titles on this theme. One in particular that illuminates these concerns (and does much more so besides) is Arun Kundnani's *The Muslims Are Coming! Islamophobia, Extremism, and the Domestic War on Terror*.

picking and choosing the so-called good Muslim, to borrow Mahmood Mamdani's framing (and I should add that Professor Mamdani taught at Columbia University). We were amplifying the voices of imams interested in learning how to be amplified, whatever their specific theologies.

We adopted a kind of theological Darwinism; we'd let the *ummah*, the global Muslim community, decide, based on its likes, shares, retweets, and views, which of these imams it most approved of. The wisdom of the Muslim crowd: we'll help you plaster your sermons and speeches all over the internets, but what happens after that is not our business. About the only condition of participation was not being crazy. But during the first few months of my employment—the first full-time job I'd had in almost a decade—my health went from congenitally bad to inexplicably worse. I was regularly in and out of the hospital. Sometimes even while traveling for my side gig as a Muslim speaker.

Worse, not infrequently, these painful episodes descended into all-out nightmares of writhing pain, hot sweats, dizziness, lightheadedness, and occasionally I even passed out.

Also my marriage stopped thriving.

BECAUSE I'D NEVER suffered so severely, never faced this kind of health crisis or been threatened by the loss of a relationship that had lasted so long, or indeed had really ever had any previous relationships, I didn't just crash. I burned. I had to ignominiously resign from the New America Foundation. If I had had a tail, it would've been tucked between my legs. As I was leaving, my supervisor, another public intellectual whose work deeply motivated me, noted that I had accomplished next to nothing in the time I'd been there. Which would've been wounding enough, except the length of my subsequent convalescence required me to abandon my academic studies too. I'd worked so hard. I'd even turned down Harvard for Columbia.

(You don't need to say anything. My own regret is sufficient punishment.)

I hope you never fall to Earth like I did. But you might. You may already have. You might already know what it's like to experience the disconnect between how people see you and how things really are. You've got a great job, a kind and accomplished partner, an academic trajectory that appears overwhelmingly promising. Many people would die for your bad days. But many people don't know your bad days. So, there I was on my downward spiral, my *kerplunk* against rock bottom, losing my trusty Toyota Camry, my rather nice apartment, my rather nice spouse, my rather nice job, my enviable if potential academic career, and everything that was in my bank account including my savings and, oh, no more health insurance either. I remember days I had nothing to eat but tortilla chips and protein cookies from grocery trips long since past.

I landed in Dubai because I had nowhere else to go. I didn't just pick an expensive, shiny, halfway-around-the-world instant city for nothing, though. My brother was there, my only sibling, plus his wife and their two sons, my nephews. My exile to the Emirates lasted ten months altogether, and while it wasn't the easiest time, it was a chance for recuperation all the same. On a tourist visa, renewed every forty days at the Omani border, I began to cobble myself together again. I realized I needed years more of this. I *needed* Dubai. *I* needed Dubai. The awesome sunshine. The beautiful beaches. The reassuring palm trees. Driving with casual abandon. Those were good things. They protected me from the bad things, one of which was social media, an ironic twist for someone who'd himself once championed it. I came to hate social media for what it did to others—which we'd see clearly during the Trump administration—but more for what it did to me.

Facebook made me feel lousy: Why was I wasting hours consuming the curated lives of others who appeared happier than me? Or pretending my life was better than it was? Instagram made me feel empty, although theoretically it shouldn't have; mostly, I followed accounts that were supposed to make me joyful. Vacations in New Zealand. Finnair. But Twitter was the worst. I spent years of my life pouring words into oblivion, watching users compete to see who could surpass the other in riling up their base and pissing off the other side. When I first considered cutting back on my tweeting, I looked up my first tweet. Rather prophetically, I surmised that I'd probably be better off dedicating the energy Twitter was sure to consume to writing a novel. I knew. I'd even written a passable travelogue before I was thirty. And then, nothing else.

Did I really want to put years more of my life into becoming a better tweeter?

Soon even the experience of consuming social media became a cause and effect of great listlessness and sadness—but I could now afford to unplug, because I was incubating a new Haroon. In short, Dubai liberated me from the public, performative me, and the demands that role placed on me. I no longer had to worry about founding mosques and expanding community centers. I could enter anonymous worship spaces and worship anonymously. And freed from the curse of social media, I began to write—seriously, that is, and in long form—trying to tell the story of my life. In the middle of this rejuvenation, it was obvious that the last and worst thing for me would've been to return to America. Which is exactly what happened. My brother was moving back to America, and I lacked the financial wherewithal to survive in Dubai—or anywhere else— on my own.

Not only did I come back to New York City unexpectedly, but I had nowhere else to go but to another relative's house.

If there was any consolation, at least I had free health insurance. Because I had zero income.

Thanks, Obama.

SOMEHOW, AT THIS INOPPORTUNE TIME—and this tells you where my head was—I decided to get married again. This was a bad idea for reasons of mutual incompatibility and personal penury. In the case of the latter, I went from having no money to postnuptially drowning in debt. I'd thought leaving New America Foundation was a minor bump in the road, that my life could and would resume moving gloriously forward. But now, beyond broke, burdened with financial obligations, married to the wrong person, I realized that maybe in each of our lives there are a few decisions that either end very well for us, or just end us.

I dwelled obsessively on the latter prospect. I began to believe I'd never recover and, if I even merited any kind of obituary, it would have been of a life that had gone tragicomically wrong.

"At every turn," you'd read, "Haroon made the worst possible choice. In this, he was like the late nineteenth-century Ottoman Empire." What brief promise I had had was indubitably extinguished. I would live on the margins the rest of my life. Never mind ascending academically or professionally. I'd never even get back to where I'd been. I was terrified and at a loss for how this had happened to me. I'd had no outsize or outrageous expectations, or at least I didn't think so. My objectives had seemed reasonable enough. Finish a degree. Teach in a university. Be part of public conversations. Have a family: Wife. Kids. House. Car(s). Live a reasonable life.

Live with purpose to die with one.

Instead, I now had precisely none of these (though perhaps that was the only way to confront the last of these); I endured several more years of medical agony, but even though I couldn't understand it in the moment, I was headed somewhere. You can't see the forest for the trees until you're past the forest and the trees. Remember that writing I talked about, the dedication to long-form composition coupled with my deliberate abstention from soul-sapping social media? I made a memoir out of the stalled momentum of my recent years. A lifetime of tidying up and skinflinting the truth was at an end; I could and should and would admit to how Muslimness had chewed me up and spit me out. Cheekily, the book was titled *How to Be a Muslim*. I didn't imagine many people would want to read it, but people plan, and God plans, and God is the best of planners.

Publication followed the 2016 election.

I had long feared Trump would win. I was mocked for it, but then he did, while losing the popular vote by the margin of Chicago.

That fact is irrelevant to this paragraph, but relevant to posterity, and the rest of the planet, which should know: most of us didn't want him. The publisher's design team for my book decided on a bright orange cover, a color I thought of warmly—the room I grew up in, in Massachusetts, was bright orange—but which was also associated with the president. I'm not sure if that helped the book's success, but Trump did. Perversely, then, while the election was rather bad for American Muslims, for America, for democracy, for the West, and for the planet, it was good for sales, because anything Trump talked about was all we could talk about.

I had more stops on my book tour than I could've imagined.

Everyone wanted to know more about being Muslim.

JUST A FEW MONTHS after my book was released, my marriage ended. (That was a very good thing.) I left New Jersey, where for some reason I'd been renting a modest house overlooking a cemetery. I moved back to New York City, living in a tiny, uninsulated one-room apartment that lacked even a stove and faced out into a weed-infested lot. (My landlord referred to this cell as a "garden studio apartment," which just goes to show you: anything can be rebranded. Take heart, Muslims.) My friend Murtaza, on seeing my living accommodations, laughed out loud. "All these people," he said, "see you on CNN, and think you've got it made, and meanwhile you can't warm up food."

Man plans, and God plans.

Ari Goldman, a reporter for the *New York Times* and author of *The Search for God at Harvard*, had previously invited me to guest lecture for a course he taught at Columbia University's Graduate School of Journalism—the place from which the Pulitzers are announced. The Mecca of media. He told me he was now interested in my joining him more substantively. Thanks to a generous grant, Ari would teach a course on reporting religion, whose students wouldn't just learn how to cover the great faith traditions but would also travel abroad for ten days. Since the upcoming year's trip focused on Israel and Palestine, he wanted to know, would I like to teach with and for him and travel with the class to the region? Among other things, that meant I'd be teaching *on* campus. I had to go back to Kent Hall and get a new ID, which (literally) opened doors closed to me for years.

The first day of that semester, I went to Butler Library and made my way through the musty, low-ceilinged stacks, overwhelmed by nostalgia and ruefulness, remembering the years I'd spent meticulously researching, translating, or editing, overcome with grand ambitions for contributing to the revival of Islam, and how it'd all come to some kind of nothing. Or at least it seemed like it at the time. And now I was at Columbia. (Again.) This time, on the other side of the classroom. Maybe it was the quality of the students. Perhaps it was the setting. But I don't think I've ever enjoyed a course so much. As you can imagine, the chance for a ten-day trip to Israel and Palestine, after which the journalism students could legitimately note on their résumés that they had reported from a crisis zone, meant there was a line to sign up. We picked sixteen students, several of them Jewish, many of varying degrees of Christian, but had only one Hindu and one Muslim applicant. In light of how rarely Hinduism is publicly discussed and how poorly Muslims are publicly represented, you understand my disappointment.

But people plan, and God plans, and God is the master of awkward juxtapositions. Steve Coll, my former boss at the New America Foundation, was by then dean of the Columbia Journalism School. I'd no idea if he remembered me and kind of hoped he didn't, what with the manner of my departure from my earlier employment. But had he asked me how I'd been faring since, I would've told him that falling apart was the best thing that happened to me. Failure made me stronger. Failure even opened the door for me to serious writing. I don't know anything else that could've done so. Even though that failure involved hurting myself and hurting others. But I am a human being. I cannot but make mistakes. What matters is what I do in the aftermath of them.

. . . .

ON THE FIRST day of spring break, I joined our journalism students at JFK's Terminal 1, mostly ready for a Turkish Airlines flight to Tel Aviv. I was nervous about one thing, though. A particular fear about teaching while traveling was how my students and I would handle ten days in some of the most contentious, disputed, and spiritually supercharged places on our planet. But the trip, as Ari conceded, if hesitatingly—he didn't want to be seen playing favorites with this class over the others he'd taught—went far better than he thought it could. Our students supported each other and learned with each other, spending half the trip on sacred sites, many of which I was blessed to see for the first time, and the other half reporting on their own stories, all of which were creative, thoughtful, and well-crafted.

We started our program at an African refugee church, went up to Haifa to see some of Baha'ism's most revered sites, crossed over to Lake Tiberias and the Church of the Multiplication of the Loaves and the Fish, and then down the West Bank, toward Jerusalem by way of the Jordan River, where I stood in the very same river Jesus may have been baptized in. I was several times religiously profiled, as were the students in the class of Arab, Muslim, or Indian origin. (This too was important for them to see, and for me to keep in mind—I had privileges indigenes did not.) We'd saved the Temple Mount, what Muslims call the *Haram al-Sharif*, or "Noble Sanctuary," at the pinnacle of which stands the Dome of the Rock, for last. I badly wanted my students to see the Haram, not only because it belies stereotype, but also because of who they were and wanted to be.

But I wanted them to see the stereotype part, too.

The Haram could very well conjure Orientalist stock photography. The woman and man genuflecting. The elder consuming her Qur'an. The ascetic and his rosary beads. Spliced between shots of radicals with guns. Bombs bursting. American aircraft catapulting off carriers. Such is the orthodoxy of our times. When you portray Islam, you must combine sensationalism, exoticism, and danger. About the only things we publish about Muslims must have something to do with terrorism, reformism, or headscarves. There's hardly any room for anything else. Let alone this kind of place. There is an energy at the Haram I have hardly ever seen in any other sacred space, a spirit you might never associate with Islam. Once, after Friday Prayers, girl scouts paraded the perimeter, a marching band right behind them. Children played soccer near where Muslims believe Gabriel announced the Messiah.

And my students would see this. The future foreign correspondents of America, who would help correct the narratives that so long misrepresented Islam and Muslims. After an awkward negotiation with heavily militarized Israeli police, the calmness of the Haram was disconcerting. Any expectations our students might have had about Islam, about Muslims, about the Middle East seemed upended, and I grew overconfident as a result, sure that this entire experience would be a smashing success. After all, a spirited boys' volleyball match was well underway. It was gym class, or maybe recess, at a nearby school. We then walked toward the rock itself, what Ari called "the foundation stone of the world." And here, in Jerusalem, at the denouement, I knew. The errors, the bankruptcies, the tragedies of my past few years were not erased by this moment, but they would at least be transformed by it. It had taken me a very long time to get here, but I was sure that here was where God intended me to be.

Don't count your chickens, though.

1
....

YELLING AT
THE CONVERTED

WE SUFFERED a most mediocre tour of the Haram, a lifeless listicle overflowing with dynasties and dates that our students probably had no reference points for. As if faith itself were the memorization of a timeline. As if you went to the Sistine Chapel and were provided the relevant bureaucratic details. As if Jerusalem was only incidental to the Islamic tradition. There are nearly two billion Muslims on the planet. Almost one out of four people—and, in decades to come, close to one out of three—descend from a legacy that began when about one hundred believers joined their Prophet on his second exodus.

The mosque nearest to my house has far more worshippers on an ordinary Friday afternoon. Why are so many people Muslim now? What moves them to remain in the faith, especially with all that afflicts their communities? That people stay attached to this religion is superficially surprising; that they refuse to cede it to those who do harm, including great harm to them and their societies, is deeply moving; and all of this is worthy of our attention. Assuming, of course, you can get past the tour guide. The best he could give us? Who was Sultan when. Who built which pillar in what corner of the Haram.

Probably because that was all that was left of his faith.

Sterile, exoteric, heartless factoids.

Only Mecca, and then Medina, are more revered than Jerusalem. The Farthest Mosque, Masjid al-Aqsa, so called because it is the farthest mosque Muhammad prayed at, stands at the southernmost end of the Haram: it is Islam's first direction of prayer. (Mecca is the current one.) The Prophet Muhammad urged those of his followers who could not afford the pilgrimage to Jerusalem to gift oil to light Aqsa's lanterns. Maintaining Jerusalem is thus a Muslim obligation. And why not? Here the Prophet-Kings David and Solomon constructed a Temple twinned, we believe, with the Ka'ba, the Meccan Temple. (Or maybe they were both mosques.) Abraham might have attempted the sacrifice of Isaac here. (Or maybe it was Ishmael, in Mecca.) The Prophet Zechariah, father to another Prophet, John the Baptist, prayed here; Mary, descended from the Aaronic priesthood, was here and in prayer when she was informed of an unusual and unusually consequential pregnancy. (Or maybe that was Nazareth.)

But that does not get to the heart and soul of Muslim Jerusalem.

If you've ever watched a news broadcast about Jerusalem, you've definitely seen the Dome of the Rock. An astonishing octagon, which grows out of the limestone of the plaza but halfway yields to vivid blue, all of it capped by a brilliant golden dome. Even if the news segment has nothing to do with Islam, the building is front and center, an ironic fact insofar as the Haram is located in occupied East Jerusalem, which would belong to a Palestinian state, should there ever be one alongside Israel.* Thus the most recognized image of Israel is of a place that, according to interna-

---

*I should note for the record I have generally been convinced, for many years now, that some kind of binational or confederal one-state outcome is superior to a two-state solution; practically every formulation of the latter has essentially envisioned a Palestinian state that is subordinate to Israel, thereby rendering it less a sovereign nation and more a dependent subsidiary, if not outright colony. While this may be better in some respects than the current condition many Palestinians endure, it is hardly the freedom or justice they deserve.

tional law and a recent and reasonable consensus, wouldn't belong to Israel. But who can blame anyone for showing it off? It is a stunning and stunningly ancient construction. The Syrian Caliph 'Abd al-Malik ordered its erection in the seventh century, in honor of an event tied to an emotion many people (including many Muslims) assume absent from Islam or, worse, expel from it altogether.

Love.

THE PROPHET MUHAMMAD lost his father before he was born, in 570, and his mother when he was just six years old. He fell to the care of his grandfather, Abd al-Muttalib, who passed away only two years later. An uncle called Abu Talib took him in and trained him to be a merchant, the business of Mecca being business. A novice in the trade, Muhammad soon came to work for a wealthy widow, Khadija, who was so wowed by his honesty and trustworthiness that she asked for his hand in marriage. Theirs was a happy union, though it would be imperiled because she was about fifteen years older than him. She would be less able to bear the oppression that was headed their way.

When at the age of forty Muhammad received his first revelation—which, as with Mary before him, came from Gabriel—Khadija, then in her mid-fifties, not only reassured him but accepted his message. She was the first Muslim. She was his rock. She never saw the angel Gabriel but believed his words over her eyes. Because she loved him. When he publicly announced his mission, the Meccans gradually progressed from incredulity to insult and then injury. But Abu Talib shielded him. Because he loved Muhammad too. Given their ages, though, Khadija and Abu Talib were especially vulnerable, and the abuse, isolation, the threats and acts of violence did them in.

Ten years in, they passed, one after the other.

Muslims call it Muhammad's year of sorrow.

Their losses left Muhammad broken and probably bewildered.

If God had chosen him for a sacred mission, if God called him His beloved, *Habib Allah*, should not God have spared the ones he most loved? Muhammad was alone, his faith a veil between him and the people who once called him their own. But Muhammad *is* Habib Allah. He was awoken later one night of that same sad year, mounted on a magical steed, and flown to the Temple Mount-or-Noble Sanctuary, where he met all the Prophets who had ever lived. Adam and Noah; his ancestors, Abraham and Ishmael; his cousins, Isaac, Jacob, and Joseph. They were joined by tens of thousands more divine heralds, all of whom had shouldered the same burdens, and they prayed together.

It is called the Night Journey, and it was followed by the Ascension.

From the very rock itself, Muhammad ascended to heaven, to God's throne; there he raised his eyes and beheld the Divine. For centuries, Muslim painters and poets have struggled to capture the intimacy of the encounter; at any visit to the Dome of the Rock, I too am overcome. Aren't we all alone, sometimes? Every person will one day find the world ripped out from under her. Every person will love and lose or be loved and be lost. Most of us will suffer enmity and enemies. Many of us will wonder why, if we worship God, He leaves us to the hardness and cruelty of the world. Muhammad must have been lost in bittersweet rapture. Up there, in heaven, yes, but he would have to return, with Jerusalem only a temporary reprieve. Return to what, though—more abuse, denigration, rejection? To a life without his wife and his uncle? So, God gave him a parting gift, Islam's five daily prayers, which recall Catholic transubstantiation; we face Mecca, but our quotidian prostration takes us to Jerusalem, and from there to God.

Prayer is the Muslim's chance to escape the inevitable heartbreak of this world, to glimpse an afterlife in which there shall be, as the Qur'an promises, neither fear nor grief. But until then? Fourteen hundred years ago, some seventy years after the events in question, an Umayyad Caliph remembered his humble Prophet's deep fondness for his wife and his uncle with a monumental structure, one of the first examples of Islam's budding aesthetics: the Dome of the Rock. A thousand years after, an oftentimes unsavory emperor, Shah Jahan—he audaciously styled himself "King of the World"—created the ethereal Taj Mahal, a monument to his beloved wife, Mumtaz Mahal, who died bearing his umpteenth child. If the Dome of the Rock sometimes stands in for Israel, the Taj Mahal sometimes stands in for India. The buildings, constructed under different circumstances, serve different purposes.

But they reflect this much in common: for a thousand years, love was at the center of the Muslim worldview.

A thousand years hence? In the face of an escalating movement on Israel's far right—dragging the entire country in its direction— to erect on the Haram a Third Temple, I found myself mourning in anticipation even as our crummy tour was underway. Maybe religions have lifespans, expiration dates, statutes of limitations; there has, after all, got to be some reason why God chooses persons to whom He reveals wisdom and scripture and then renews the message through another. Between Jesus and Muhammad, six centuries had passed. Between Muhammad and the end of the world, how many?

There was a mosque next to the last apartment I lived in in New York City. But I didn't go there. For years, I didn't have a regular mosque in Manhattan, never anything more than a prayerful pit stop, if I could get myself to stop—and I'd lived in Manhattan for the better part of twenty years.

The Islamic Center at New York University, which I had helped to develop during and after my college years, was all too often a communal and cultural project for me. While it shaped me, and I shaped it, nevertheless, it never reached me where faith is supposed to take root. Something was stopping me, and I still don't know if it was outside me or inside me. But the Ramadan before our Columbia class trip to Jerusalem, I discovered something in the places I often do—the unexpected ones. In this case, the basement of a sales office for a luxury condominium tower. There I found a Shaykh—a Teacher. Despite a life lived with Islam, it was only near my fortieth year that I connected to Islam on a deeply personal, internal, and intimate level, finally understanding and transcending (without abandoning, and indeed instead increasing) ritual and prayer.

The objective in the Sufi circle I found in that basement is closeness to God, not token adherence—the form is the means to the end. We learn and remember God together. We pray together, with the men on one side of the room and the women on the other side. Ever since I've joined this Sufi space, most mosques have lost their appeal to me. It's not that I don't feel God in them, but that these intimations are muddled by real injustices and ethical blind spots. The separation of the genders as it manifests itself in most Islamic spaces makes me self-conscious (which makes it self-defeating) and uncomfortable. My problem is not that men and women are partitioned from each other, but that women are partitioned from faith—which is equated with men—and thus relegated to a secondary status. If it was about the equality of the sexes before the Divine, the reality of modesty reflected in the physical organization of the space, I would be more than okay.

But when men force women out of sight and out of mind, how can I pray there?

Fortunately, Jerusalem's Haram is, relatively speaking, among the more open and egalitarian spaces I have experienced, something I've found in few other places.

But even then, the Haram suffers the great flaw of modern Islam.

We Muslims make a lot of noise these days. Some of us confuse protest and agitation for effort; we are consumed by all-or-nothing, and since you can never get everything, you end up with nothing. I had only three days in Jerusalem, and I planned, in the obsessively deleterious way I always do, to spend a part of each day in worship, meditation, and supplication—at the Haram. Mostly this was going to be supplication, because it's easier for me to ask God for things than to praise Him. But, well, day one was the tour, and I spent most of our time on the Haram frustrated by the badness of that experience and then looking after one of our students who'd gotten sick.

Day two, and my second chance was Friday Prayers, which in the Muslim practice is a two-part sermon followed by two cycles of prayer. Really motivated, I got to the Haram a full two hours before the sermon was scheduled to begin, because I needed a space in the Aqsa Mosque—it fills up, and I mean really fast—to do my own thing, Islamically speaking, until the main event was underway. Stupid, stupid me. When I got there (and got my precious seat), the Imam was already giving a sermon. Not *the* sermon, but a sermon nonetheless. Kind of like Friday Prayer pregame show. Regrettably, there were no commercial breaks and no panel of speakers that might enliven or enlarge the conversation.

Since this Imam was stuck, like so many Imams are, in outrage, I couldn't do my own thing. I couldn't even hear myself think. Maybe that's the point. He was pissed off. Yelling. Hectoring and badgering the congregation, which already agreed with the basic premises of the religion under question. I'm not sure why he thought anyone wanted, let alone needed, to be subjected to this. Of course, I understand that Aqsa isn't just Aqsa. It's a symbol of the Palestinian aspiration for freedom, for dignity, for sovereignty. But why, then, hassle and harangue and practically verbally assault your audience? It's bad enough that the women and men present must go through the burdens of occupation.

On top of all that, they had to listen to an Imam choking on his own furiousness, magnified by the worst invention ever afforded modern Islam, the microphone.

YOU'D THINK THAT, if anyone needed to be uplifted and empowered, reminded of the value of their efforts in the face of tremendous suppression, it'd be this tribe of my co-religionists. This inability to experience or communicate any emotion other than anger isn't exclusive to the Middle East. Once I gave a rather hastily assembled sermon at an American mosque that had asked me to take the original preacher's place at the last minute. A young man came up to me afterward, astonished. "That's the first sermon I ever heard where the Imam didn't yell." The standard for success now: the avoidance of aggression. Extra points for rationality. I have repeatedly been invited to speak on panels about "Islam and women." When I suggest that perhaps women should be on a panel about women, I am occasionally met with unfeigned surprise. One such contact responded enthusiastically, "That's a great idea!"

Beyond this, there is racism, ethnocentrism, sectarianism, the deadly politicization of religion, the belief that the purpose of moral law is secular administration, the expulsion of spiritual consciousness from culture and creativity, where there still is culture and creativity. Because now, where we build, we do so imitatively. Not to reflect our values, to support, nourish, and shape our societies in positive and inclusive directions, but to cater to the wealthy. Or to compete in the construction of anonymous glass towers that reveal values not only foreign to our own, but hostile to them. Or we construct idolatrous cults of personalities and practically deify permanent presidents—can you imagine anything more hostile to an uncompromising monotheism that preaches humility before the universal fact of mortality? Or we buy weapons and use them against our own. And still the mosques are full. There is a silenced majority, a great many of the world's almost two billion Muslims, fed up with the above and more. Who are sick and tired of the way things have been. Who haven't yet begun to articulate how they want things to be.

Who never got their turn on the microphone.

MY LAST BOOK was about my journey through my Muslimness, learning how to reconcile myself and my religion. This book begins, as of course you know by now, in Jerusalem, combining the autobiographical and even the comic to tell a cosmic story, something much bigger than my life. I recognize in telling a story about Muslimness generally, I am claiming authority for myself and my opinions. So let me be fully clear. I am not a scholar of Islam. And I do not pretend my own take is the only one, or heaven forbid, that it should be.

That said, I still aspire to something audacious and outrageous. This book describes what Islam has been and what it is, who its heroes are, what its big ideas are. Not only to tell you about the past or the present, but to create a future. This book prescribes outcomes. It advocates for a way of being Muslim in the world. It offers Muslim thoughts for coming generations, fashioning an interpretation of Islam of and for the years ahead, the kind of religion we deserve, with echoes of the confident faith we once had. For Islam was a religion of love and, more than anything, I want it to be (itself) again. I want that vulnerability, that longing, that bond of kinship, and that tug of romance to be at the very heart of my faith.

My hope is that *Two Billion Caliphs* helps us get there.

IN THE FOLLOWING fourteen chapters, I will bring together theology, history, and philosophy to present the core ideas through which Islam explains and explores the world and, out of them, sketch a foundation upon which a Muslim tomorrow can be built.

In chapter 2, "What's the Big Idea?," I examine the Islamic idea of God, which begins with what is probably widely known—Islam preaches that there is only one God—and graduates to what is less widely known—that not only is there one God but that God is Oneness, too. From there, we will mine the idea of worship in Islam, namely, that there is an intimate and direct connection between the one God Who is Oneness and His creation, including, but not limited to, humans. But as I will point out, there are consequences to this theology, the principal of which has always been a personal stumbling block for me: the idea that the omniscient and omnipotent God is watching us. And will then judge us.

In chapter 3, "Standing for Torah at Sinai," I explain how the teaching I have received about other faith traditions—specifically, Judaism—repeatedly conveyed to me the centrality of core covenants and historical moments. That pedagogy inspired me to understand and communicate Islam not through facts and figures but through critical occasions, the central one of which is called the

Covenant of Am I Not? In short, that Covenant describes a scene outside of space and time, when the souls of all human beings were gathered to testify to God's Lordship—as well as the judgment that proceeds therefrom. The Lord Who can always watch us *is* always watching us, and will reward or punish us for what we did.

In chapter 4, "Anakin Skywalker Is the Devil," I talk about a second covenantal moment, the emergence of humankind in material and temporal terms with the creation of Adam and Eve. Crucially, our species is described as God's Caliphs on Earth, drawing our attention to a term with multiple meanings, including some controversial ones today. Having discussed something of God in chapter 2 and the relationship of God to humanity in chapter 3, I will explore how Islam views the human being—crucially, for example, as an individual, with wisdom and moral agency, as well as a susceptibility to moral amnesia. This is, without a doubt, one of the most reassuring, moving, and surprising components of the Islamic worldview.

It is also, as I will argue, at the heart of the destiny I fervently hope for my religion, one in which each believer's moral agency is returned to her, such that each and all of us come to see ourselves as Caliphs—God's deputies on Earth.

Only from there can we address the challenges of a global future.

In chapter 5, "Flood from a Machine," we move from Adam, the first Caliph (and, as I'll have explained, the first Prophet), to Noah, who might have been the second named Prophet. This chapter, therefore, concerns itself not with God, or humankind abstractly or individually defined, but the living relationship between God and our species as channeled through Prophets, all of them teachers and warners, but not intermediaries or clerics. Through Noah, we understand the formation—and unlikelihood—of moral communities, juxtaposing the very distant past with the less distant past. And through Noah, we arrive at the Prophets Abraham and Muhammad, whose lives and legacies are formative for Islam—and the subject of the next few chapters.

The story of Abraham, and especially Hagar and Ishmael, Abraham's wife and firstborn son, is critical to understanding both Muhammad's life and how Muhammad understood his life. In chapter 6, "Twilight of the Idols," I explore the significance of these historical figures, their relationship to one another, their place in the Islamic worldview, and, in a nod to the Kierkegaardian, how Abraham's relationship to his father helps us to make sense of the enormity of the Ishmaelite sacrifice. Namely, why would God ask Abraham to do something so apparently awful, and what does that have to do with—going back to chapter 2— the conversation between the individual and her Creator and— returning to this very chapter you're now reading—the theme of love in Islam?

The embodiment of that theme is Muhammad.

It is through his life that Islam is most fully humanized.

What, then, is his life? What did it mean in the context of his times, and how does that apply in our time? Why does Muhammad sometimes strike some of us as such a challenging religious figure, and is there any substance to the allegations sometimes leveled against him—principally, but not exclusively, of an excess of worldliness, unbecoming of a Prophet?

Chapter 7, "Friends, Romans, Countrymen," attempts to present an overview of Muhammad's life in the context of seventh-century Arabia; after outlining the various milestones of his biography, and the tremendous impact of some of his decisions, we come to a thornier subject: the question of Islam and politics. To make the case that Islam is a religion of love, as well as, as I will argue, intimacy and proximity, I must address the fact that Islam has been presented—sometimes by misguided Muslims—as a project for the pursuit of territory and power. Rather, as I will contend, Islam was forced by circumstances into political postures; in the absence of such circumstances, Islam can return to what it was meant to be: an ethical vision, a spiritual journey, a means of establishing closeness between the One and everyone (else).

Of course, Muhammad is unfortunately also misunderstood in other ways, which prevent us from appreciating his genius, distort our understanding of his spiritual qualities and tendencies, and, when those misconceptions are acted upon, mutate our understanding of Islam.

I turn to several of those next.

Chapter 8, "What's Past Is Prologue," briefly touches upon three facts. First, Muhammad is one of those rare figures who does not merely shape a religion but shapes how we think of religion. Second, while we might be tempted to force Muhammad into the categories of twenty-first-century Western morality, this would be unfair to him and unreasonable of us. And third, most of the Muslims I am most attached to and affected by, the Muslims my family and my descendants are and will intimately remain connected to, are minorities in and of the West.

They—we—live in secular democracies, however imperfectly our societies live up to those descriptors. All of that is to say, how Western Muslims choose to interpret Muhammad's life and legacy will likely differ from how Muslims in majoritarian contexts do—and that's okay.

Chapter 9, "Adam and Eve and Eve and Eve and Eve," foregrounds three of the subjects on which Muhammad is most misunderstood and with which Western Muslims will have to do the most demanding work to overcome external (and sometimes internal) misconceptions and misunderstandings. Namely, these are polygamy (Muhammad was a polygamist); slavery (Muhammad never banned the practice outright—or did he?); and heteronormativity (Muhammad practiced and preached a morality that appears to leave little room, if any at all, for many sexual orientations and expressions that are increasingly celebrated today). If Muhammad is the embodiment of the values of Islam in the world, what then do these three facts say about the place of Islam in our modern Western world?

Chapter 10, "The Fable of the Stable Theocracy," directly addresses the idea that Muhammad intended to establish a state. I do so by exploring how some (Sunni) Muslims understand the immediate, post-Prophetic era versus how that period should actually be historically comprehended; the gap between the two reveals the "fable" of the chapter title, the idea that the Prophet meant for a theocracy to be pursued and maintained. I go so far as to argue that not only did Muhammad never intend a theocracy but that the very structural conceit of Islam—that Muhammad is the only normative embodiment of Islam that the tradition recognizes—makes theocracy practically impossible and inherently unstable.

Chapter 11, "The Empty Throne," returns us to the theme of chapter 4—the Caliphate—except not in its scriptural iterations but its historical ones. When Muhammad died, the community around him largely coalesced around a so-called Caliphate of Muhammad. Following the tumultuous and contested emergence of this office, I survey the history of classical, premodern, and precolonial Islam, when versions of this political Caliphate ruled over or symbolized the might of Islam in the world. I point out how this legacy was formidable—as well as how this legacy hobbled Islam and harmed Muslims. Finally, with the ultimate collapse of the Caliphate in 1924, I ask whether the time has not come to imagine a new Caliphate.

In chapter 12, "The Case for the Caliphate," I argue that, because the ummah—the world Muslim community—is beset by huge problems, it requires some mechanisms to bring it together to translate its potentials into possibilities. With the scale of the challenges facing contemporary Islam, there is an urgent and desperate need to activate the strengths, talents, resources, and commitments of modern Muslims in ways that convene our potential clout. As I discuss especially in chapter 10, political Islam is essentially and inevitably unstable—worse than this, in the name of unity, it creates division, moral exhaustion, and spiritual burnout. Contemporary Islamic communities need an organic, proactive, deeply compassionate, forward-facing ethos of fraternity and sorority.

In other words, a new kind of Caliphate.

But because there can be no authentic future of Islam that does not respect and reflect the present, past, and prehistory of Islam,

I propose that this new kind of Caliphate be, in many respects, a revival and reconstruction of the Caliphate of God introduced in chapter 4.

Instead of focusing on collectivizing, totalizing, nationalizing, and globalizing visions—which are remarkably perilous in a fast-growing and gigantic ummah—we should go small. We must stop dreaming about uniting Muslims globally and start thinking about empowering Muslims locally. That means we build into our education, institutions, and respective visions a new emphasis on the idea that each human being is empowered and indeed commanded to uphold the Divine order through her agency.

That, above all else, is the meaning and purpose of the old-new Caliphate.

That we be empowered stewards of and on Earth.

And that we recognize, in each other, this equality of status and dignity.

CHAPTER 13, "THE END," communicates what the histories, theologies, philosophies, ontologies, and epistemologies of the previous chapters together amount to. Namely, if Muhammad is the embodiment of Islam, and if Islam is a religion of intimacy, proximity, and love, what then does this mean for the contemporary practicing Muslim, who has inherited the complex, contradictory, confusing, and contentious legacies of Islam, colonialism, modernity, and the West? Without dismissing the importance of these factors and forces, I propose that the purpose of Islam is still to enable the individual and the communities she is embedded in to approach and engage the Creator—and I describe, in very personal language, my own attempts at such engagement, my experience of Islamic spirituality through a Sufi community.

Chapter 14, "Sermon on the Mount," draws together the ideas discussed thus far with a provocative conceit. Perhaps, as some Muslims fear, the Muslim world is headed for a civilizational collapse. I cannot say that such a fear is apocalyptic because no person knows the final hours, but I can agree that the times ahead look existentially worrisome. Or not. Some collapse, after all, leads to rebirth. Out of the ashes, something perhaps rises. It could be that our job is to tend to our gardens. To do what we can and trust that the result is not only out of our hands but has never been in our hands. That might strike you like a position of powerlessness, but Islam neither condemns powerlessness nor considers it a permanent condition.

Once, Islam was a Prophet Muhammad mourning an uncle who stood between Muhammad and the world and a wife who held Muhammad at his lowest and saddest. Once, Islam was Adam and Eve, expelled from the Garden, forced to live out life on Earth, even though this was their victory. Once, Islam was Noah, preaching fruitlessly. Once, Islam was Abraham, chased out by his father, forced to leave Hagar and Ishmael in the desert. Once, Islam was Hagar, raising a son alone, building a city, founding a civilization; she is one of the most consequential figures in the history of humanity, and yet she is rarely celebrated, even by those who claim her. Once, Islam was Mary, beside a tree, giving birth alone, wishing she was forgotten and could forget herself.

These are not stories introduced into our tradition. They have been forgotten from our tradition or crowded out of it. The destiny of Islam is not a reformation. It is a counter-reformation. A restoration. Once, Islam was hundreds of millions of people and they had forgotten their strength. When I used to speak publicly about Islam, until very recently the question I heard most often from people who weren't from my faith tradition was, "Why don't more Muslims condemn terrorism?" One correct answer is that we do—it's just that most people aren't listening, or don't know where to look to see those denunciations, or that mainstream media outlets have comparatively less interest in rather dull pieces about reasonableness and decency. But the other answer is a lot harder to face.

How is it that one in four people on the planet do not have the institutional wherewithal, the political strength, the social capital, the cultural influence to be known for something beyond what a small minority of the community represents? Yes, there are Islamophobic forces arrayed against us. But it's not like we lack for money, or numbers, or passion, or talent. What we lack are ideas that can become practices, visions that can reenergize cultures, leaders that deserve followers. Because I want Islam to survive, yes, but also to thrive. I believe it deserves to. Because the world needs the connectedness to God that we offer, the vision of God that we preach, the personality that Muhammad presented.

All religions are valuable, but all religions are not all the same.

BUT THAT IS NOT how *Two Billion Caliphs* concludes.

Chapter 15, "Why I Am Not a Sufi," is a kind of epilogue—and perhaps a prologue, too.

THE PUBLICATION OF THIS BOOK was inevitably delayed by the awful coronavirus pandemic. During that time, I experienced the culmination of a series of spiritual apocalypses, the realization of profound and, worse still, systemic shortcomings in the Sufism I had enthusiastically embraced and thereafter endorsed in the original draft of this book. By the time the manuscript had entered review, however, I was no longer a participant in the Sufi order I was once inseparable from. I could not in good conscience conclude the book without admitting as much and offering an explanation as to why.

However, while this process of disillusionment was at times crushingly disappointing, it was also constructively enlightening. For I had concluded that, in much the same way political Islam arrogates authority specifically reserved to the Prophet Muhammad, so too do many professedly apolitical forms of Islam, suggesting that to live Islam now it is not nearly enough to shrug off politics and otherwise carry on as always, as the first iteration of the book might have seemed to suggest. We must disabuse ourselves of all forms of special dispensation and unchallengeable authority, for these are hostile to the very spirit of Islam. To live as Caliphs of God in communities of God, we must actively experiment with new kinds of authority, neither dismissing the inevitability of some forms of hierarchy nor the expertise or other benefits they provide, but all the same tempering the worst features of these. Because Islam is not a solitary faith, and because no faith restricted to the individual can survive—humankind is not meant to be atomized, as capitalism and liberalism endlessly learn to their surprise—we must search out new forms through which we understand, realize, and access not just Islam as identity but Islam as spirituality, morality, and intimacy.

The prescriptions are not always as definitive as you (or I) might sometimes hope.

But prescriptions aren't always meant to be.

The world is, after all, divided between different answers to the same questions. Islam has its own various answers. Permit me to offer some of them here, whether you believe in them or not. Take them to enhance what it is you understand of the belief system of almost two billion people. Put them in conversation with the answers you've already received, whether or not they suffice you. A moment of contemplation is worth a lifetime of genuflection. Learning how to turn back the way you came, which you can only do if you think—if you reflect on where you started, where you went wrong, and how to get it right again. If you ask the right questions.

Who am I?

How did I get here?

What am I meant to do here?

And what was so damned special about that tree?

2

WHAT'S THE BIG IDEA?

SOME FOLKS DEFINE Islamophobia as discrimination against people who happen to be Muslim. And some Muslims do indeed happen to be Muslim. But for me, at least, I don't just happen to be born into Muslimness, or not only that. I chose Islam, and I choose it, with varying degrees of commitment, every day. (I could drift from the faith when my practice of it slackens, and I know that because when it does, I do.) There was a brief time in my youth when I embraced atheism, but then, finding it unconvincing, I contemplated other faiths. I considered Catholicism and Zoroastrianism. The former was hard to square with early Christian history, and the latter seemed practically impossible; i.e., I did not know any Zoroastrians. But what kept me in the doorway to Islam was Muhammad. I was convinced that he was upright and sincere, and therefore that the message he brought was true, and as such I was obligated to it. But that doesn't explain what sustains me in the Islamic tradition.

Some people these days like to call themselves spiritual, not religious; sometimes, they do so because they see religion as divisive. And it certainly can be—just watch the news. But what else can happen with incommensurate truth claims? Either Jesus is the son of God, or he is not; either I am right, or you are. (Either I am wrong, or you are.) However, this does not mean that all religions do not have tremendous and particular value: if they didn't, religious diversity wouldn't be a thing worth pursuing and preserving. Without a range of religions, the world would be a poorer, less interesting, and less moral place. It does not follow, however, that because all religions are precious that they are the same, for each religion has its own particularities. In the case of Islam, it is not Islam's big(gest) idea that reinforces my faith, but its consequences. Some of those consequences, however, have made it hardest for me to remain a Muslim. Got that?

With that established, that big(gest) idea is absolute monotheism.

It's outlined in the *shahada*, the testimonial of Muslim faith. It's elaborated on in the Qur'an's 112th chapter. We'll talk about both of them here, but devote more attention to the latter than the former because, although that chapter's sundry implications appear at first blush to be counterintuitive, they incidentally explain (and also explain away) one of the most significant misunderstandings of Islam.

That Islam is a religion of coldness, hardness, and distance.

What a far cry from how Muslims (should) experience their faith.

BEFORE HE WAS A PROPHET, he was a merchant. But a disillusioned one. Outside of his business and beyond his wife and growing family, a middle-aged Muhammad spent more and more time in meditation, troubled by many of his fellow Meccans. The Qur'an would call them *mushrikun*, or associationists, for while they believed in an all-powerful supreme deity, *al-Ilah* (contracted to "Allah"— meaning, simply, God), they transferred some of His powers down, to lesser deities, while elevating various forces, spirits, and beings, real and imagined, to intermediary positions between man and his Creator. They associated. They muddled monotheism.

However, a few of the Arabs of the time did not so associate; they called themselves *hanif*s. Muhammad may have been considered (or considered himself) one of them. He'd often retreat to the caves outside Mecca to think about where his society had gone wrong (and not just in theological ways: he was upset by the patriarchy, classism, and racism running rampant through mercantile Mecca).

On one of his contemplative retreats, as per usual Muhammad was alone in the darkness. Until he sensed he was not alone. An alien presence filled the cave and commanded Muhammad to read.

Muhammad responded that he couldn't. Like many Arabs of the time, he was illiterate.

The forty-year-old was squeezed hard in response and asked again. Told again. Read! Muhammad replied the same.

This happened once more, and then the voice sang, "Read: In the name of your Lord . . ."

The voice recited five verses of rhymed poetry, although Muhammad was not interested in this communication. He had bigger concerns on his mind. Like his fear of descending into insanity. When Muhammad exited the cave, distressed and breathless, he saw, over the horizon, consuming the sky, a massive thing that repeated itself like a broken record, "I am Gabriel and you, Muhammad, are the Messenger of God." *

This panicky occasion is the beginning of the Qur'an, the words of God, almost always via Gabriel, to Muhammad, sent down piecemeal over some twenty-three years, and unchanged from revelation down to the present. To give you a sense of how the Qur'an is (not) structured, these first five verses don't appear at the beginning of the Qur'an. Rather, they are the first five verses of the 96th of the Qur'an's 114 chapters. In total, there are over six thousand verses—the Arabic word for which, *ayat*, means "signs"—and many of them, especially the earlier ones, return overwhelmingly to several core themes: God is One. Injustice is bad. Charitableness is good. You'll live, you'll die, you'll live again. In heaven or in hell. Purify yourself if you want paradise. God is One.

That monotheism thing is a very, very big deal. It's the essence of Islam. The theological position the religion most strongly

---

* I wrestled for a long time with this one. In Arabic and the Islamic tradition, Muhammad is almost always referred to as *Rasul Allah*, "the Messenger of God." But in English we call him "Prophet Muhammad," which title has connotations—of prophecy and prophesying—that the Arabic *Rasul* does not communicate. In the end, however, I stayed with "Prophet Muhammad" in the hopes that that would be more familiar.

condemns is the absence of monotheism. "Associationist" is not a term of praise or of endearment. Islam has five pillars, and the first of them is the shahada, the aforementioned testimonial. *La ilaha illa Allah*, it begins.* The first two words, *la + ilaha*, represent an Arabic form that might be called absolute negation: "There is *absolutely* no god." Then comes *illa Allah.* "But God." The same three letters that spell "Allah" in Arabic, "a," "l," and "h," are the only letters required to spell out the shahada. If someone wishes to convert to Islam, all she needs to do is recite the shahada. (While intending by it to convert—just because you read the above doesn't mean you've become a Muslim; unless, of course, you want to be.)

That is, in my opinion, Islam's big(gest) idea. That there is one God, and only one. And that, furthermore and by association (sic), this God is meant for all people. All you have to do is attest to that truth, and you join a massive global community. But the shahada, as important as it is—and it is really, really important—leaves other critical questions unanswered. Who is this only God that Islam wants you so very badly to acknowledge?**

---

* The second half of the shahada is *Muhammadun Rasul Allah*, or "Muhammad is the Messenger of God."

** In the Islamic tradition, God is not only not a father, but not a parent of any type, and not only not a son, but not anyone's offspring of any kind. But I refer to God as "He"—even though English has gender-neutral language available ("it," for example, or "they," which these days is used singularly as well as plurally)—because God refers to Himself (sic) as "He" (*huwa*) in the Arabic of the Qur'an, which book is, we believe, the eternal word of God. This choice of translation was and remains a difficult one for me, not least because the English "He" conveys many things *"huwa"* does not. Arabic, for one thing, has no gender-neutral pronouns, but rather assigns masculine or feminine genders to all nouns. ("Book," for example, is masculine, even though no one thinks books are literally or substantively male—readers familiar with French or Spanish will get this.) Still, God chose in the Qur'an to refer to Himself as "He," not "She" or "They," and because the Qur'an is immutable, I am being conservative and sticking to a faithful translation of the pronoun. Given my own disquiet, however—not least because in Islam God is both beyond gender and possesses stereotypically masculine and feminine attributes (and often esteems the feminine ones over the masculine ones, by the way)—I have tried where possible to refer to God in more neutral language, such as "the One," "the Divine," and so on, which I believe is true to the Islamic tradition.

It should also be noted that Arabic has no capital letters. So, I debated whether I should capitalize "God" and any other references to the Divine. In the end, I chose to capitalize because I believe it is more traditional and respectful.

What are the implications of absolute monotheism?

For that, we need to look to the Qur'an. The Prophet Muhammad said that its 112th chapter, *Ikhlas*—"Sincerity"—which is only four verses long—was worth an entire third of the Qur'an. Since the Qur'an is not twelve verses long, something about this chapter must give it enormous significance.

Its seventeen words are so powerful and so definitive that they are where our journey begins.*

Say, "He is God, One.   *Qul: 'Huwa'llahu Ahad.*
God, [the] Eternal.   *Allahu as-Samad.*
He begets not nor was   *Lam yalid wa lam yulad,*
He begotten,
And there can be nothing   *Wa lam yakun lahu*
like Him."   *kufuwan ahad.'***

Ikhlas opens with a command: "Say: 'He is God, One,'" from which we learn it's not enough to acknowledge that there's just one God, as the shahada does. To be purely monotheistic, we must go from accepting that there is one God to believing that this one God is One. Indivisible. That which is one is, furthermore, also unique.

---

* It may mean something or it may mean nothing, but Muslims pray seventeen cycles of prayer a day, grouped into five prayers (the first is three cycles, the second is four, the third is two, and the fourth and fifth are four cycles each).

** There are many excellent English-language translations of the Qur'an; the most popular is probably still Abdullah Yusuf Ali's *The Meaning of the Holy Qur'an*, although S. H. Nasr's *The Study Qur'an*, a massive volume that gathers together Qur'anic commentaries with an English translation of the Qur'an itself, seems to have made some serious inroads among many Muslims. For the purposes of this book, all translations of the Qur'an, and of Arabic, are my own. I studied Modern Standard and classical Arabic in academic institutions for five years, six months of which were intensive immersion programs, three of which were in Egypt, and six additional months of which were dedicated to the Qur'an and to pre-Islamic and early Islamic poetry. I only underscore this because Muslims take the Qur'an very seriously, and the act of translation too. To help me out, I have consulted works such as *The Meaning of the Holy Qur'an*, *The Study Qur'an*, and translations by A. J. Arberry and Muhammad Asad, as well as the excellent work by Gabriel Said Reynolds, *The Qur'an & the Bible*. Where necessary I have also spoken with scholars of Arabic and Islamic studies more knowledgeable than myself.

God, One. God, Unique. The Divine is singular and, as many Sufis have it, alone and lonely for it. Desirous of being known.

Which, on an initial reading of Ikhlas, might seem impossible.

For if you scan the four verses of this "third of the Qur'an," what you appear to get is a picture of a God utterly unlike humanity, a Divine so alien, so different, so *unique*, as to be in some sense incomprehensible and perhaps therefore unapproachable. As I and others before me argue, however, God is advertising the potential for closeness between us and Him, albeit in a manner that appears, on its face, counterintuitive.

That doesn't mean that these four verses don't articulate who God actually is, but concretizes particular experiential possibilities, too.

The second verse of Ikhlas is just two words: "God, [the] Eternal."

Because He depends on no one, He is Eternal; because He is Eternal, He depends on no one. Indeed, *all* depend on Him. He has all power over all things.

The final two verses of Ikhlas only underscore that sempiternity. "He begets not, nor was He begotten," the Qur'an continues, "and there can be nothing like Him." The immediate reference in the third verse appears to be a direct knock on the Christian idea of the Divine, dominantly Trinitarian. The fourth verse returns us to the first, with the repetition of "Ahad"—God is One. Nothing else is (so purely itself). "There can be nothing like Him." Theologians who read these verses divine their implications and construct creeds therefrom. That's important work, but more relevant for me are the implications of these verses, not just in what they say, but also in what they *do*. If it is true that God is One, that He is Eternal, that He is neither a parent nor a child, that He is completely unlike us, and indeed anything that we can conceive of, then there are consequences.

ONE OF THE MOST common tropes about Islam is that it's not a religion, it's a political ideology. Or, if it *is* a religion, it's not a religion of love, like Christianity, but a religion of rote ritual at best and primitive servility at worst. An ungenerous reader of these four verses might be tempted to the same conclusion. God, different, singular, distant. Whereas I have learned that God's difference from me is what makes me (think I can) come close to Him.

As Islam sees it, God exists and has always existed. He *has* to exist. He knows *why* He *has* to exist. Before anything existed, before it even made sense to say "before"—when time and space were only thoughts in the mind of God (and even this language fails to convey the distinction; we find it nearly impossible to think outside our spatiotemporal boundaries)—there was God. He created us from nothing, and He can do so because only pure and necessary Being can donate, gift, or lend existence to anything else.*

No matter what we achieve, no matter how vast, wonderfully beautiful, and complicated (and yet, elegant and precise) our universe is, from the micro to the macro, all of it exists because God endlessly renews its existence by a constant donation of existence. We have being. We are not Being. This is part of Islam's trouble with the Trinity: the notion that God is anything but singular—He is not divisible—or that Creator and creation can coexist in some space. (All of creation is separate from, and distinct from, God.) This awesome powerfulness that is the unique, singular, matchless God is at the heart of Islam.

But of course, Islam has theologies. It is not a theology. It is a way of being in the world, with something unique to offer. That isn't just that there is one God, but that this Oneness is a gift to humankind.

IN THE MUSLIM TRADITION, there are three kinds of prayer. *Salat* is the ritual, five-times-a-day, must-face-Mecca physical performance

---

* One of the few works that accessibly makes this point clear is (Eastern Orthodox theologian) David Bentley Hart's *The Experience of God: Being, Consciousness, Bliss.* The book is organized into three parts, each of which is dedicated to a quality named in the subtitle; the section on "Being" is directly relevant to the discussion here.

that is the most famous form of Muslim prayer. *Zikr* is the repetitive invocation of God's names and qualities. And *du'a* is supplication, the act of asking God for specific things. One could also say there are two faces to prayer: the petitioning and the praising. The petitioning is just that—here's what I need or want. The praising is just that: minimizing the self and maximalizing the Self. For me, the first of the two, petitioning, has always been significantly easier. This is probably because even though it requires a humbling of the self—an admission that I am not enough to realize what I want, that I am not the author of my destiny—it nevertheless involves fulfillment of the self. I can *ask* for things I want. Sometimes these are substantive. Paradise, for one. A life of nearness to Him. Contentment. Freedom from oppression, anxiety, fear. Sometimes these are mundane.

I've prayed for: a road trip across Tasmania, the chance to do *The Lord of the Rings* tours in New Zealand, a vibrant life connection to Los Angeles and/or Montreal, a visit to the Gaspé Peninsula—I am sure you can see a trend here—as well as particularities that are cool to me and definitely weird to most everyone else. I like the corporate aesthetics of Finnair and would like to take the airline to Helsinki. I began this pattern of expansive, worldly petitioning when my life was going every way but mine; asking for things I wanted, no matter how seemingly inappropriate—the Alfa Romeo Stelvio appeals to me—forced me to think about all the things I liked about the world, all of which became reasons to pick myself back up again. I notched each achievement (I got to sit in the Alfa Romeo SUV at the Los Angeles International Auto Show) as one more blessed memory to turn to when I got down on myself. In that respect, God is a hand to hold on to. A rope to remain attached to.

Because while I can let go, He won't ever. I believe Islam is true, yes—but I sincerely appreciate and, what is more, need what Islam does for me. I couldn't worship a Being in need of anything; I am too in need of everything. I couldn't orient my life around someone as fallible as me; I've let myself down enough. I'd rather dedicate my life to the cultivation of a relationship with He Whose ears never tire of hearing, Who possesses such richness beyond measure that He can create, and create, and *nothing* of Him is depleted. For because He created all things and sustains them, He is aware of all things that happen in this universe, and any other universe, at every moment. From the steps every ant in every ant colony takes, to the precise place at which every wave on every beach broke, breaks, and will break, to the melting of comets, the burning and exhaustion of stars, the endless chatter of each and everyone's internal monologue—even cataloging it feels exhausting. Yet it is not just a matter of sustaining a world, but unfolding worlds upon worlds, an existence of unfathomable complexity that evolves, changes, grows, transforms, inflates.

This is why the Qur'an says, "God is closer to you than your jugular vein," a sign that incidentally raises some interesting questions as to where you are in relation to you in the first place. In the Qur'an, He is called *Rabb*, or Lord. Meaning also: Master, Provider, Nourisher. He depends on nothing, which is why we depend on Him. This is the great misunderstanding of Islam. Sometimes Islam is called a religion of mercy or a religion of (social) justice. Those categorizations have ample truth to them. But I believe Islam is, above all else, a religion of intimacy. That absolute monotheism applies to all people in intention and activation. Anyone can reach out to God and approach Him for help, because the Divine is always available.

Sometimes you hear people decline to pray for their own needs because, as they put it, "God has more important things to do." But He does not. We humans only need to rank things in order of priority because our own capacities are limited. The omnipotent Divine has no need to conserve energy—He created it and creates it ever anew. There is literally nothing so important that God cannot attend to something allegedly minor at the same time, such as, potentially, my interest in returning to the south of Spain behind the wheel of a rental car. (As for the transactional quality of my prayers, well, that doesn't suggest much intimacy, but that is my shortcoming, and not the Divine's.) This is the lesson of Ikhlas.

The unexpected consequence of God's differentness isn't distance, but closeness. Total otherness makes total intimacy possible.

If God is One and Unique, that is because He is Eternal and, because He is Eternal, He is Self-Sufficient, and because He is Self-Sufficient, He can always be there for us, come what may.

It sounds, on the surface, like a very good deal. Worship the One Who is in need of no one. The One Who will always be there for you. Except. It isn't just that there's one God, unlike any other. Or that God is One. It's not even that God knows everything or has to know everything. It's that it kind of works in the opposite direction too. You and I, and all people, have always known God, and because of that, God can judge us. Because we've been warned in advance. The rules of the game were set down before you were born. And when He does judge you, He'll judge you for everything He knows about you.

Which is everything.

3
....

STANDING FOR
TORAH AT SINAI

IF YOU GROW UP marginalized in America, you may think you know a lot about the people around you. You've no choice but to. As against being powerful, which makes you lazy—explaining why, as of writing, many young Americans might be shocked to know a competent white president. But this would be wrong. Take my supposed comprehension of a kindred faith, Judaism. I (thought I) knew a lot about Hanukkah and Passover, relatively speaking. I kind of understood the High Holidays and was proud to vaguely appreciate their greater importance. But I hadn't even heard of Shavuot, which, on one occasion, a Jewish friend and scholar, Yossi Klein Halevi, described as the birth of his people. How had I never heard of this holiday? I wondered. To borrow from the late Donald Rumsfeld, former United States secretary of defense, there are things we know we don't know, but there are also things we don't know we don't know.

We Ishmaelites have only two consensus holidays, the names of both of which are contracted to *Eid*. The first, Eid al-Fitr, is preceded by a full month of fasting, Ramadan, meaning that the festival commences with feasting but is ended by mid-afternoon, when most of the Muslim world has descended into gastrointestinal distress. The second holiday, Eid al-Adha, marks the end of the *hajj*, the pilgrimage to Mecca, and honors Abraham's (almost) sacrifice of Ishmael. The two holidays are just seventy days apart, meaning we can spend most of the year in unrelieved routine. Campaigns to introduce new holidays usually end in charges of heresy, so I'm not going down that road. It's so bad that you might be excommunicated for feting the Prophet's birthday. And the Islamic New Year, Ra's as-Sanah, our Rosh Hashanah, is about as important to the wider world as my birthday is. It is mostly ignored by Sunni Muslims, while it occasions a period of deep mourning for Shia Muslims, the first ten days of Muharram, which are concluded by Ashura, our Yom Kippur.

Ashura is, like Yom Kippur, the tenth day of the first month. It is the day Muslims believe God parted the sea for Moses—and not so much for Pharaoh's host. (It is also the anniversary of the martyrdom of the Prophet Muhammad's noble and courageous grandson, Imam Husayn.) There are other apparent convergences between the Jewish and Muslim traditions. The last ten nights of Ramadan are especially sacred in Islam. One of these is the Night of Power, or *Laylat al-Qadr*, which marks the first revelation of the Qur'an at the Mountain of Light. The aforementioned holiday of Shavuot features a parallel tradition: Jews celebrate the revelation of the Torah at Mount Sinai. But again, it is not an exact match. Muslims believe the Archangel Gabriel brought the Qur'an to Muhammad, for God meant to speak to the whole world through the Prophet, whereas the revelation of the Torah at Mount Sinai wasn't to Moses or Aaron, but to all of the Jewish people. Including, in some interpretations, every single Jew who has lived or will ever live. All of them testified there to receiving communication from the Divine.*

---

* See Gabriel Said Reynolds's commentary on this verse: "Verses 172–74 reflect an opinion expressed in the Babylonian Talmud (Shevu'ot 39a) that the covenant on Mt. Sinai was made between God and all later generations, not only those who stood on the base of the mountain." Reynolds also draws a productive contrast to Joshua 24:22. See *The Quran & the Bible: Text and Commentary*, p. 286.

Abraham may have wed Sarah, and she gave birth to Isaac; from his son Jacob, we have the Twelve Tribes; Moses led his people out of Egypt and toward the promised land. But Yossi called Shavuot the night when the Jews became a people, and this moment of peoplehood is central to Judaism. In Islam, there is of course a concept of peoplehood, too: it's the ummah. But it is religion that creates, undergirds, and provides the boundaries for peoplehood. We didn't birth Islam. Islam birthed us. If you renounce Islam religiously, you cease to be a participant in the ummah. (At least, that's how it's been traditionally—the rise of secular Muslimness, or cultural Islam, complicates matters.) In Judaism, peoplehood precedes and succeeds religion. You can be Jewish without believing in Judaism, a position Muslims would not have historically recognized. As a teacher of Islam and Muslim experiences, I have often found such differences to be rich sources of conversation and reflection. Learning someone else's faith helps you know your own.

That thought reigned in my mind for years, as I was repeatedly called on to introduce Islam to audiences very unfamiliar with it, and my answer—if I'm honest—kept evolving. Increasingly, I have used the parallel of Shavuot as a place to start from. For, if I start with the idea that God is One, this is usually not particularly surprising for most American audiences, most of whom are, or are descended from, Christians (and, in places like New York City, often Jews as well). What I like to stress instead is the Islamic idea that we, as in all of us—all of humanity—have always known that God is One. Islam, like Judaism, features multiple covenantal moments. There is one that parallels Shavuot, although there's no holiday attached to it. But in my religion's defense, we'd have no clue when to celebrate it. It occurs outside of time and space as we understand them. It is our moment at Sinai. *Ahd-e Alast*, the Covenant of Am I Not?

> And when your Lord took from the Children of Adam, from their loins, their progeny, and made them testify concerning themselves. "Am I not your Lord?"

"Yes, we so testify," they said.

This so that you would not say, on the Day of Resurrection, "Of this we knew not."*

There's no introduction furnishing a when or a where because, adverbially speaking, there is no when or where for when or where this happened. (I like to think that God prefers to keep the Qur'an as universal as possible; this is another reason why Islam is disinclined toward human representation and horrified by it in the religious context.) The important part isn't the details. It's the overall thrust of the moment. Namely, God takes the souls of everyone who will ever live and asks them a pretty simple question: "Am I not your Lord?"

God doesn't ask us if we recognize Him as God. (I suppose that much was obvious.) He asks, instead, if we recognize God as our Lord. God is God. But God is also Rabb, or Lord: Master, Provider, Nourisher. God asks—okay, asked—if you knew who God was *to you*. That's why the Arabic contains that "to themselves"—you're testifying to and for yourself, for when, after everyone who was ever meant to live has died, and the world has ended, we stand for judgment. Standing there, before God. Reminded. Oh yeah. Oh God.

Because yes, we're souls. Especially in this Covenant, when we're only souls. But we'll enter bodies. Live out lives, here on Earth. Die. The Jewish people at Sinai. Humanity at somewhere. The word "religion" derives from the Latin for "binding" or "obligation." In Arabic, the corresponding word is *deen*, which can convey a debt. What you owe God: all the things.

Some Muslims use the word *kafir* to refer to anyone who isn't a Muslim. Some Muslims use this word to denigrate and dismiss other peoples, other faiths, other traditions.

---

* Qur'an 7:172.

Worst of all, the jihadists use it to condemn whole categories of people (including plenty of Muslims) and legitimate violence, even genocidal violence, against them.

But the kafir isn't a person who isn't Muslim. The kafir is the one who knows God is One, and who moreover knows we owe a debt to God—that existence is a gift, that our individuality, our uniqueness, our distinctiveness, is a blessing and a privilege—and yet buries that knowledge. And sometimes works to deny others that knowledge. Muhammad had knowledge of who was guilty of such a crime, but now only God knows, which is why the term is not particularly helpful, and its use should be severely restricted.

THE FIRST LESSON I draw from the Covenant of Am I Not?

Universality.

Everyone who's ever lived, who lives right now, and who will live, was there for this one. Black or white, male or female, rich or poor, Muslim or not. Every. Single. Person. Including you. Which means everyone who's ever lived, who lives right now, and who will live, is aware of God, not just in the vague manner of acknowledging a higher power, but in a very specific sense. We know God is our Lord. Master, Provider, Nourisher. Why might you not remember it now? We come into the world with this primordial knowledge still a part of us. This primordial condition is called the *fitra*, and it explains why it's so easy for children to believe in an invisible, all-powerful deity. Because they remember better.

The distractions, obfuscations, and temptations of the world muddle the monotheism for us and lead us, as Islam would have it, away from God. What is the purpose of religion? Is it the outcome of acknowledging the debt we owe to God? The consequence of not just apprehending monotheism, but implementing it? It's the Muslim belief that a life of petition and praise, of the constant invocation of God, polishes the mirror that is the soul, removing the gunk and the grime that makes it hard for us to intimate the overwhelming nearness of God in every aspect of our lives, thereby restoring us to our fitra. And since *all* people are born into the same fitra, including those who aren't Muslim, all people are inclined toward transcendence. This brings us to a corollary of universality, my second takeaway. Pluralism.

Since this inclination toward transcendence is part of human nature, the religious impulse can never be obliterated; at best, one can play whack-a-mole. Crush religious expression in one iteration, and it pops up somewhere else, in another vernacular. It may be that we evolved to see the world religiously, which doesn't mean that religion isn't real—God could've evolved us to *want* to look for Him. If God created humankind to worship Him, as the Qur'an underscores, He can do so by any means He chooses, including seeding a preference for religion in our genetic code, which He, incidentally, also came up with. This expansive universality is one of my favorite parts of Islam and the source of the vigor it demonstrated in its early history.

When we reached outwards to embrace. I recognize that while universality is a lesson of the Covenant of Am I Not? that might be widely shared, the inclination to see pluralism in this, at the very heart of the Muslim worldview, might surprise some, Muslims and otherwise. But isn't it kind of obvious? For if humans are preternaturally inclined toward theism, every religion is an expression of a common human yearning to discover the origins and purposes of our selves. You can't know God without knowing yourself, and you can't know yourself without knowing God. This is why mystics of every faith report similar experiences, as do individuals of no theistic faith. Various religious traditions can nurture us and bring us back, in some way, shape, or form, to our fitra, which is to say, where we were at the Covenant of Am I Not? Every faith waters the soul, and for that we should honor the complexity of individual faith and the varieties of collective faith. I certainly hope this perspective is embedded into the Islam of the future, to cure us of the ills of supremacism. The legacy of an imperialism, as the philosopher Muhammad Iqbal put it in his Allahabad Address—that early post-Prophetic Islam snuck into the evolving superstructure of the faith.*

THE THIRD LESSON of the Covenant of Am I Not?

"Am I Not Your Lord?" God asks. It could be meant rhetorically, answering by way of asking. God's saying, "You already know this—I'm just emphasizing it by turning it around on you." Before our bodies were ensouled, before our souls were embodied, in whatever place and space we existed, we knew God made us and we knew He'd sustain us, because we were right there. That's why God could ask us a rhetorical question. In this life, in this world, it's sometimes hard to believe in God, because at least for the novice there is no direct experience of God. You can't point up to Him as you do to the sun in the sky. But back then, in that realm, there He was, and you could no more reject Him than you could tell someone that the sun isn't overhead at midday.

But there's more than one way of looking at a question.

"Am I not your Lord?" might mean the very opposite. It could be that we doubted it. Yes, the sun is in the sky, but for a long time, many societies believed that our star orbited our planet, and not our planet our star. Maybe we had a tendency to forget God even then, or rather forget that God was our Lord; or perhaps God knew that all of us would at some point down the road lose track of this, which is why He had to ask, in the hopes that the answer would echo inside us for those times when it'd be hard to hear anything of

---

* Muhammad Iqbal, also known as Allama Iqbal, was a South Asian philosopher, poet, and political thinker who helped to shape the movement for an Indo-Muslim homeland; that is, the country we now know as Pakistan. He was one of the most original, compelling, and creative Islamic intellectuals of the modern era, whose writings—largely in English, Urdu, and Persian—spread across the world. In his Allahabad Address, delivered in that city in 1930, he outlined to a Muslim audience his conception of a Muslim-majority territory in the northwest of the Indian Subcontinent, laying the conceptual groundwork for the sovereign nation of Pakistan, although he neither lived to see that country's independence—nor the horrors of Partition that marked it.

the Divine. Hard even to believe in the possibility. Is this an apparent contradiction, between a primordial condition of monotheism and a primordial condition of forgetfulness?

This is the problem with extremism, or rather the cause of it, which is also a consequence of it. Extremism simply cannot fathom that religion can be complex for one of two reasons. It is either because extremists are not capable of admitting that they are complex people, which would be why their religiosity manufactures boredom at every level and also produces such lifeless art, tacky architecture, and a mimetic aesthetic—or because extremists are not capable of complex thoughts. (In which case, extremism isn't their fault, even if it's our problem.) Religiosity that cannot accommodate complexity, that does not possess tensions between competing impulses, is a brittle thing. It will snap at the first sign of pressure. Or snap people at the first sign of difference. As a teacher of mine from another tradition once put it: "The more rigid the belief system, the less room there is for faith." It's a simple truth.

Human beings are messy.

Take an action you embarked upon ten years ago, assuming you can remember back that far. Consider a marriage you entered into that ended in divorce. Did you marry the wrong person? Was it your fault, or your partner's? Could things have been fixed, or was the relationship doomed from the get-go? Did you change, or she change, or nobody change? Not only do we find it hard to understand ourselves—I know using social media is bad for me, but there I am, late at night, swiping mindlessly through empty virtual calories—but *how* we understand ourselves changes. Every worldview that wishes to survive beyond a few generations has to accommodate shifting circumstances, stretching and bending, pressing down and yielding, because that's how life goes. Sometimes you're strong, and need to be humbled. Sometimes you're weak, and need to be nourished. Sometimes you need the God of wrath. Sometimes you need the God of love. Maybe some people will prefer the former meaning, and others the latter. And that is okay.

But here's a head-spinner:

Two things can be true about some texts—at the same time. At least two. There's not always a conclusive way to determine which one is more correct. Especially if they're questions and not answers. Texts are multivalent. No single human interpretation can capture the depth and richness of a text that, if we are clear in our creed, is meant to last from the early 600s until the end of this world. A primordial condition of monotheism, framed rhetorically. You already know this. Do I, being God, Who you recognize as God, really need to tell all of you? So I'll pretend to ask. Or a primordial condition of theological amnesia. We forget not just who we are, but where we came from, even when God is literally right there in front of us, or we're at home, in our real home, the only home our progenitors knew—I mean paradise—and we're willing to throw it all away—for a tree, at that, "and a kingdom that never decays." That we have to be told about the Covenant suggests we need(ed) a reminder. We're no longer in God's presence. We're embodied.

Our bodies have physical limits.

Expiration dates.

I've always found monotheism to be the easiest part of Islam, the thing that most attracts me. All prayers end up in the same inbox. All of us are equal before Him. The hardest part is the Covenant of Am I Not? Not just that I've always known this—that part is nice, really—but that I'm *responsible* for it. If I don't live up to its implications, I might go to hell. How have I come to terms with this? Not easily and not consistently. But I tell myself that if existence is a gift, if living religion is the means of paying back the debt for the gift of our individuality, for our self-hood, and the chance at self-fullness, the opportunity and obligation each of us has to become more fully ourselves, then there has to be an afterlife with judgment, where true fairness is realized. Because in order for there to be individuality, there has to be difference, and in order for there to be difference, there has to be contrast, and if there is contrast, there is inequality. Some people will have more power than others. I can't accept that the wrongs in the world will never be righted.

When Muslims are asked how they're doing, many of us reply *Alhamdulillah*, which are practically the first words of the Qur'an, not in the order they were revealed, but in the order Muhammad told us to put them in. "All praise is God's." It might mean we're doing just fine, that we recognize that whatever good there is comes from God—and, a little superstitiously, we're hoping it stays that way—or we're admitting that, no matter how poorly we're faring, there's still blessing in how we're doing. It's a good way to answer a question or end a conversation.

From one God we traveled to one Covenant, and from here we move on to one Caliphate. Or, rather, one concept with countless iterations, beginning with two, a man's and a woman's, a template for everyone else, from here to the end of the world. Because I'm going to tell you a story with five actors: There's God, of course, because it wouldn't be Islam if God wasn't in every encounter. There's the angels. There's Adam and there's Eve. And there's a very powerful creature whose backstory we know very little about, except that he sought out and sipped from the fountain of youth, except that he was so praised for his piety that he began to assume he was the chosen one. His name was Anakin Skywalker.

And he is the Devil.

4

ANAKIN SKYWALKER
IS THE DEVIL

I'M NOT SURE which of us—my mother or me—started watching the show first, but we both watched it regularly. Religiously. *Star Trek: The Next Generation* wasn't just mind-bending, it was heart-warming. You got the feeling that the crewmates were actually mates. They trusted, supported, and loved one another. There wasn't a need for an outsize personality—a team of remarkable individuals could pull off what no one could do on her own. And although the show was set in the future, it vibrated with the best of our past. It was about decency, creativity, curiosity, and a robust commitment to reason. The bright lights of the bright bits of the Enlightenment. On a spaceship. For a sick kid, as I used to be, *Star Trek* was more than just a balm for my psyche, though. It was a salve for my soul. My limits were not always going to be limits. There could be solutions to problems that plagued me, if even I might not live to benefit from them. And so, along the way, I fell for the science that made the show feel plausible, and my mother warmly encouraged me.

When I went to college, I thought seriously about studying physics, or astrophysics, or cosmology. I wanted to know where the world we lived in came from. I wanted to know what more there was to know. I believe(d) we had a future out there, far beyond the stars. Even today, I spend too much money buying (and usually reading) books about these subjects. Many of these passions were my mom's as well. It is, therefore, likely that she, like me, felt somewhat homeless. My mother also took religion seriously, though she was much more practicing than I have been. She loved the traditions of her pious ancestors; she was invested in poetry and literature, travel and history, and law and religion. Still, she felt very strongly about medicine and science too.

I am her child, perpetually an outsider like her, committed to spaces between which there is no longer much, if any, overlap. I find many people of faith alienating, even though I'd like to think I'm a person of faith. I find many people of science alienating, even though I almost pursued a life of science. For many people of faith, science is taboo. Evolution is a false god. For many people of science, faith is taboo. Revelation is an artifact. At no point, though, did either my mother or I experience our passions for the Creator and His creation as contradictory, but instead, and this probably doesn't sit well with many, we felt them to be mutually supportive. Science and religion thus weren't competitors, but partners. They still are. The more I learn about the universe, the deeper my faith becomes.

Some of the people who look at me skeptically when I say I believe in an unseen God superintending the universe take *Star Trek* not as outlandish fiction but as a possible future. But some of the people who look at me skeptically when I say I take the theory of evolution seriously take it as an article of faith that God creates all, however He chooses to, operating on levels of complexity we could never fully fathom. How could a religious person believe benevolent intelligence designed the universe, but in ways designed to mislead people of intelligence? That we evolved to be capable of discovering the order that pervades the universe demonstrates to me that this evolution was guided, with interests in particular outcomes, and in a clear direction: toward greater knowledge. Beyond that, it seems unlikely—and to me always a little bit incomprehensible—that physical laws alone could fully explain physical reality. We're just stuck in a series of tautologies.

There is always a first cause, a place you stop at, and it is hard to conceive of any believable cosmology that does not endow that first cause with at least some foresight and unique capacity. There is nothing that science can uncover that would make my faith waver, nor is there anything that religion can preach that challenges a scientific mind: the Qur'an all but says so. The Qur'an esteems, reflects, and above all else, nurtures knowledge about the world. Muhammad Iqbal said that the Qur'an describes three types of signs, the contemplation of any of which will confirm and deepen faith. They are the natural world (science), history (more broadly, I would say, the humanities), and revelation itself (religion), for which reason the Qur'anic word for verse means "sign." It's practically the seal of a prestigious university: *Scientia, historia, fides.* In other words, watching *Star Trek* is a way to know God.

I may believe that Jean-Luc Picard represents a tradition of statesmanship, maturity, and democracy that we'd be blessed to have in the White House but, tangents aside, his exploratory instincts are deeply spiritual. The *Enterprise*'s discoveries produced in me awe before the Divine. How is that any different from Rumi's poetry? Or a reverential *qawwali*? Some people date the conflict between religion and science to Galileo Galilei and his hammer blow against geocentrism. But that'd only be a problem if you believe scripture literally describes the structure of the solar system (or should). Some people date the conflict between religion and science to Charles Darwin's theory of evolution. But that is only a problem if you think that God's creation of a thing cannot unfold according to laws that, incidentally, He also set in place. I find it hard to understand why it is beyond an all-powerful, endlessly creative being to set a universe in motion that unfolds in infinite directions all at once, underneath which are laws humankind can discover and benefit from.

Some people who are keen to see faith disappear—they take *Star Trek* a little too prophetically (it might be spiritual; it isn't scripture)—propose that although belief in the supernatural hasn't yet gone extinct, it soon will. Perhaps the final defeat wasn't Einstein's or Marx's or Freud's (whoever still believes in him); rather, it will come with the discovery of alien life, a last nail in the creedal coffin. But that's only if you believe religion has no space for intelligent life beyond us.

Indeed.

God, and then beings "made" of light, smokeless fire, and earth.

THE FIRST SENTIENT species that God appears to have created were the angels; they are heavenly messengers made from light, which probably explains how they transport from place to place in the blink of an eye. Although they visit Earth, bring news to us and take information from us, they are not actually from Earth and may well predate our planet, if not our universe itself. They exist in a realm imperceptible to us, despite being inseparable from our ultimate destiny. They also do not have moral autonomy. They hear, and they obey. They can question God, meaning they can ask questions of Him, as we'll soon see, but they cannot act on doubt or sow confusion. They are obedient servants. This distinguishes them from another sentient species, the jinn, who were created from smokeless fire, but who, despite transcending the limits of our perceptible and sensual, physical reality, are (mostly?) terrestrial. They live among us.

Jinn have been limited in the Western imagination to genies, as in the kind who live in lamps and grant wishes in the triplicate. Disney's *Aladdin* captured something of the pop North American Muslim genie, although insider Muslim baseball makes jinn less Magic Kingdom, more X-Files. The Arabic word "jinn" comes from a trilateral root, J-N-N, which means "to cover" or "to hide";

madness, or insanity, is *junoon*—you might see the relatedness of the word, insofar as madness is the veiling of reason. The jinn derive their name from this root because they are hidden from us. They can act on us. We are mostly helpless before them. These aren't the only two words derived from J-N-N, of course. Another is *Jannah*, which means garden, as in the Garden, as in Heaven, the Garden of Eden, Paradise, all of which are probably the same space. The connection? Gardens, in the Islamic tradition—including *the* Garden in the afterlife—are walled off, and thus hidden from view; anyone who's driven through an upper-middle-class suburb in the Muslim world gets this.

We're going to get to the Garden in a second, because it's where the story of the original Anakin Skywalker unfolds.

THE ANGELS AND THE JINN share this much in common: they're well acquainted with one another, and share between themselves something of the relationship of the Valar and the Elves. (Tolkien's Age of Men arrives with Adam and Eve.) We poor humans have no sophisticated sensory apparatuses. Ordinarily, we can't see angels, or interact with jinn. Every North American Muslim knows the terrible pleasure of staying up late telling jinn stories, true to the folk Muslim belief that jinn can be crafty, and prone to terrifying pranks, stalking, haunting, and playing with their human peers-cum-prey. Because jinn share something with us that divides them from the angels: they, like us, are morally autonomous. We can recognize good and evil, but we don't have to pick one or the other. It's reasonable to assume that the Covenant of Am I Not? also applies to all jinn because after death they, just as with humans, will be resurrected, judged, and found wanting or wanted. Which is important, because somewhere way back when, there was one jinn in particular who was very pious, and very interested in immortality, and found the confluence between these two when he made a prayer for life until the end of this world, and that prayer, on account of his fidelity, was answered.

If prayers are wishes, or wishes are prayers, then be careful what you prayerfully wish for. Palms raised up to the sky, Muslims ask for blessings to be sent down, balms for our fears, treasures for our debts. Genies grant wishes.

He was delivered a burden.

"Make not your own hands," God warns, "the source of your own destruction."*

A LONG TIME AGO, in a Jannah far, far away, God had an announcement to make. Before the angels assembled round His throne, God declared: "I am making a Caliph on the Earth."

The Arabic word the Divine uses for "Caliph" is *Khalifah*. You might instantly think of Caliphates, of (tyrannical) governments or (medieval) monarchies, but that's because in the Islamic tradition we use the same word for two different things.** The *Khilafat Rasul Allah*, or Caliphate of the Messenger of God, is a political office, invented by human beings to meet a communal need; these Caliphates included dynasties like the dazzling Abbasids or fearsome Ottomans and, of course, the recent perversion of the logic of the Caliphate, the ISIS iteration. We'll get back to the Caliphate of the Messenger of God, but that properly belongs to post-Muhammadan, secular history. The Caliphate we're talking about here is the *Khilafat Allah*, the Caliphate of God.

It applies, very much like the Covenant of Am I Not?, to everyone who's lived, lives, and will live, beginning with Adam and Eve. In this context, a Caliph is someone who acts on someone else's behalf. Thanks to the preponderance of South Asians among Anglophone Muslims, and the strong desire instilled in us, by centuries

---

* Qur'an 2:195.
** The relationship between a "Caliph" and "Caliphate" is similar to the relationship between a "King" and a "Kingdom." But, of course, as we see here and subsequently, the former terms can have very different meanings. While all human beings are Caliphs of God, only a select few were Caliphs of Muhammad; the former denotes a moral and existential status, whereas the latter refers to a political officeholder.

of colonization, to make the Qur'an sound like the (King James) Bible, "Caliph" is often translated as "vicegerent," a word that I have literally never seen in any text anywhere in the world except in certain English renditions of Muslim scripture. (In case you're wondering if this is an isolated instance, I invite you to look up "supererogatory," an adjective that [a] I have likewise never seen outside Anglo-Islamdom and [b] sounds like an enhanced interrogation, but actually describes things you should do but don't have to.)

"I am making a Caliph on the Earth," God says.

He means a Caliph for *Himself*—God's representative on Earth.

Our story began with a simple exchange: God makes an announcement. The angels not only don't have the ability to act against God, but they also have no *desire* to—they are not morally autonomous creatures of light in metaphysical chains. But they are still sentient and free to ask questions, a capacity that may help them better understand the commands they are so eager to implement in the world. That seems a fair use of their sapience. The angels come across sounding rather like center-left Nordic Europeans when they follow up the Divine's Caliphal announcement with a curious question: "Will you make [a Caliph] who sheds blood and causes corruption?"

No background material of any kind precedes this story. In fact, the Qur'anic verse immediately preceding this story about Caliphs is addressed to hypocrites and kafirs, who are, respectively, people who pretend to believe Muhammad is a Prophet of God for reasons of cowardice or convenience, and those who pretend Muhammad is not a Prophet of God even when they know he is, and act vigorously to suppress his message, for reasons of cowardice or convenience. In both cases, people who are publicly dishonest about their private beliefs.*

---

* It is possible that this also subtly refers to the Devil who, prior to his fall, was possibly a hypocrite and who, after his fall, becomes a kafir.

God lambasts both categories of people for spreading corruption on the Earth, then proclaims His own omnipotence and omniscience, and then? "I am making a Caliph on the Earth." In light of this statement, the angelic query of the announced Caliph—are you making a violent, venal thing?—is a bit curious. Why would God talk about the evils of hypocrites and rejectionists, and remind us that He knows everything and can do anything, only for that to be followed, a few verses later, with the angels making their concern the very same one God had for hypocrites and rejectionists?

I said the Qur'an jumps from story to story.

I never said deeper threads of meaning didn't run through them.

A PROMINENT SYRIAN scholar referenced an early interpretation of this exchange at a course offered at the Islamic Center at NYU many years back. His reading—and it's a rather likely one, in retrospect—has profound implications for whether a Muslim worldview can be reconciled with current and future scientific knowledge. Now, Muslims should be okay with aliens. We already believe in the angels, for one. And we're fine with other forms of intelligent life on Earth—the jinn—for two. We should likewise be okay with evolution. We might have a reference to it right here, in the question the angels ask.

The only reason the angels expressed this concern, the Syrian scholar told us, was because—it might've been obvious to you already—God had already made a Caliph (or two, or three), and that hadn't gone so well. Maybe they'd been bloodthirsty and unscrupulous. So who was to say Caliph 2.0, or 3.0, or whatever iteration we are (on), was going to be any different? Otherwise, why would the angels ask such a thing? In the Islamic tradition, the angels would *never* doubt God's wisdom or capacity, which means they were very likely bringing up something from the past. It was their way of saying, "That's interesting, but remember the last time this happened?"

Maybe these previous Caliphs were other hominids; for example, according to some scholars, Neanderthals appear to have believed in an afterlife. And then Neanderthals were displaced and replaced by the waves of modern humans on their way out of Africa approximately fifty thousand years ago.* But maybe they were species on different planets. Maybe these were creatures we can't capture in any category. The Qur'an's point isn't for us to get lost in the possibilities, but to learn the lesson that is immediately relevant to our spiritual and ethical cultivation. God answers the angels' concern in the way that only a Perfect Being can: "I know and you do not know."

For a very long time, I considered this response very much the same way I considered the interpretations some religious folks provided for the Biblical Job's travails. In other words—and here's something I couldn't bring up with many Muslims—I felt something was missing. After responding to the angels, God then fashions Adam—who, in case you didn't see it coming, is the Caliph God speaks of—and teaches Adam "the names of all things." But what are the things? Suppose Adam is a stand-in for every human being, and not a modern, actually individuated person, in the way you and I are. In that case, this might mean God is present for humanity, in its synecdochic form, learning everything it will ever know. With our arrival on Earth and the beginning of our measurable history, we recover, in bits and pieces, what we once possessed in spades. Or this might mean Adam literally knew all things, and the coming fall from grace causes him to forget. Or maybe Adam

---

* In *God: A Human History*, Reza Aslan argues that belief in a soul precedes a belief in the idea of the Divine. Although, of course, I cannot as a Muslim hold this belief, nevertheless it seems true all the same that, for a very long time, ancient humans, and apparently some of our earlier hominid cousins, believed that some part of our self survived the physical death of the body.

In his work *The Qur'an & The Bible*, Reynolds notes that, in the Qur'anic exegesis, *Tafsir al-Jalalayn*, the Caliph of God, Adam, is "successor" to the jinn, who spread corruption on the earth. This interpretation helps to explain Anakin's furiousness over Adam's grand appointment. Keep reading.

is an actual person—the interpretation I prefer, and that concurs with orthodoxy—and God is either underscoring that what distinguishes humans from other species, and makes us worthy of Caliphal stature, is our ability to name things. Or maybe there's some truth in all of these interpretations.

Still, I proceed with the belief that Adam was a living, breathing human being, and while perhaps he was different in many respects from you and me—after all, he was designed to be immortal, and to live in paradise, not here on Earth—he was still real. And that opens up another possibility. Maybe God's response to the angels isn't just "I know, and you do not know." Maybe the verses that follow after, too, are part of His response. If the angels are skeptical of God's design of a Caliph, perhaps because God has gone down this road before, then certainly God might want to show them something about this new Caliph that distinguishes him from his predecessors. What things Adam is naming might not be mentioned because what matters is the act of naming itself. Our ability to use language to double back on ourselves, become aware of our own thoughts, process, categorize, and progress, might make us unique among other earthbound species (excluding jinn, of course).

Some summers ago, I was at a University of Chicago event to hear Steve Brusatte, a paleontologist and evolutionary biologist, reading from his book *The Rise and Fall of the Dinosaurs: A New History of a Lost World.** During a wonderfully illuminating discussion—of a compulsively readable work—we got to the question of what made humans different from (other) animals. Professor Paul Sereno, a University of Chicago paleontologist, noted that dinosaurs evolved bipedalism and opposable thumbs, and the only thing that distinguished us from them is our use of symbolic language. Read paleontologically, therefore—which is an approach to the Qur'an I'd like to think I'm the originator of—showing the angels that Adam can name names is a way of showing the angels

---

* On July 18, 2018, at the University of Chicago Seminary Co-op Bookstore.

what distinguishes Adam from previous Caliphs.* (Because, after all, the angels themselves are capable of symbolic language.) Of course, I'm not arguing that dinosaurs were Caliphs, although I'm not *not* arguing that either.

Suffice it to say, it's not clear what's being named. Rather ironically, and amusingly, God tells us He knows, and the angels don't, but in this case, we, the descendants of Adam, don't know either. The point of Qur'anic storytelling is primarily moral, ethical, spiritual. Maybe the absence of information is meant to remind us of our shortcomings, or maybe I'm wrong, and the gaps in the Qur'an, the spaces where God could provide details and doesn't, is meant to push us into exploring further and trying to find meaning and wisdom for ourselves. Or maybe both are true. As you know, I like that answer. The act of naming things—all things—speaks to the larger lesson of this story. It is the difference not just between Caliphs old and Caliph new, but between this Adamic being and the angels. Some creative curiosity drives human beings to go where no one has gone before and makes us qualitatively different from the rest of creation. Religion is not about constraining the mind; it is about disciplining the mind—to liberate its capacities.

Islam believes that earlier generations of Muslims were closer to the Prophetic spirit, and it is not coincidental that, relative to their time, earlier generations of Muslims were far more advanced than many of their peers in fields as disparate as law, ethics, philosophy, agriculture, ophthalmology, geology, astronomy, chemistry, mathematics, and aesthetics. We were better at naming things.

We were better Caliphs.

---

* The Qur'an is not a document that should be crudely mined for scientific truth—it is a religious text, not a curriculum textbook. I am also well aware that our scientific knowledge grows and changes over time; in matters of our belief, we should be chary of relying on any convergences, real or desired, between Qur'anic language and the state of our scientific knowledge. Still I can't help but contradict myself, in the spirit of paradox, and recommend David Reich's *Who We Are and How We Got Here: Ancient DNA and the New Science of the Human Past* to the reader curious to further consider this line of thinking.

. . . .

ONCE GOD HAS established Adam's superiority over the angels, He orders them to prostrate themselves to the new Caliph, which they all promptly do. Except that one jinn. You remember, I hope: the jinn who asked God to live forever so that he could worship God forever. That jinn is called Iblis in the Islamic tradition—cognate, perhaps, with the Greek *diabolos*, though it appears unlikely. I like to call him Anakin Skywalker, at least up to a point. (There's no Luke Skywalker rising here.)

Told to join the angels in bowing down to Adam, Iblis refuses.

Here is where Iblis goes from brooding Jedi apprentice, pugnacious but full of promise, to the heartless and genocidal Darth Vader, voiced by James Earl Jones. Elsewhere in the Qur'an, Iblis makes clear why he refuses to bow to Adam: "You created me from fire, and him from clay." * I've heard some Muslim commentators argue that this is the first instance of racism in history. Except, of course, racism is about some humans elevating themselves over others on the basis of certain physical features, which have no correlation to our capacity for, say, decency, rationality, or wisdom. Racism is a social construct with real and devastating consequences—but racism is also about baseless arrogance. At the end of the day, all are human. In this case, though, we have two different species, and Iblis is right—physically, at least, he is superior. While Adam can only lumber around on two legs, Iblis can dash from one end of the earth to the other.

Jinn have powers humans can only dream of.

So why isn't Iblis, aka Satan, aka the Devil, aka Anakin Skywalker, the Caliph on Earth? Doesn't he deserve it? Isn't he the right candidate for the job? And that's the point. Iblis had done all the right things. I mean, he was so prayerful, he was up there praising God like only the angels could—and he wasn't forced to. He was

* Qur'an: 7:12–13. This portion of the seventh chapter complements Qur'an 2:30–40 with an extended discussion of the tale of Adam, Eve, and Anakin Skywalker.

invited into the most elect assembly in existence, in recognition of and as a reward for his pious accomplishments. He knew the precise time of the day when prayers would be granted and used that moment to ask for life until the world ended and judgment commenced; he hoped, apparently, that he would pray for years and years and years and never stop praying. An endless life of prayer, the aspiration of every ascetic: to be speaking to God eternally. So when he'd heard God was making a Caliph on the Earth, he probably tilted his head to the guy next to him and whispered: "I won't forget about you when I get down there."

I mean, who else would it be?

God not only doesn't pick Iblis, though, but produces Adam, a new creation. How can He give such a tremendous responsibility to someone neither tried nor true? And if Adam wasn't really new, if the angels had really been referring to Adam as a newer iteration of a Caliphal creation that had been tried and found wanting, then why give such a mighty promotion to someone whose predecessors had been so thoroughly disappointing? Iblis is aflame. All his piety is washed away in one moment, which may signify that "envy burns up good deeds like fire does wood," as Muhammad said, or it may signify that Iblis's piety was simply self-righteousness all along. Put my forehead to the ground for this ugly bag of mostly water, Iblis asks? It's like a redux of the Covenant of Am I Not?, in that God is right there, before him, undeniable. But Iblis not only rejects this command, which God literally issues to his face, but he doubles down, vowing to bring Adam low, thereby proving that he is superior, that he would've been the better choice, that any jinn beats any human, any time, any place.

The stage is set.

GOD TELLS ADAM, and his partner, elsewhere named Eve (and yes, she drops in on this story unannounced; welcome to the Qur'an), to dwell in Jannah, to go wherever they like and eat from whatever they like, except of course for this one tree, which is off-limits. Naturally, what do they do? Satan whispers in Adam's ear, or in both their ears, and convinces them to go for it. He even talks up the tree. "Shall I lead you to the tree and to a kingdom that never decays?" Which is an odd invitation, given that Adam and Eve are already immortals in an undying Garden, but maybe Satan was just an outstanding salesman. Maybe he's promising them something more. Maybe they just want to know what'd happen if they eat from the tree. Just as with God's order to Satan, He issued this order to their faces, and now God appears to be 0 for 2. Maybe they willfully disobeyed. Maybe they slipped up, forgetting, sinning—a catastrophic, earth-shaking oops. Maybe the reason why doesn't matter that much.

So far, as you'll note, Adam, Eve, and Satan don't have much separating them, even given that they are from two different species. Because Adam and Eve ate from the tree. (In the Islamic version, this is not Eve's fault; either they are tempted together, or Adam convinces Eve to make the most consequential decision in human history with him, but rest assured, many Muslim men, like many men everywhere, will not be deterred, and will find other excuses to subjugate, oppress, and denigrate women.) On taking a bite, Adam and Eve become aware of their nakedness. They already were conscious, but now they feel the sting of conscience. And God confronts them. He knows what they've done, but He still has to voice His disappointment and explain what happens next. They are to be cast out, to live lives on Earth, full of hunger and need, but He doesn't abandon them to themselves.

He teaches Adam words of repentance; Adam repeats these, and he's absolved.

Eve, too.

They made a mistake. They recognized their lapse in judgment. They apologized. God doesn't say they can come back to the Garden, that everything can go on like it did before. But He does wipe their particular slate clean—the consequences of the error are inherited, while the error itself will not count against them in the afterlife—and their descendants will be born blemishless, free of fault and stain. Islam has no original sin. Jesus is our Messiah, but he does not need to die for our sins. All we have to do when we go astray is ask God for forgiveness, and we know how to because God teaches us how—He promises to be in touch with Adam, Eve, and their progeny, from time to time. That's the origin of prophethood; revelation kicks in when humans err, out of arrogance or amnesia or what have you. God teaches the same basic truths to people from every time and place, the broad outlines that Muslims believe inform the original editions of the great faiths. Hence Noah, Abraham, Moses, Jesus, and John the Baptist, among many others, were Muslims of a kind.

But before we get ahead of ourselves: God being God, He already knew they'd fall. Remember what God said to the angels? "I am making a Caliph on the Earth."

But he made Adam and Eve in Jannah. When the angels said, "Will you make one who sheds blood and causes corruption," little could they have imagined what God meant when he said, "I know and you do not know." Adam and Eve only end up on Earth when they fall, and land, disoriented and confused, on the planet we now call home. The one the angels should've been worried about was the worshipful one who was treated as one of them, even if he was a jinn.

Which is how Anakin Skywalker comes in.

THE NINE *Star Wars* movies have been of radically uneven quality; the original three are widely considered the best. While I personally consider Episode VIII to be outright heresy against Luke Skywalker, the series really began to go downhill with the prequel trilogy, which tells us the story of how Anakin Skywalker, promising Jedi, became Darth Vader, menacing Sith. To save you several hours, here's the premise. Young Anakin Skywalker is born with an unusual awareness of the Force. He's very talented, but the Jedi Order is wary of training him. Still, they eventually take him on, and Anakin does indeed become a formidable Jedi. But there is anger in him, fear, doubt, and even despair. He begins to have dreams that the woman he loves, the mother of his children, Queen Padmé of Naboo, will die.

He doesn't know how or when, but he believes it'll happen.

Chancellor Palpatine, who is in secret the wicked Darth Sidious, has had his eye on Anakin for a long time. He wants to turn him to evil, to support him in his bid to conquer the galaxy. Because he can't do it alone. Palpatine first strikes up a relationship with Anakin in his tween years, and in Anakin's adolescence Palpatine becomes the supportive mentor and champion the young man believes he lacks among his fellow Jedi. Bit by bit, Palpatine whispers evil to Anakin, and when Anakin reveals that he believes his wife is going to die, Palpatine has what he needs. Anakin's weak point. At an opera (or maybe a giant bubble show, it's not really clear), Palpatine drops hints that he knows about the dark side of the Force, and only the dark side of the Force can save Padmé from death. Events are set in motion, and Anakin eventually attacks the Jedi to defend Palpatine from certain death—because only Palpatine, as he's come to believe, can save Padmé.

The desire to do good leads to evil. But that's not the worst of it. Anakin's turn to evil leads his wife to confront him, and, in a fit of rage, he attacks her; she, wounded and inconsolable, either dies of her injuries or of a broken heart. Anakin set in motion the very chain of events he had set out to prevent. His desire to save Padmé from death is the very thing that caused her to die. He lost his soul and lost her anyway. Many science fiction movies flip our sense of causality in this manner. This is kind of what happens in the Qur'anic story of Adam and Eve. Satan, worshipful and obedient, gains access to long life. He gets what he wanted. But, upstaged by Adam and Eve, the Caliphate usurped—especially galling since other Caliphs appear to have failed before Adam—Satan sets out to prove Adam and Eve aren't worthy of the title they are promised. But it is Satan who causes Adam to fall, and it is the fall that leads to Earth, and it was on Earth the couple are meant to be Caliphs. Satan's desire to deny Adam the Caliphate is the very thing that causes Adam to become Caliph. God never told the angels that humans won't be flawed.

He tells them that there's more to the story.

What distinguishes Adam and Eve from Satan is not moral agency, nor even innocence. Adam and Eve make a mistake. Right after being told exactly what not to do, they go ahead and do it. But unlike Satan, who vows after his disobedience to prove God wrong—a rather blockheaded strategy, given that the latter is omniscient—Adam and Eve fess up. That's what makes humans Caliphs. Not that they don't make mistakes. Not that we won't screw up. Because we will falter, fail, hurt, wound. But we can make up for it. Our repentance doesn't change the harm we cause. But in admitting our wrongness, we rise to the stature God gave us. Because perfection is reserved for God and, in admitting our imperfection, we understand Who God is. To know oneself is to know one's limitations. And to know one's limitations is to know God—the limitless. As God told Muhammad, "I was a hidden treasure, and I wished to be known."

Adam never had what Satan had. He lacked those powers, those abilities. His strength was his honesty about himself. That is the first virtue. It is hard to look in the mirror. The second virtue is to keep looking. It causes discomfort, but life itself is characterized by a persistent, unavoidable discomfort. I used to think that this anxiety, this leftover cosmic background radiation originating in our fall and exile, was precisely because we had been pushed out of home, and we walk around, even now, with the unease of someone uprooted. Now I think it is something else, or maybe something else in conjunction with the first thing: maybe the anxiety is a gift, a feeling instilled in us by God—and perhaps His mechanism was the evolutionary causation mentioned before—to remind us that this is not where we belong, that we have another destination, that our end is our return, and so nothing, no matter how long it lasts or how intensely we feel it, will ever be enough to fill that hole, to ease that pain, to reassure that troubled soul.

During a very low point in my life, the story of Adam, Eve, and Iblis gave me strength. I repeated it to myself as if it were a kind of zikr.* Who knows how many tens of thousands of years separated us, and yet, for me, for a believer, the story of Adam, Eve, and Iblis is more than just a chapter in prehistory. Their example resonates today, if even that means shining light on the parts of ourselves we'd rather nobody else have a glimpse of. Much of my thirties had been the struggle to find myself after a string of unfortunate events and ill-thought-out decisions. Who was I really? Who was I supposed to be? What did my future hold? And I was astonished by the mistakes I had made in the course of my adulthood. I'd wasted years. I'd squandered much of a decade. Maybe there was no fixing these mistakes. Maybe I made a mess of my life, and that was that.

It took me a while to realize that, at the heart of the Muslim narrative is this fascinating idea that to be human is to be meant for a great destiny—to be a Caliph of God on Earth. But to become the first Caliphs, Adam and Eve had to be forgetful and even dis-obedient. And so I made mistakes, yes. I would continue to make mistakes, true. But that did not mean that I was a mistake.

Because I was made to make mistakes.

---

* Like *salat* (ritual prayer) and *du'a* (supplication), *zikr*—meaning "remembrance"—is a specific and Prophetic form of Muslim worship. It is especially favored in Sufi circles, but by no means limited to them. In many forms of zikr, the worshipper repeats, concentrates on, or meditates about specific names and qualities of God in order to draw herself closer to the Divine, purify her soul, and better understand herself, the universe, and the Creator.

5

....

FLOOD FROM A MACHINE

ON THE INSTRUCTIONS of the Prophet Muhammad, Muslims mark their calendar by the cycles of the moon. The first crescent moon is the first day of the lunar month, each of which is 29 or 30 days long. (The lunar year is 354 or 355 days long.) Some Muslims believe that the date can be calculated astronomically, whereas others—and I am in this latter camp—believe astronomic calculation is necessary, but insufficient: visual sighting of the first moon phase is also required. In the first camp, people will go with a calculation alone. In the second camp, my camp, people will wait up the first possible night on which the first crescent can be seen, but unless someone sees it, the new month will have to wait for the next day. Of course, it must be a scientifically plausible sighting, too. In the year that I write this, Ramadan is either April 12 or 13. If someone claims to see the new crescent before these two dates, we can confidently dismiss this report (or assume some grave cosmic event has changed the relationship between Earth and moon, but that is less likely, even if also a plot device from H. G. Wells's *The Time Machine*).

If nobody sees the first crescent moon for April 12th—and usually observatories and experts are involved in making and confirming the sighting, not Abdullah, the generic and universal mosque

· 67 ·

announcements guy—then April 13 it is. Incidentally, every Abdul-lah also embodies resilience. Every week without fail, after Friday Prayers, when most worshippers are busy with their supererogatory devotions—or rushing out the door, back to their jobs, for while our interfaith conversations might be increasingly Abrahamic, our weekends remain resolutely Judeo-Christian. At that inopportune time, an Abdullah makes the official announcements. Invariably these announcements include dire warnings of the penalties to be incurred by nefarious double-parkers, but invariably nothing ever happens, except, of course, for the same thing: continued double parking and continued threats of penalty. But Abdullah never loses hope. He could live 950 years, and he would keep making the same announcements. After his death, there should be no announcements for at least one Friday in honor of American Islam's Chick Hearn.*

But back to Ramadan, the ninth month of our calendar, the name for which derives from or signifies intense hotness, which, when you keep in mind that the religion emerged from a scorch-ing desert, must imply something wickedly warm indeed. But that might not be the first thing that comes to mind. If Ramadan is fa-mous and infamous for anything, it's intentional deprivation. No smoking, no sex, no food, and no drink—no, not even a sip of water—throughout the daylight hours. So you get it in while you can. One of my favorite Ramadan memories is one from child-hood: I'd stumble downstairs, only nominally awake and, in legal terms, hardly conscious, and scarf down a breakfast that was as necessary—you have to carb-load and overhydrate to survive the

---

* A longtime announcer for my beloved Los Angeles Lakers, the late Hearn passed away in 2002. What do the Lakers have to do with a book about the future of Islam? "Who controls the past controls the future." When my father came to this country, many of the sports were no doubt unfamiliar, this being the early 1970s, well before the age of satellite television, to say nothing of the internet. He gravitated toward basketball and specifically the Los Angeles Lakers, precisely because two of their prominent players, Jamaal Wilkes and the legendary Kareem Abdul-Jabbar, were Muslims. My father was not alone in his fandom: In western Massachusetts, in a corner of a state otherwise populated by fanatic Celtics fans, there is a cluster of believers in our Lord and the purple and gold. May the Divine give us victory over our enemies.

day—as it was disgusting. Have you ever gorged before sunrise? Then I'd pray, try to fall asleep on a bloated stomach, suffer the gas and the cramps, until, by late afternoon, I wished there were just something, anything, in my body at all. And then repeat.

For medical reasons, I can no longer fast, which has changed my experience of the month. Because I do not partake in the evening *iftar*, the break-fast meal immediately after sundown, more and more of my focus is on the spiritual side of the month, which increases in significance as the end of the month nears. When the fasting person's body is at its most depleted, when their most basic physical needs are increasingly going unmet, that is the moment their door to God is open the widest. Islam is not a religion that rejects, or denigrates, sensuality—for example, we have no taboo on birth control, we celebrate sex for its own sake, and the vision of paradise we put forward is sometimes erotic—but Islam does preach that, in this world, an excess of food, drink, sex, or money works at cross-purposes with spiritual intimacy. Perhaps an apt analogue to the overall structure of Ramadan is an inverted Russian nesting doll. Inside one is another, larger one. Tucked inside Ramadan are the blessed last ten nights, one of which is the Night of Power, Laylat al-Qadr.

It is a night the Divine and the world He created are at their closest.

If Islam is a religion of intimacy, this night is the zenith of it.

MUHAMMAD WAS DULY informed which specific night of Ramadan was the Night of Power, but on his way to announce the good news to his community, he encountered two of his followers bickering and was so distraught by their contentiousness that he forgot the date that had just been vouchsafed to him. (One wonders what he'd have to say to all of contemporary Islam.) Suffice it to say that God decided not to send him a reminder. The best Muhammad could do was tell his community that it was one of the last ten nights, and my co-religionists, as fearful of uncertainty as any other faith-based community, decided to pick one and run with it.

For Sunnis like me, the Night of Power is presumed to be the 27th night, even though we might have made that up. Others argue it is the 21st, or the 23rd, or the 25th, or the 29th. (Why no even-numbered nights? Muslims prefer odd numbers, insofar as God is One—peerless and pairless, He is odd.) The upshot is the same: the spiritual seeker should stay up as long as possible, and as many of these nights as possible, for that Night of Power is, as the Qur'an reports, "better than a thousand months." That's four-score-and-three years. Meaning that, with all those Ramadans, Muslims live longer than they'll actually live.

WHEN I WAS YOUNGER, however, the deep significance of Ramadan was not entirely or even meaningfully apparent to me. I surveyed the landscape and timescape of Islam and felt overwhelmed by the tasks set out for me, which were eagerly communicated to me and added on to as if learning ten more things we had to do was a good thing. Why burden me with more responsibilities? Why give God more reason to punish me if I fail? Why is there a prayer for exiting the bathroom? Why are there so many days and nights—especially nights—when prayer is recommended above and beyond its normal value? Seriously, the bathroom? Initially, I found this extensive spiritual apparatus to be oppressive, and I'm sure many other people do too. Unsurprisingly.

If you're told that if you don't do something, you'll go to hell, then you marvel at all the things you have to do just not to get yourself ceaselessly incinerated. God comes across as a capricious tyrant. As I've grown older, I've come to see that these various sacred practices and blessed moments (and consecrated spaces and lands) are points of entry, ways to infuse our lives with meaning, serenity, and grace, and that numerous different options are offered not because all of us are expected to do all of them (we all fall short), but because each of us has various spiritual strengths and weaknesses.

Maybe the command for prayer is meant as a form of mercy for those for whom it is easy, giving them succor and nourishment, even as there are those for whom it is difficult. For them, I have come to believe there are other ways to the Source. I can't forget the scene in *The Autobiography of Malcolm X* when Malcolm Little—the future X—learning (Nation of Islam) Islam in prison, is told to get on his knees to pray, but he can't bring himself to. It's a relatable moment for, as I write this, it's a peaceful evening, if a little cold, because the landlord hasn't turned the heat on yet. I can pull a Qur'an from the shelf and read. I can do some zikr, though I haven't done the daily litany of zikr my Shaykh has assigned me.

But I haven't prayed. It feels like the hardest thing I can do. There is so much lethargy in me—maybe a consequence of all my sins, maybe resentment from having been forced to pray as a child, maybe disgust with all the people I see praying who never seem to change but practice and communicate a prayer-based self-righteousness, suggesting that one can only be a good person through religion— that is as disgusting as it is off-putting. But maybe these other points of entry—namely, Qur'an and zikr—exist so that I still have some easier means of intimacy with God. I'm pretty sure that doesn't excuse me from the many days when I fall short of praying all my prayers, but at least it keeps a door open, and I'm still talking to Him.

I also see further value in differentiating days and months into hierarchies of sacredness. Otherwise, life gets weighty and weightless at the same time: time sinks into a slow-moving sludge as the interminable hours of each day press upon you; but time also flies by as indistinguishable days fuse into a forgettable haze. The Urdu poet Dard wrote, "Ho 'umr-e khizr bhi to kahange be waqt-e marg: hum kya rahein yahan? Abhi aye, abhi chale."* (Even if we were to live forever—literally, live to the age of the Immortal Khidr, mystical teacher of Moses—still, at the moment of our deaths, we would ask: What time did we spend here? We just got here, and now we're leaving.) There are weeks that bleed into months, months that bleed into years, days that never seem to end, but whole stretches of our lives that are over before we can even appreciate them.

---

* As far as I can tell, all Urdu poets took noms de plume; Dard's is my favorite. His meant "pain."

What can infuse this time with richness, purpose, meaning?

For someone who might be in the middle of his life, and caught in an avalanche of obligations, these temporal interruptions are literal godsends, because they give me moments when I can get a little closer to God and a little farther from the drudgery of routine and the blandness of too much of everyday life. This world is crisscrossed by currents of piety, rivers into which we can jump, all of them pathways to the ocean, invitations to swim in the majestic Infinity of Oneness. Indeed, as the mystics say: "The Sufi is the son of the moment." The offspring of the instant in question. We will have time to talk about Abraham and Ishmael, Hagar and Muhammad, but first, we should stop to see a man who tried for a very long time to get his people to go along and mostly failed.

Because all of this still has much to do with the life to come.

And the life that gets you there.

NOAH IS ONE of the most revered figures in the Islamic tradition. Yet his life was, by the standards of our frenetic world, rather dull. At least the antediluvian portion. That inundation came much later, though, and before that his life, by any secular measure, amounted to a spectacular stretch of nonsuccess. By the Muslim reckoning, he preached 950 years before God decided to flood at least the part of the world in which he lived (the Qur'an does not suggest a global catastrophe), and in many of those nine-point-five centuries, preaching submission to God was Noah's primary function, his heavenly burden, his metaphysical calling, and no one answered.

He couldn't even get his whole nuclear family to go along. You'd think his kith and kin would come along if only out of pity—because, after all, nearly a millennium of fruitless exhortation should at least provoke some sympathy. I sometimes talk about the things I nowadays wish I'd learned back when I was in Sunday school, although in fairness what makes sense to a forty-one-year-old probably wouldn't have carried much water for a fourteen-year-old. I don't mention enough the many things I was taught that I am very grateful for, that made sense back then and make even more sense now.

I should.

One of the stories I was taught concerned Islam's founding generation's response to Noah's track record, a story I can make much more of now, in the long spells of listlessness that characterize (my) middle age. Muhammad's companions didn't ask how Noah kept up for so long or why he had so few followers, or at least not that I'm aware of. The early Muslims appeared, of all things, envious. Envious! Because Noah had more *time* than they did. They calculated that, given their shorter lifespans, they could never be resurrected before God for judgment with as many praiseworthy deeds as Noah and his few followers accumulated in their very long lifetimes.

This was, my Sunday school teacher taught, one of the reasons why Muhammad's community was made aware of the Night of Power, when it is not only the case that Satan is restrained, as in the rest of Ramadan, but that the angels, and the spirit, dwell among us. It is when a command of peace comes down from on high, which Muslims are so concerned to be present for that we spend the intervening days asking each other how the previous night felt, to see if it gave off those special Night of Power vibes.

We even like to study the weather for portents—what did the sunrise evoke? Was the temperature hot, cold, or mild?

Did the air feel calm and peaceful?

Thus the heart of Ramadan compensates Muhammad's Muslims for our failure to experience a rather unusual achievement: hardly anything at all. We are reminded that the point of the action isn't the outcome but the intention. That we may spend years or even more of our lives pursuing what we believe to be the right thing, but never bring anyone around to our point of view. That we can believe passionately that there is a cause worth fighting for—it might be bringing people of different faiths together, undoing the generational scars of racism and bigotry, or the liberation of our people from occupation—and yet we might, time and again, just slam into a wall, or be slammed into a wall. It might be the overheating of our planet, which makes the scientists into Noahs, warning of disaster, unheeded, even as some of the people who insist Noah was flesh and blood deny that there could be any flood at all.

I suppose, in our day and age, when there will be no more Prophets to warn us, someone has to explain to us that the flood-waters are coming.

And yet, on we go.

Even if we never get there.

At least, all of this is the theory.

SO MUCH OF ISLAM'S foundational aesthetics, our law and litera-ture, dates to a time when we were, if not necessarily the majority, still the dominant culture. Because of the circumstances of Islam's birth in the world, a triumphalist and even imperialist note has crept into many of our interpretations, and above all the Sunni ones, which are mine; beyond the dubiousness of this kind of worldli-ness, it is manifestly irrelevant in a world where many Muslims are marginalized or minorities. We have very few resources for making sense of times when we are in disarray. We are not a people who have gotten ourselves used to not shaping norms and values. This take on Noah—not of the flood, not of the victory of God over His enemies, but the long stretches of repeated failure—might offer us a way to look at Islam anew.

Yes, I am concerned to convey what Islam is. But I should also convey what Islam could be. In that, I have little patience for the unicorn of reform, that magical thing that somehow will solve all our problems. The way forward is behind us. Not in inventing new stories but creatively and thoughtfully returning to our oldest stories. The same lesson I have so much trouble internalizing is the same lesson I think I need most, and it is the same lesson I think modern Islam would greatly benefit from. I am, after all, a modern Muslim; my problems aren't that special. Muhammad's companions wished they had had as much time as Noah to worship and to venerate and to do good works and received the Night of Power, worth a thousand months, as a compensatory gift. We should have the same attitude, writ large. The world is not something to simply get through. Even, and maybe most of all, when it wounds. When it isn't going our way. Contentment is to hold two opposite truths in your head. That there is good in the moment, even if it feels bad. And yet, the moment is not enough. More must be done.

One of the most understudied lessons of *Star Wars* is that the most dangerous Sith Lords often start off as the most promising Jedi. Satan asked for the same thing Muhammad's apostles did. He knew that there was a time of day when any prayer would be answered, and what did he ask for? Immortality! So that he could worship God until the end of the world and the judgment of each and all. But what happened? The gift he asked for turned on him—either because his piety was all for show or because, at the first shock to his system, his piety evaporated and was replaced with twisted enviousness. Instead of a life spent in the achievement of good, he burned through his decency with resentment, jealousy, and rage and will spend lifetime upon lifetime calling men and women to terrible acts. *Ho 'umr-e khizr bhi*. Even if we were to live forever. We Muslims believe that anyone with a speck of goodness and decency will eventually be liberated from hell. But we don't believe you'll be exempt from it just because you wear faith on your sleeve. Go to heaven, and you're set for eternity. Fail to make it there, and your eternal future is dicier. In the classical Sunni tradition, the less you know about God, the Qur'an, and Muhammad, the more likely you are to go to heaven. Because we're a classical *Star Wars* religion. (*Star Wars*, like Islam, was better in its infancy.)

In an age when some Muslims have arrogated to themselves the right to punish people based on their perceived moral status, it is instructive that our founding tale isn't about people of other faiths. Satan was the embodiment of the perfect Muslim. Anakin Skywalker was a Jedi. I understand why classical Islam was so tremendously, even paralyzingly, cautious on, for example, questions of moral status and final, eschatological outcomes. Can God actually judge you if you've never received revelation? Conversely, if you have received revelation, then acting against it is spitting in His face, even as it's also setting a terrible example for those around you, who are vulnerable to the authority and power wielded by men (usually men) of faith. Contemporary Islam is overrun by people who take exactly the opposite lesson, who believe their divinely inspired mandate is to bludgeon folks over the head with their fundamentals. It's unfortunate because it's going to drive people out of faith en masse and leave the Muslim world facing a terrible scenario. Like a city with a declining tax base, unable to restore its fortunes until it can invest in itself, but every year losing the citizens who could fund that restoration, we might be a religion in serious trouble.

We are suffering from a dearth in spiritual, institutional, and material resources to confront our challenges, which pushes people out, which in turn makes fewer resources available, and one day the trickle becomes the flood. Inundatio ex machina. That is why Noah matters so much. Yes, he knew there would be an ark and that he would be on it. But he also knew that the people he loved, his own flesh and blood, wouldn't. His preaching? Failed. His example? Not enough. Still, he persisted. Maybe God decided to flood Noah's people after they reached the point of no return; that is, even if they were to live forever, they would continue on their path of obstinacy and heedlessness. So God intervened to end them. Noah did not. Noah didn't have the right to punish, let alone the luxury of walking away. God acted, but God's is the judgment, for only God knows what path a people would remain on, just as He knew who Anakin Skywalker would've been ever after. One of the reasons I found *Star Wars: The Last Jedi* so appalling was the ruination of Luke Skywalker. He'd been a hero. He was transformed into a petty, whiny, irresponsible recluse.

But you don't have to win. Yoda died in exile. Obi-Wan Kenobi spent much of his life a fugitive. They knew they couldn't defeat the Empire. But they also knew that Luke could, that perhaps there was a chance for redemption despite all their tremendous failures. After all, their own decisions and actions, Obi-Wan in letting Anakin live, and Yoda in failing to stop Palpatine, had helped to bring about such conditions. It's not whether you win or lose. You might lose. The question is what you do in those days, for better or for worse. Satan's countless centuries became the doom of his life. God already knew which choices he'd make. Muhammad's people admired Noah for using the time he had in this life for preparing for the next. But they also admired him for using the time he had to try to save others. They wouldn't have wanted a flood for Mecca, and not just because they loved their hometowns. Once Muhammad was told by God who the hypocrites in his community were; one of Muhammad's closest lieutenants was worried he was one of them. Today, he's revered as the second Caliph, yet his greatest concern was that he was not really a genuine Muslim. They would've been afraid the flood might come for them. Not your sins, but our sins.

The second half of Islam's shahada is *Muhammadun Rasul Allah*—Muhammad is the Messenger of God. The last of them. Not the longest lived of them. There were lessons in his life. There were lessons in each of the Prophets' lives. Lessons about the value of life. Noah's is the lesson we must take, not just about the value of life, but of destiny and free will. Islam was born in triumph, but did it have to triumph? What if Islam had been born differently? What of those religious heroes who are not victorious—whose lessons might mean more to us now, in our present condition, when we ask ourselves if we are on the road to terminal extinction or in a dawn we cannot yet perceive?

It might feel fairer to stop excluding Islam from Judaism and Christianity, as terms such as "Judeo-Christian" do, and stick with "Abrahamic," because we share this great patriarch with other faiths. What makes Islam Islam isn't (just) Abraham, however—for we share this Prophet with other faiths. It's Hagar, the African woman, the Egyptian who might've been a princess and could've once been a concubine, who is the founding mother of our faith, and ours alone.

Judaism and Christianity not only trace themselves through Sarah but dismiss Hagar and her son Ishmael (and in turn Ishmaelites, who stand in for Muslims). They are wrong to. Very few people survive leaving their home for foreign lands and the consequent decline in status. Never mind to then leave again. Very few people wed a Prophet. Raise a Prophet. Anticipate the mercy bestowed on all the worlds. Survive in a desert. Oversee a city. Shepherd a destiny. Birth a civilization.

Hagar can say she did all of these things.

6

TWILIGHT OF THE IDOLS

WHEN IT COMES to Abraham and his partner, Hagar, and their child, Ishmael, we must rely on what the Bible says and where the Qur'an interjects. Take Hagar. She's Egyptian, at least. In her Nilotic life, she might have been Pharoah's daughter, a maidservant, a concubine. We don't know because the Jewish and Christian traditions overwhelmingly overlook her—indeed, today they overlook her importance even in the Bible—pushing her, mythologically speaking, to the margins, whereas the Islamic narrative begins her story with what happens after she leaves Egypt and joins Abraham's caravan (under unclear circumstances). The Qur'an doesn't provide a lot of detail, but then again, there's plenty of room for us to fill in the gaps, which, in this case, we surely should. She is too fascinating and too important to be left on the sidelines. Islam does not make sense without her.

In the Judeo-Christian tradition, Pharaoh gives Hagar to Sarah while Sarah and her husband (Abraham) are still in Egypt.* Hagar

---

* The Jewish and Christian traditions spend a lot of time on this story, although not so much on Hagar, may God's peace and blessings be upon her. Many Muslims, meanwhile, also often overlook Hagar. This lack of curiosity about our own history has been endemic to contemporary Islam and is one of the reasons why I write.

becomes Sarah's maidservant and then a surrogate mother; because Sarah cannot conceive, she urges Abraham to take Hagar as his consort, at least until she becomes pregnant. At birth, though, the child will become Sarah's. When Hagar starts to show, however, Sarah begins to regret her plan: what's to say that instead of giving her child to Sarah, Hagar won't be taking Sarah's place in the family—and that Abraham, overcome by his love for the child he wanted for so long, won't go along? Sarah launches a preemptive strike. Somehow, apparently, she convinces Abraham to banish Hagar, the mother of his child.* However it happened, the Qur'anic narrative really takes off here, with Hagar about to be abandoned.

The Bible locates the place of banishment, Paran, somewhere beginning in or near the Sinai and extending southward into Arabia. The Muslim tradition informs us of a specific location in Paran, a place called *Bakkah*, which later generations began to call *Makkah*, which came into English as Mecca.

Of course, there's nothing there at the time. Nothing at all.

ABRAHAM (BORN ABRAM) was raised in a Mesopotamian city of associationists; his father, Azar, was not just a fellow traveler on the polytheistic path but even made idols, too. Abraham stuck out like the proverbial sore thumb. He suspected that the Creator of the heavens and Earth was not any of the gods his people worshiped, and he searched exhaustively for Who that Creator must be. He looked to the moon, the stars, and the sun but soon came to believe that God could not be as inconstant as celestial bodies that rose and set. Whatever was behind the cycles of the universe—it is a fascinating conclusion—had to endure unchallenged and unchanged.

Abraham brought all the zeal of a convert to his community.

---

* All the same, Sarah comes across, in some Islamic traditions, as a rather unlikeable figure. In one source text, the Prophet Muhammad even says—and this is unusual—that his explanation of Sarah and Hagar's story is drawn from Jewish texts; ordinarily, Muslims believe that God instructed Muhammad as to these histories and personalities, and they were not drawn from Muhammad's prior or concurrent experience of Judaism, Christianity, or Zoroastrianism (another religion Islam believes was founded as an earlier iteration of itself).

His people, however, were not too keen about his newfound spiritual enlightenment.

So, in a brash display of teenage enthusiasm, making the kind of religious decision only an adolescent would think compelling, young Abraham went to his people's temple and took an axe to all their idols. How to proselytize with a hammer. He left the chief idol standing, however, and tied the axe around its neck. When the people discovered what had happened, they were horrified—but their suspicion fast fell on Abraham, who'd been asking all those impious questions. When Abraham was confronted, however, he mischievously proposed they ask their chief idol what had happened. I like to imagine he cocked a Spockish eyebrow as he made the suggestion.

"You know he"—the chief idol—"can't talk," they said. And anyway, the idea that their god had actually lifted an axe and chopped away at fellow idols was absurd.

Abraham responded, "So why worship a god who can't speak, let alone defend itself?"

This was not appreciated either. Abraham's people met his blasphemous behavior with a death sentence. They kindled a fire, just for him. Abraham must have been terrified, but devastated too. His father joined in, picking his faith over his flesh. Was he worried what would happen to him if he didn't? Did Azar have other children he had to think of? Or did he so love his faith and hate his errant son that he was in accord with Abraham's accusers?

God intervenes, though; the Divine has been watching Abraham all this time, moved by the young man's curiosity, his bravery, his ardor, no matter that it is immature and unformed. There is great promise there.

So God cools the fire.*

Abraham is thrown in, but he doesn't burn.** The flames cackle and rage all around him but never harm him. For days the fire goes,

---

* Qur'an 21:69.
** Qur'an 29:24.

and for days, Abraham sits in the center of it, untouched. Now it's the townspeople's turn to be terrified.

They banish the fireproof firebrand.

In the Biblical tradition, Sarah (who was known at first as Sarai) was his relative before their marriage (as indeed in many premodern and some modern societies, marriages between relatively close relatives, second or even first cousins, are not uncommon). So Abraham isn't entirely alone; still, he's lost nearly everything he's known. He moves across the Middle East, spending years crisscrossing the terrain, growing older—and lonelier. Sarah can't provide him an heir, or he can't provide himself an heir, or both. The precise reason why doesn't matter—what matters is he's getting on in years, and maybe he wants a son to prove he'll never be the kind of father his own father was. Maybe, he wants his own world to repopulate in place of the one he's lost.

One should not ignore how important children were either, especially in a time when there were no social safety nets. Nobody wants to grow old and frail in solitude, but it was all the harder when there was nothing else you could rely on. (His father and mother were long since dead, his extended family was probably not too keen, and he couldn't go back. Wouldn't go back.) We sometimes read these people as almost superhuman. We forget that they had to leave so much behind, and entire lives and worlds went on in their absence—lives and worlds I imagine they must've wondered about, childhoods they would've missed, families they would've grieved over. This is where Hagar enters the story.

Hagar isn't just a figure of Qur'anic importance; she herself is a kind of walking Qur'an. In most Qur'anic stories, after all, there are hardly any of the details we expect in typical narration, and the same can be said for hers. In the Muslim tradition, it's assumed that Hagar and Abraham are married, but whether or not they were—or theirs was another kind of intimate relationship—she becomes pregnant. So she, not Sarah, becomes the one who gives Abraham the heir he always wanted, while Sarah remains childless. The healthy baby is called Ishmael, for "God hears," because God heard Hagar's prayer. In the Arabic, *Isma'il*. (The "el/il" is cognate with Allah.) And no sooner are they celebrating the good news than God asks Abraham to give it all up. To get on his mount, ride deep into the harshest desert, well beyond any hope of survival, to go there and stop there. To abandon his Hagar and his Ishmael in the waterless wild. Prove to me you love Me as much as your father loved his idols, God says. Will you leave your son in the searing heat as your father left you in the searing heat?

I WAS FIRST and only told this story from Abraham's perspective. Ishmael can't have much of a perspective, of course. He's a baby. Hagar, on the other hand, was mostly absent from the story I heard, a bit player, even though she should be the headliner.

Abraham abandons Hagar and Ishmael in the desert valley that now hosts Mecca but which was empty at the time. That must have been impossibly hard for him—knowing his loved ones seem doomed while he gets to go back to food, water, shelter, Sarah, the rest of his caravan—but Hagar is the one actually being abandoned. With a child. Her child. Her little, little child. She must've been furious and frightened all at once. Because there was nothing. No shade, no trees, no nourishment, no persons, not for countless miles. After all, they'd ridden down there, the three of them, together, and seen nothing for a long while. And then they dismounted, and Abraham just hopped back on his ride again and meandered away. He's going slowly, as I imagine it, but too fast for them to catch up. She can't exactly run with a baby in her arms. He speeds up. She's falling behind.

She screams after him, and the camera zooms out; there are two little specks, her and him on his ride, one blurry shape a little fatter than the other, set against dusty rock mountains that reach unfathomably high. It's scorchingly hot. There's no one else around. What had she done to deserve this? Did he plan this all along? Did Sarah? Hagar calls after him, but Abraham won't turn around, and then she knows it. She's dead. Ishmael, crying, is going to be dead soon too. At least he'll die first. She had left Egypt.

Maybe she never knew her family. Maybe she knew them and had to leave them behind. Then she had this family. Then this family breaks into pieces? What kind of destiny is this? Which is when she thinks it, feels it, knows it. She understands her Abraham well enough to know that he couldn't—wouldn't—do something this drastic, this inhumane.

Like Khadija, the Prophet Muhammad's first wife, she believes in his character over what her eyes are telling her. Hagar is not just a professed monotheist but trusts deeply, almost unbelievably, in God, to a degree many people today would find impossible, even absurd. "Did God order you to do this?" she asks the silhouette of her husband as he rides north, back to Palestine. She asks this three times, demanding an answer. He is forced to admit that God is the reason he's leaving her and Ishmael behind.

And what does she say in response to this discovery? "Then He is sufficient for me."

Here's a woman with no clear social status. In the Islamic tradition, she's referred to only cryptically; Sarah is called Abraham's wife, but Hagar is called Ishmael's mother. And?

I'm okay with you leaving me alone, she says to Abraham.

AND WHEN HAGAR and infant Ishmael become alone, Abraham having disappeared back the way he'd come, she notices two high hills set off a fair distance from each other, and she decides to use those as lookouts. It'd take her too long to climb up the much taller mountains, and of course, she can't climb up either with Ishmael, but she can't exactly run from one end of the valley to the other with him in hand, either. So, imagine this. She's nearly delirious from the heat and the thirst. She wants to save Ishmael but he hinders her plan. So she sets him down. Down. By himself? By himself. And rushes, climbing the heights of the hills known to us as Safa and Marwa, looking for something, anything, someone, anyone. She knows God'll help her. But she knows people of piety don't wait for miracles. They help themselves until God helps them.

She might not understand how she'd be redeemed, and maybe, as the day grew darker and the temperature threatened to drop well below what anyone could tolerate without blankets or furs or tents, she ran more and more desperately between these little mountains, screaming for help.

MAYBE GOD HAD TOLD Abraham to ride south to a particular point, to move at a particular speed, to not pause for explanations or reevaluations, because all of this had to be timed perfectly. Ishmael began to wail, but as the story goes, he kicked his feet against the ground, or an angel's wing struck the earth just then, and water from a spring to be called Zamzam gushed out of the ground. This, at least, meant they would have some sustenance for some time, even though water in the desert is not enough: you need food, shade, companionship. Or just God.

A flock of birds passing by caught sight or sound of the water (I'm not actually sure how birds sense water) and began circling, drawing the attention of the Bani Jurhum, the Children of Jurhum, a tribe of Arabs who were right beside mother and child all this time. Their caravan was making its way just past the Beccan valley, but they wouldn't have had any reason to ride into a valley lacking food, water, and shade, or anything else of value. Until they saw birds circling—and that's the kind of sign, the kind of *ayah*, that you want when you're out in the desert.

It could be carrion or, better yet, water!

They sent out a search party and came across a babbling infant and a panting woman of unclear origin. Think for a moment how strange that must've been. How much it must've felt otherworldly, like these two were visitors from another universe. Sent to them. In a moment of desperation, when a weaker person would've caved entirely, Hagar stayed strong. She owned the well, she insisted, outnumbered, but the Bani Jurhum had her permission to water their camels and rest their weary bodies besides.

And word spread.

Soon a settlement grew up around the well of Zamzam, which Hagar oversaw, and she raised Ishmael there—Ishmael, who would become the patriarch of a new lineage, *al-'Arab al-Musta'riba*, or the Arabized Arabs.

The Arabs of what became Becca, and later Mecca, have Ishmael-ite origin, and they dispersed out across the Peninsula. Legend has it that Arabic itself emerged when Hagar's Egyptian and proto-Semitic tongues mingled with the Jurhum's related proto-Semitic, and out came the language we know today. I don't put so much stock in that, but I do put stock in the rest of the story. When I said that what makes Islam Islam is the Hagarite history—much of which either becomes uncreative and uninteresting hagiography or gets overlooked altogether—I should stress my intended expansiveness. It is not just about who Hagar is, or what she does, but in addition to these things, it is what she represents, the values and lessons of her life story. Hagar was expelled from Abraham's family not because she was found wanting, but because God knew her to be of strength sufficient to handle the task presented her.

Alone.

She raises Ishmael in a foreign land, she founds Mecca. She is a kind of ambling Islam. Or running, in this case, from one side of the valley to the other. She represents what we must come to represent. Our formative history is expulsion, migration, relocation, reinvention. Leaving home isn't a sign of meaninglessness or a problematic rootlessness, as blood-and-soil nationalists would have it, but an indication of divine favor: exile and displacement can be marks of chosenness. In Islam, being pushed out of your home isn't a suggestion God hates you; it's the strong hint that God believes in you. Even loves you. Didn't He adore Muhammad? Muhammad, a merchant taking caravans north to Palestine and Syria, a descendant of the Bedouin, a product of the Ishmael whose own mother and father weren't just non-Arabs, but of different ethnic origins from each other. This may be why the Prophet said the whole planet is a mosque. Other than a few places—bathrooms, graveyards, associationist houses of worship—believers can worship wherever they please.

Pray with your head on a polished wood floor or an open field. It's the same. It's why I'm so protective of our Western, liberal order: because citizenship isn't defined by blood or by ancestry, but by adherence to a common set of values, an extension of a spiritual perspective to a social reality. There's something deeply Islamic about the idea of a government under which people are accorded rights because of their agreement with a social compact. The color of their skin, the sound of their language, the heritage of their ancestors doesn't and shouldn't matter. All men really are created equally—by God. The story of Hagar, like the story of Adam and Eve, or Jesus and Mary, or Muhammad and Khadija, is a story of how God means for people to achieve great things beyond where they come from, beyond what you'd think they'd be able to tolerate, beyond their limits, where they find no limits.

Mecca is born as a fusion, an embrace between several different places and heritages. Though Hagar and Ishmael are immigrants, so too are the Bedouin. Hagar becomes a dominant influence in the city, while Ishmael is raised in an Arab milieu and organically takes on their language and culture. They, in turn, bring monotheism to the Jurhum. We have evidence dating back to early Hellenic cartography of a sacred city at the spot where Mecca is now located; among its ancient names is "Macoraba," which might be related to local terms for "blessed," or "sacred," or even "temple." For while it is true that Abraham had abandoned Hagar and Ishmael to this place, he does return, on several occasions, and makes Mecca more miraculous still. For one return, it is to join Ishmael in building the Ka'ba. For another—or, rather, what I presume is another occasion—it is for more distressing reasons.

Abraham was ordered to take the life of his only son.

Both of these stories are important; the first because the construction of the Ka'ba is the erection of the centerpiece of Muslim religious life, a structure that was a major, even topmost, concern of the Prophet Muhammad. The second, because it leads to a question every religious person has probably pondered. Namely, if God is good, why do bad things happen? In this case, though, it is more grievous—if God is good, why does He *command* a bad thing? Does that mean God is good, or religion is evil, or that religion can just as easily go one way as it can the other? Intermingled with these questions are assumptions. That good and evil exist only because God, and religion, label one as such and the other its antithesis. That good and evil depend on what God commands, and that what can be bad—bowing to someone or something other than God— can become good (for instance, when God commands the angels, and Iblis, to bow to Adam). Others believe that good and evil exist inherently, and the purpose of revelation is not to tell us what is good and what is evil but merely to remind us of the difference, because deep down, we've always known. There have been Muslim schools of thought that have come down on opposite ends of this debate, or occupied centrist positions. I wish this was a debate that was recovered and refurbished for today.

MUSLIM LEGEND HAS it that when Adam and Eve were exiled, they arrived at different points on Earth. Eve landed in Jeddah, Arabic for "grandmother"—as in Eve, our grandmother—while Adam surfaced in Sri Lanka. Somehow it was fair that the two of them would meet in what became Mecca, which is, of course, incomparably closer to Jeddah than to southern South Asia. But then again, since Adam's the one who ate from the tree, and convinced Eve to go along, I suppose it wouldn't be unreasonable to expect him to walk a little longer. When they finally met in western Arabia, they constructed the first iteration of the Ka'ba, what we might call the seminal Temple, the original House of God on Earth.* That

---

* The *New York Times* reports on what the historical record reveals about ancient Arabia: "Fossils from long-extinct elephants, antelope and jaguars paint a prehistoric scene not of a barren wasteland, but of a flourishing savanna sprinkled with watering holes." Nicholas St. Fleur, "When Human Relatives First Visited a Green Arabian Peninsula," November 2, 2018, www.nytimes.com/2018/11/02/science /arabian-peninsula-green.html.

structure quickly fell into disrepair, and it was many thousands of years later, when Ishmael had come of age in the new town of Mecca, that his father returned with a mission: to (re)construct the Ka'ba, to create a second Temple, which was never as formidable as the Temple in Jerusalem, but maybe that's because Adam and Abraham were humble Prophets, neither the mighty, monarchic Prophet Solomon nor the resplendent King Cyrus.

There's even a story that Adam and Eve put up a second Ka'ba, this one in Jerusalem, some forty years after the first one in Mecca. This pattern—of Mecca coming first, in the instance of Adam, of course, but also of Abraham, well preceding King David—reflects God's order of priority, with Jerusalem second to Mecca. When Abraham and Ishmael complete the Ka'ba, the legend is that the elder stood atop it and called out to the nations of the world, his voice amplified by God; according to some, all heard this invitation to God's House, which Muslims take up in the form of the hajj pilgrimage.

This means two important things. First, while there were many Prophets, most of them, indeed almost all of them, were meant for specific peoples. The Prophets of the Children of Israel were sent to the Jewish people; to this day, Judaism is largely not a proselytizing faith. (There were historical periods of exception, of course.) Even Jesus, in the Muslim tradition, was a (Jewish) Prophet chosen to preach to the Jews. He would return one day—he will return one day—for he is the promised Messiah, but in his (first) lifetime, his concerns were not, apparently, universal. Abraham is an exception, and a straight line can be drawn from him to Muhammad. We remember the rituals of Abraham, the running of Hagar, Ishmael's well of Zamzam, in the hajj.

The sacred days come to an end with the Eid al-Adha holiday.

Eid al-Fitr is the holiday at the end of Ramadan. It's not a hard one to make sense of. But Eid al-Adha is the bigger holiday, and in recent years, young Muslims have increasingly talked to me about it with serious disquiet. For it is "the Feast of the Sacrifice," the celebration of Abraham's willingness to heed God's improbable, disconcerting command. Why, these young Muslims wonder, more and more openly (and good for them for talking about it), are we celebrating God asking Abraham to murder his son? Sure, in the end, he isn't sacrificed at all. But still. God asks.

More than asks. He commands.

Isn't that Divine directive an enormity in and of itself?

As if it hadn't been painful enough leaving his infant Ishmael to apparently certain death not so many years back, now Abraham is asked to slit his son's throat as if he were no more than an ordinary animal, prepped for the kind of sacrifice that was common at the time. The future Prophet Ishmael is still just a boy. But Abraham has to tell him all the same, and Ishmael responds to this bewildering decree with uncanny calm: "You will find me, *inshallah*, patient." As if he is saying, I can't say for sure how exactly I'll react, but I know how I *want* to react. At the last moment, when Abraham's sharpened knife is up against his son's soft neck, a ram is placed in Ishmael's position, and the boy (and the father) are spared a horrific and barbaric charge, the animal taking the blade instead. I don't blame you if you now furrow your brow and ask who would want to believe in a God who asks such things.

But the story only makes sense if we see it from the larger view of Abraham's life and the still larger sweep of human evolution thereto. Abraham proves he is willing to give up his son, on God's command, just as his father had been willing to give up his son on his (false) gods' command. But that's not enough, God is saying. Prove to Me, it appears He's adding, that you love Me more than you love anything in the world, more than your father loved his deities. Don't just let them burn your son. Burn him yourself. It is not an expectation lightly placed on anyone; our task in the world is to love God, to put Him before all and each. So, so much easier said than done. Few of us can really adore God. There's a reason, after all, that Hagar is Hagar. The clue is in Ishmael's response to his father—"You will find me, *inshallah*, patient"—which echoes his mother's response to Abraham, "God is sufficient for me." There's a reason Abraham is Abraham. Power might demand responsibility, but responsibility invites the possibility of power. Maybe this was easy for all three of them. Maybe they're so besotted by God that they can't help but reflexively agree to whatever it is they are asked to do, which is why juvenile Ishmael is so equanimous—he, therefore, will also receive revelation.

He is a Prophet in his own right. Though this specific status is particular to Islam, nevertheless, all three religions consider him a formidable character.

They have his mother to thank for this.

IN THE BIBLICAL NARRATIVE, Ishmael, possibly wed to an Egyptian, himself of half-Egyptian and possibly half-royal ancestry, fathers twelve sons, each of whom becomes a prince. The oldest two were Nebaioth and Kedar, and Muslims usually posit that Muhammad's ancestry can be traced through either of these two sons.

When Muhammad was born, the Ka'ba still existed. Control over it made his tribe, the Quraysh, the first among (Arab) equals, assuming a pride of place within the Abrahamic lineage. The Arabs had no overarching polities, no kings or queens, no empires or governments of the kind their great Persian, Roman, and Ethiopian neighbors enjoyed. They had a kind of unity regardless. Even as they fought among themselves to an almost habitual degree, they all streamed to Mecca to pay annual homage to the Ka'ba. Still, there was a difference. The Arabs of the Peninsula recognized God as the ultimate Creator; nevertheless, most all of them associated deities with Him (a sin the Qur'an also lays at the feet of Trinitarian Christians). When the Ka'ba was built by his distant ancestors, it was empty; by the time Muhammad was born, many centuries later, there were 360-some idols inside.

Muhammad's mission as Prophet can be seen as a many-sided conversation with previous Prophets, or rather, I should say, with their followers. It was about reminding Christians that, while Jesus was the Messiah, miraculously and immaculately conceived, he was also no more than a Prophet of God. A very special but very human human. It was about reminding the Children of Israel of their covenant, but making it clear it was time to reunite the lines of Abraham, turning Jewish particularism into a boon companion of Muhammadan universalism, a journey as philosophical as it was spiritual. It was about reminding the Arabs generally of the primordial monotheism they'd once practiced. Clearing the Ka'ba of its idols and making it a shrine dedicated to God alone—again. It is, in that respect, a most ancient building, yes, but also a curious one. For it is very different than what Muslims ordinarily consider to be sacred space. It is the first of its kind, and now the only. There is no more Temple in Jerusalem. Only the Temple in Mecca. And what of it?

WE MUSLIMS CAN pray anywhere, but mosques are specially reserved for the five daily prayers to be performed congregationally. So, a lot of Muslims prefer to pray in mosques, free of distraction and alongside other people in worship, all facing the Ka'ba at the heart of Mecca's grand Sanctuary Mosque, or *al-Masjid al-Haram*. The perceptive reader will remember that the Temple Mount in Jerusalem is *al-Haram al-Sharif*, or the Noble Sanctuary. There is a reason the same word, Haram, is used: these two sites are twinned. As a very tall cube, draped in black, the Ka'ba also resembles few, if any, mosques, which are usually known for their domes, their arches, elaborations of the Greco-Roman architecture the Byzantines had brought to the Middle East. (How's that for a clash of civilizations: most mosques are cousins of the US Capitol). What does this cubical shrine remind you of except the Temple in Jerusalem, which was built, as a colleague, Rabbi Sarah Mulhern, once described it to me, in concentric cubes? There were outer layers that were more public and inner layers that were increasingly more exclusive until you reached the Holy of Holies. At the innermost sanctum of the Jerusalemite Temple, only a select few were permitted to enter, and only on specific, sacred occasions, such as Yom Kippur.

Unlike a mosque, you don't enter the Ka'ba to pray either. It's not that you can't enter, but that, practically speaking, there is no reason to enter except out of curiosity (or for maintenance). For one thing, what direction would you pray in? (There's only one other point on Earth where you can pray in any direction: the Ka'ba's precise antipode, which, Nuh Ha Mim Keller notes in his book, *Port in a Storm*, is helpfully located in a landless expanse of the South Pacific.) Too, there's *nothing* in it. The building is the House of God. It isn't God. And why would God need a house? He doesn't live anywhere. Islam, being an abstracted religion, does not believe God should be represented in physical form. If I may be so bold, the Ka'ba is a kind of emptied temple, but when I say "temple," I don't (just) mean a structure like the Jerusalem Temple; I mean the term we use to refer to everyday structures within which people of many faiths worship. If anything, the Ka'ba represents an inversion of the religious order to which Abraham had been exposed in his childhood.

Take the house of faith you grew up in, turn it upside down, and shake vigorously. It is no longer full of gods or goddesses, but of nothing at all; it's not to be entered but, at most, to be prayed in the direction of. Prayed at. A curious young Abraham, as I remarked earlier, found his people's religion insufficient to his sense of the order of things and rather brazenly modeled his discontent by marching into a temple and defacing the idols therein. Abraham represents a hinge moment in history, a pivot from one kind of morality to another, a rupture from an old order to a new one just beginning. It is not coincidental that Abraham wanted, above all else, a son; he who lost a father wanted desperately to be a father. To right a wrong. Then, given Ishmael by Hagar, he is asked to actively sacrifice Ishmael, an act worse than his passive abandonment of mother and child years before. How does one reconcile Islamic morality with a request for an action that should be considered heinous, and yet is feted on the most important festival day of the Muslim calendar?

There is an indication of what God was asking in a *hadith* recorded by Ibn Arabi:

> O child of Adam, each of you wants you for himself, and I want you for yourself, and yet you flee from Me. O child of Adam, how you wrong Me!

Or in this one:

> O child of Adam, it is your right from Me that I be a lover for you. So, by My right from you, be for Me a lover.*

Do you love Me, God asks? If so, prove to Me that you love Me as much as your father loved his idols. He was willing to let his son be killed for them. You should be willing to kill your son for Me. Exceed him in love for Me! Allah throws it out as a challenge; Abraham accepts. God replaces Ishmael with a ram at the very last moment, for He rejects the act as monstrous at the same time as He asks for it. Two truths can coexist right alongside each other, temporally speaking, the one ending where and when the other begins. This is why we feast on this day. Not just to honor the depth of Abraham's piety, the extent of his sacrifice, but also the condemnation of an act that subordinated human life to creedal belief. Yes, God asks: Do you love Me?

But He also asks: Do you really think you're supposed to be your father?

---

* For these two specific hadith, see Stephen Hirtenstein and Martin Notcutt's translation of Ibn 'Arabi's *Mishkat al-anwar, Divine Sayings: 101 Hadith Qudsi* (Oxford: Anqa Publishing, 2004), 44, 46. Of course, this does not answer the question of what a hadith is. In the Islamic tradition, we derive our moral code—shari'ah—from a robust, thoughtful, and principled engagement with the two sources of revelation, the Qur'an, which has already been introduced, and the life and example of the Prophet Muhammad. The latter is effectively communicated to us through what are called hadith, or "reports," which are either things Muhammad said (memorized and passed on by his followers) or things Muhammad reports God Himself said, as in the current instances.

And the trial is over. Ishmael is spared. The rituals that become the hajj are set in motion. The Ka'ba will be constructed. Not an endorsement of barbarity, but the very opposite—embedded within Islam, in the core of our calendar, the most important holiday of our year, is God's refusal to accept a human life for His sake. Even the life we take, the life of an animal, is consecrated through its distribution to the poor and the needy. From taking a life, we are giving life. That's what makes the Ka'ba empty. "It is not the flesh," God says in the Qur'an, "which reaches Him." God doesn't need things because God's not, to be crude, a thing. God has no form. God doesn't want action for the sake of action. God wants action by intention, and action to benefit the self and others. Do you love Me? God asks. Then never harm another human for Me.

Growing up, I was sometimes taught Islam as a story that began with all the Prophets setting the stage for the last of them. They became bit players, mere signposts on the path to Muhammad, as opposed to heroes in their own right, with historical circumstances and spiritual significance unique to them. Indeed, Muhammad once compared the collective enterprise of all the Prophets to building a house, in which one brick is missing; I am the last brick, he told his followers. A house of God, abstractly speaking. You have to understand these men on their own terms. And understand the women on theirs. Abraham could not have built the Ka'ba without Ishmael, but Ishmael would not have been up for the task if he had not been raised a Muslim, and he wouldn't have been raised a Muslim, let alone survived the desert, were it not for his mother.

In the opinion of many Muslims, Hagar and Ishmael are buried in a partial enclosure immediately outside the Ka'ba, an honor accorded no others. In some Muslim cultures, women aren't allowed to attend burials, but here is a woman, buried at the fulcrum of the world, the direction in which we pray whenever we pray. When Muhammad doubted himself, panicked after his first revelation of the Qur'an, it was Khadija who steadied him. She was his elder, then his employer, and then the foundation stone of his life. When she died, he was plunged into sadness and sorrow.

The only way God could console him was by briefly raising him up to heaven.

The only sustained description we have of paradise in the Islamic tradition comes from Muhammad's journey to Jerusalem and thereafter to God, passing through paradise on the way. Who did he meet? Other Prophets, like Abraham, Ishmael, Isaac, Jesus. Especially Moses. What did he get out of it? Prayer, five times a day, and communion with God. Many crude understandings of Islam dwell on the fact of sex and sensuality in our visions of paradise; it is telling, therefore, that those elements of heaven (which are, to be fair, present in the Islamic tradition) are nevertheless absent from the most famous Muslim story about heaven.

Instead, it's all about spiritual fraternity, mystical engagement, and love. Familial love, romantic love, Divine love. Some people say Islam needs its own Reformation. I would just say it'd be nice if we looked at the religion we actually have. Women are not objects but agents, not wallpaper but title characters, and often the cause of spiritual revelation. Earlier I asked if it was easy for the great heroes of Islam to meet the tasks that were delegated to them, or if it was a challenge. Mary gives us one answer: she was worshiping at the Jerusalem Temple—an honor she was eligible for, given her priestly, Aaronic descent—at the moment Gabriel approached her and announced the birth of Jesus.

When she was suffering the pains of her pregnancy, alone, cast out, unwanted, and terrified of the burden of bringing a child into a premodern world without a father—not that single motherhood is an easy thing now, either—she cried out to God: "I wish I was forgotten, and forgot myself." She was desperate, scared, solitary. But not by herself. Even as she wished she could disappear from herself and the world. Which is a pretty bleak way of putting it. But her love was enough for Jesus, who had no father, who turned out fine, who's the Messiah. Moses, too, was raised without his father in the picture.

Muhammad came into the world after his father passed out of it. His achievements are remarkable, although they are so rarely

heard or acknowledged in the West. Out of a small band of followers, he built a world; out of a city on the margins, he inspired a culture that sought to stitch together a planet; an orphan, he attracted
a group of followers that grew exponentially and may soon surpass
Christianity to become the world's largest faith. All because of a
woman, in a desert, with an infant to take care of, and no one to
take care of her. God chose her, because He knew she could handle
the task. Maybe she had in her what Abraham didn't have in him.
Maybe that's why the task fell to her and not to him. Maybe there's
something in that story we don't know. Maybe she was abandoned
at some point, and God wanted to see if she could do what He later
asked Abraham to do. To prove she loved Him more. We don't
know. We have no prologue. She took that to her grave, and every
day, pilgrims, repeating Abraham's cry—"Here I am, my Lord, at
Your service"—pass by her, over her and her body at the farthest
point of their circumambulation, and I know that she hears them,
and marvels at the shuffling of naked feet once over sand and now
over marble, millions of them, coming, and coming, and coming.

7

FRIENDS, ROMANS, COUNTRYMEN

CENTURIES AFTER ISHMAEL, a man of his line, now known to us as Hashim ibn 'Abd Manaf, was born. (Hashim wasn't his given name, but hardly anyone remembers that now.) He would be so influential that a clan of the mighty tribe of Quraysh were named after him—the Banu Hashim, or Children of Hashim. Like the rest of the Quraysh, their responsibilities and privileges included overseeing the maintenance of the Ka'ba, running the hajj pilgrimage, and governing Mecca. Much of that prestige is attached to them because of Hashim's efforts. The man was a skilled diplomat, a talented merchant, a born leader.

Hashim obtained trading privileges for Mecca in the Byzantine Empire, known to itself and its contemporaries as the Roman Empire. His skill abroad paralleled his prestige at home: he embodied the virtues of the noble Arab, which included generosity to neighbors, wayfarers, and strangers. Once, when Mecca was afflicted with famine, he spent so much of his wealth to alleviate the general hardship that he earned his honorific, "Hashim." It means "tears apart," alluding to how much meat and bread he tore into digestible pieces to feed his suffering homeland. But then, while leading one of his caravans through Roman territory, Hashim fell ill and died, and was buried in Gaza.

Hashim's nephew, a son by his brother and Yathribite sister-in-law, came to be known as Abd al Muttalib.* That wasn't his given name either. It means "slave of Muttalib," because he was once confused for an attendant in his father, Muttalib's, retinue. Not quite the honorific, but it stuck. Muttalib the younger was so widely respected that he personally oversaw the maintenance of the Ka'ba, and even rediscovered the miraculous well of Zamzam, the spring that had first popped up in the ancient Beccan valley to save Hagar and Ishmael. Abd al Muttalib had a son named Abdullah, who married Amina, also of Yathrib. She became pregnant, but Abdullah died before the child was born.

That son was supposed to be called Ahmad, an Arabic name that means "highly praised," except that the infant's venerable grandfather chose differently. Born in 570, the child was named Muhammad. This more intensive form of the same Arabic root foreshadowed Muhammad's legacy in the world—a Prophet who would be endlessly and intensely praised.

ABD AL MUTTALIB would be famous enough just on the strength of his sustaining the Ka'ba and unearthing the well of Zamzam, which heaped still greater praise and prestige on the Quraysh tribe. But there is another respect in which he was signally important, and it has to do with the rather convoluted politics of sixth-century Arabia. We will be jumping into some messy history, full of what are probably unfamiliar dates, likely cumbersome names, and often vexing religious and political intrigues, but all of it is worth it if we can do something outrageous: find new meaning and still more value in Muhammad's life, which would further his relevance to our time.

I don't mean to negate his life or revise it beyond recognition, but I do want to be more honest about the context in which he lived,

---

* Yathribites were the residents of Yathrib, two hundred miles north of Mecca.

to not only more accurately understand history—which is a good on its own—but to liberate Islam from that curse of the modern age, the conflation of faith with politics. Much of this has to do with how Muhammad's life is misunderstood. Whether in democracies, monarchies, authoritarian dictatorships, illiberal populist regimes, or "Islamic" Republics, Islam and government are often forced into an awkward embrace, which is bad for the religion and bad for the state.

But, paradoxically enough, one of the reasons Islam is hyper-politicized is because understandings of Islam are insufficiently conscious of its formative political context.

These understandings assume that Islam craves power because they refuse to realize or acknowledge how early Islam had no choice but to respond to the politics of the time.

The Arabian Peninsula of the sixth century was a kind of backwater, surrounded by great powers and their rivalries. To its northwest were the Christian Byzantines, the inheritors of Rome, who governed from Constantinople (today's Istanbul). To the northeast, Rome's great nemeses, the Zoroastrian Persians. Theirs was the Lakers-Celtics rivalry of that time. To the southwest was Christian, Axumite Ethiopia, which often acted in concert with its bigger Christian cousin, even though their varieties of Christianity were different. As you can probably expect, all of these entities politicized religion, or religionized politics.

Although for several centuries Jews had rarely been in power, going back to the fall of the Second Temple in the year AD 70, there were exceptions. One of these could be found in Yemen, in the southwest corner of Arabia itself, right across the sea from Christian Ethiopia. In or around 520, the Jewish ruler of Yemen, Dhu Nuwas, went to war with the Ethiopians and the Christian Arabs allied to them. The armies of Dhu Nuwas put large numbers of Christians to death, often in gruesome ways. This provoked predictable retaliation; with some help from the Romans, the Ethiopians sent an army under a viceroy named Abraha and conquered Yemen, retaining it for the Christians.

But nothing that happened in Arabia stayed put in Arabia.

Think of how the Cold War worked. The Soviets viewed any success by America's allies suspiciously, even if Moscow initially had nothing to do with the conflict in question. Likewise, the powerful Persians were discomfited by the success of the Christian Ethiopians in Yemen, and soon a pattern developed across Arabia. Many Jews and associationist Arabs fell into the Persian camp (while others, to be fair, sided with Rome, or even became Christians on top of siding with Rome). This particularly applied to the flourishing Jewish communities of Yathrib, which would become critically important to Islamic history in AD 622.

BUT BACK to that viceroy, Abraha.

Separated by the Red Sea from the Ethiopia that had dispatched him, Abraha declared independence and set out to establish his own Yemenite Christian dynasty. As part of his initiative to secure himself great power, Abraha set about to reduce—in the militaristic sense of that word—rival centers of influence and power. Religion and politics were so intertwined in the premodern age, a point we would do well to keep in mind as we study this history, that religious targets were political, and political targets were religious. Going to war with an enemy often meant going to war with his faith. Abraha tried hard to make Christianity the dominant faith in Yemen, which meant pushing back against a Jewish community with deep history in the region. (Some trace their presence all the way back to Solomon and the Queen of Sheba.)

There were other religious challenges to his quest for spiritual supremacy. Abraha built at least one grand church, but wasn't getting the kind of love the Ka'ba was. Associationist Arabs, who were still probably the overwhelming majority of the peninsula, preferred to go to the Ka'ba, disinclined as they were to attend church services. So Abraha decided he would destroy the Ka'ba.* Sans

---

*I have also read some scholars report his grand church was attacked by Arab tribesmen, for which he singled out the Ka'ba for retaliation.

Ka'ba, maybe the hajj pilgrimage could be redirected to Yemen, and the power and prestige that accrued to the Meccan Quraysh would be transferred to Abraha. In the Muslim sacred history that has come down to us, it is said that in or around the year Muhammad was born—in 570, but possibly very much before—Abraha sent a grand army to invade Mecca, destroy the Quraysh, and pound the Ka'ba to ruins. In the chapter of the Qur'an called "The Elephant," God explains how this scheme failed.

Abd al Muttalib, Muhammad's grandfather, was then the de facto ruler of Mecca and ordered the majority of Meccans into the high hills around the city, retreating before Abraha's mighty war elephants and many soldiers. Meanwhile, he and some followers kept guard at the Ka'ba, in what likely appeared to be a suicide mission. But Muttalib believed God would intervene to protect His shrine and, as the Qur'an records it, He did, dispatching a flock of birds that pelted Abraha's army with stones, scattering his formidable forces. According to some, Abraha died in the assault; others say he was fatally wounded. The point is, he lost; the Ka'ba stayed standing, and Muhammad was born in an Arabia bruised by the rivalries of associationists, Jews, Christians, and Zoroastrians. Much of the years before and after him were consumed by war— wars he tried to escape but never could.

Muhammad's life can't be separated from this context, and shouldn't ever be.

His father died before he was born and his mother, Amina, when he was only six. He was an orphan. Abd al Muttalib took him in, but he lived just two more years after that. One of Muhammad's paternal uncles, Abu Talib, then embraced the eight-year-old, raised him, taught him to be a merchant. This was tough stuff all the same. In a very tribal society, to not have close blood relatives didn't just mean you were an outlier. It meant you were especially vulnerable in times of hardship. This being a desert, there were also plenty of opportunities to suffer hardship.

Muhammad combined a deep concern for the poorest and weakest in his society with a profound dissatisfaction with the general order of his time, the inegalitarian and patriarchal instincts of which deeply dismayed him. His compatriots thought highly of him all the same, and not just because of his noble, Abrahamic ancestry—despite his disinterest in their religion. When Meccans embarked on long trading journeys and had to leave property behind, they left it with him. They trusted him implicitly and explicitly. He was honest, decent, and kind. He was nicknamed "Amin," the trustworthy.

He practiced asceticism mixed with the necessary emphasis on commerce. He was a trader who meditated often. He worked for the aforementioned Khadija, who eventually proposed to him. At the age of forty, Muhammad experienced that encounter I shared with you earlier. "Read," the Archangel Gabriel demanded of him, and then continued, in perfect rhymed Arabic verse, "in the name of your Lord, Who created man from a clinging clot. Read, and your Lord is the most generous, Who taught by the pen—taught humankind what it knew not."* Muhammad thought he'd gone mad and rushed out of the cave he'd been quietly reflecting in moments before, only to see the awesomely terrifying spectacle of said angelic messenger spread out across the sky. Muslim angels are not modest creatures of adornment in their primary form, but more formidable presences. In this case, what he saw stretched the horizon, but at least helpfully identified itself: "I am [the Archangel] Gabriel and you, Muhammad, are the Messenger of God."

Muhammad ran home to his wife and confessed to her what had happened, but she reassured him that he had not lost his mind. Because he was a good person, she argued, this being must not intend harm, and could only be who he said he was. Gabriel.

Ipso facto, you are who he says you are. Muhammad's life was turned upside down.

OVER THE NEXT THREE YEARS, Muhammad received a stream of melancholic, provocative, and gorgeous revelations, most of them in short bursts of rhymed verse, each generally circling one

---

* Qur'an: 96:1–5.

of several themes: Feed the poor. Protect the orphan. Pray. Give in charity. Learn lessons from those who came before you. The world will end. Sooner than you think. You will come back to life. You will be judged. You can go to heaven. The existence-to-come lasts longer, and is better, than this one you're living in now. God is One. God is One. God is One. These messages described themselves as a continuation and reaffirmation of the messages God sent to Adam, to Abraham, to Moses, and to Jesus. Hagar's run between the hills had not been in vain. These were, all the same, dangerous and subversive messages.

Fortunately for Muhammad, he could preach in secret.

The first Muslim was a woman—Muhammad's wife, Khadija, who believed in him before he believed in himself. Then there was Ali, the Prophet's cousin and later his son-in-law, who was barely a teenager at the time but destined for great things: he would be Sunni Islam's fourth Caliph and Shia Islam's first Imam. There was Abu Bakr, Muhammad's best friend. Zaid, who was Muhammad's adopted son. Until, in the year 613, after three years of quietly transmitting his message to this small group of followers, Muhammad was ordered to proclaim God's words to the Meccans en masse. So he gathered them and asked them: If I told you there was an army beyond Mecca waiting to march upon you (shades of Abraha v. Abd al Muttalib here), would you believe me? And they said yes because he was truthful. But when he told them about Islam, right after they demonstrated they'd believe anything he said, even if they had no evidence of it themselves—none had, after all, seen this army in question—they laughed in his face. Even his closest relatives laughed. One of his uncles damned him.

This set the tone for the next several years. Muhammad preached; Meccans mocked. He told them that, contrary to their beliefs, they were not mortal; that Allah—God—was One and the only One. That their entire social system was unjust, oppressive, unfair, too. They snorted. Uneasily. Not only was their religiosity being dismissed, their faith being undermined, but so were their social order and what appeared to be their livelihood. If there were no idols, they protested, there would be no hajj pilgrimage. If there was no hajj pilgrimage, wherefrom the lost revenue? If there were no idols, there would be no prestige attached to Mecca, and the tribe of Quraysh would become markedly more vulnerable in the brutal politics of Arabia. Fortunately, for the associationists of Mecca, the new religion didn't seem to spread. At first. It was restricted to women, slaves, the low-born—the undesirables by their social standards.

The problem was that this new religion gave these undesirables dangerous notions—of equality, of the right to dignity, of the choice to turn down marriage proposals. Soon uncomfortable mockery became outright humiliation, and humiliation became abuse, and abuse became brutal violence. A pattern emerged, the understanding of which cannot be bolded, italicized, and underlined enough—every text effect you can think of, save strikethrough. How can Muhammad be a Prophet, people ask me, if he went to war, commanded armies, oversaw sieges, punished whole tribes? (Their model for a religious leader is Jesus.) But you can't understand Muhammad's choices—guided, as they were, by God—if you won't understand the circumstances he was forced into. You can't understand the circumstances he was forced into unless you understand this: the Meccan elite, the aristocrats of the Quraysh, who led opposition to early Islam, often assumed Muhammad was motivated by the same things they were. That he wanted what they wanted.

It was a miscalculation of fatal consequences, though these were not apparent at the time. Stop preaching Islam, the Meccan notables pleaded with Muhammad, and we'll give you what you want. What is it you want, anyhow? They thought he wanted what they did. Women? You can have the most beautiful women. (And no, they'd have no say in the matter.) Riches? We will pour our wealth upon you. (Wealth that was often ill-gained and illegally obtained.) Power? We will make you our king. That one might have been the most surprising at all. If all the Meccans wanted was to maintain their power and privilege, it gives you a clue as to how threatened they were by Islam that they offered Muhammad the right to rule over even them, to create an office the Arabs of their region had never had. All to stop the undoing of their social order. It's enough to feel bad for them, until you remember what they represented: Misogyny. Vulgar capitalism. Bigotry and prejudice. Even slavery.

The Qur'an made clear: "To you, your religion," God told Muhammad to say, "and to me, mine." That's important to dwell upon. Muhammad didn't want to take away their right to worship as they pleased; he would not, however, cease to preach what he believed was correct.* They could practice their religion, he explained, so long as he could also practice his own. The Meccans refused, in part because his religion was the one gaining converts, albeit very slowly (at first). So the Meccans singled out the most vulnerable of the tiny ummah of the time, and went after them, whipping slaves for being Muslim, torturing those with no tribal connections, even killing a female slave for refusing her owner's orders to renounce her understanding of God. How did Muhammad respond? Not by fighting back—he refused this. He declined to allow his community to even speak back with the same kind of language deployed against them. Indeed, he had a novel response.

Running away.

Muhammad, conscious that he could not defend his community from vindictive Meccans, searched desperately for safe harbor, somewhere, anywhere, to moor his community. He found a refuge for some of them, but it was a fateful choice.

IN 616, MUHAMMAD sent the weakest of his followers to Ethiopia to seek shelter under the benevolent shade of its Christian king. Why Ethiopia? For one thing, it was a country that Meccans, the Muslims among them included, knew of by way of commerce. For another, it was powerful, far more powerful than Mecca. Its king was known for being fair and kind. And finally, Muhammad calculated that, given their shared love for Jesus and Mary, perhaps

---

* The Qur'an considers the question of the relationship of the Prophet Muhammad's community with associationists in great detail; the 60th chapter is a good example.

the king would be partial to the Muslims and shelter them. He was right. The king did.

The Meccan elite, however, did not interpret this as the desperate escape of vulnerable Muslims who just wanted to be left alone. Remember those power politics of the time? The Meccans saw the Muslims sail to Ethiopia and open negotiations (for asylum) with a Christian power with whom they, the Meccans, had had their own diplomatic relationships. Recall that they interpreted Muhammad's baseline motivations as material; perhaps he wanted power. And perhaps he appealed to a greater power so he could undermine the Meccans' power and political standing.

And anyway, wasn't Ethiopia Christian, like Rome, and didn't Muhammad claim to be like Jesus? Maybe they were all in league with each other. Unsurprisingly, the Meccans, and later groups who would share the Meccans' skepticism of Muhammad—most especially the powerful Jews of that town of Yathrib—inclined to the Persians. Indeed, at that very time, while the story of Islam was unfolding, a war between the Persians and the Romans raged in the background. The Persians had launched a massive assault on the Romans, successfully seizing not just Jerusalem but also carrying the true cross back with them. The Jews who had been so mistreated by Christians returned to Palestine with the Persians, shades of Cyrus once more, and visited revenge upon their Roman enemies and oppressors.

A whole regional dynamic was unfolding, implicating Muhammad, as much as he might have wished not to be. Many associationists and Jews took the side of the Persians, though a revelation in the Qur'an promised, as all of this was happening, that though the Romans were now losing, soon—in "three to nine years"—they'd win. (The Qur'an was right.) Of course, the Meccans didn't believe that prophecy and felt reassured by the apparent direction of events. If the Muslims really were even only sympathetic to the Romans—and that much they were—it was a good thing their side was losing. But the experiment in Ethiopia, though necessary, was insufficient. Muhammad could not, for reasons I do not understand completely yet, send all of his community to Africa; it may have simply been that Ethiopia could not absorb them all, or God did not want him to yield the right to worship at the Ka'ba (a right that existed, thanks to the Meccans, more in theory than in practice), or that Muhammad did not want to make undue demands of a foreign king. He kept searching, while the Meccans kept escalating. It became a kind of self-fulfilling prophecy. The Meccans forced Muhammad into the very actions they claimed he was pursuing all along, with more than a few echoes of Anakin Skywalker, Adam and Eve, and the Caliphate.

They were bringing about the very thing they were concerned to prevent. Muhammad didn't want power, but they were making him see the necessity of it.

AROUND 616, the Meccan elite did the unthinkable. They placed the entire Banu Hashim under sanction. That included Muhammad, Khadija, and Ali, of course, but also Muhammad's uncle Abu Talib, who, according to Sunni Muslims, never converted to Islam. Everyone. No one could trade with them who was not of them, and neither could they trade with anyone other than themselves. In a society that lived and died by caravan commerce, this was a death sentence. And the Meccans knew it. Slow-motion mass murder. When I talked about the Dome of the Rock earlier, I told you how it recalls the Night Journey and Ascension. I said that that miraculous journey to Jerusalem and then to Jannah was sparked by the deaths of Abu Talib and Khadija.

This is when they died. This is how they died. Muhammad was heartbroken, and harried, and hurried. He had to find some way out because he could sense that the Meccans were now willing to go to lengths until then unimaginable. During this time, though, Muhammad continued to insist that there be no retaliation: Muslims were to answer unkindness with kindness, cruelty with mercy, mockery with compassion. He was a Prophet of love, a "mercy to all the worlds," as the Qur'an characterizes him and his mission. Indeed, the incremental revelation of the Qur'an continued throughout these years, building an Islamic edifice even as the circumstances of the nascent Muslim community grew ever more urgent, the environment ever more toxic.

In 619, pressure from other tribes, horrified by what Mecca was doing to an entire clan—both associationists and Muslims—finally forced the rest of the Quraysh to lift the sanctions. It made some difference, but not enough. The same vituperation was there. Two more years of searching for safe haven turned up nothing. But then, during the hajj pilgrimage, a small delegation of associationists from the city of Yathrib asked to meet with Muhammad. Their mission was a curious one, as it seems to strike as a bolt out of the blue. When I was younger, I perceived this as the kind of divine intervention people of deep faith might deserve, but now I think that to say so is to underdetermine the event: It was miraculous, insofar as God intervened; *how* He intervened, however, also matters.

The Yathribite delegation admitted to being overwhelmed. Their city was composed of two large associationist tribes, the Aws and the Khazraj—don't worry about those names—and at least five Jewish tribes (although these were ethnically and culturally Arab). The former two kept feuding violently, dragging the Jews in with them. What were the chances Muhammad would help them out? We, the associationists, will convert to Islam, they pledged. Unify us through the new faith and your moral leadership. In exchange, we'll shelter and defend you—you, and everyone from your community. Cue upswell in the music.

Muhammad had received the first revelation of the Qur'an about a decade earlier. He had thus only been preaching that long. Numerically, at least, he had modest success.

This request changed everything.

And it is a superficially strange request, insofar as it's unprecedented. It was one thing for Yathribites to want to become Muslim. But to offer Muhammad, who had thus far never ruled over anyone, control of their entire city, fertile with lucrative date farms and located near trade routes headed to Rome and Persia, seemed something else. Then again, if you believe God's speaking to Muhammad, and you join his religion, how could you not expect him to determine your affairs? It's not clear if the Jewish tribes had any say in this, or if they simply had to accept it—perhaps with no small measure of unease—as a fait accompli. Because now, their erstwhile Yathribite ~~opponents~~ rivals were unified. In 622, the Muslims of Mecca made plans to emigrate, to make a second exodus to Yathrib in the north, which would soon be renamed Medina, short for the City (of the Prophet).

At almost the exact same moment, the Romans, who'd lost the wealthy province of Egypt and much of the Near East to the Persians, made a bold, desperate bid to retake the initiative by launching a strike inside Persian territory.

These two events, one major and the other apparently minor, might not be disconnected.

THERE WERE TWO factions unhappy with Muhammad's planned move to Yathrib, which from here on out I'll call Medina. The first were the wealthiest Jewish tribes of Medina, who must've been threatened by the consolidation of their associationist rivals. These Jewish tribes apparently affiliated or sympathized with Persia, and wondered if the Muslims did not carry with them a whiff of Roman intrigue. (What happens in Ethiopia doesn't stay in Ethiopia.) The second were the Meccans themselves. You'd think they could finally show some decency and let the Muslims leave. After all, they were effectively exiling themselves.

But the Meccans must have wondered what was leading Muhammad to Medina in the first place and feared that his governing a city-state so close to their trade routes, one that was relatively fertile and much more agriculturally self-sufficient than their own, would give him the power to choke off Mecca's livelihood. And didn't he have reason to? Amusingly, the Meccans feared Muhammad might seek revenge for how they treated him. So they couldn't just let him leave. They decided to assassinate him. They hired youth from every major tribe to strike him in his bed while he slept; such a distribution of culpability would make retaliation impossible.

On to the plot: Valiant Ali took Muhammad's place in bed while the Prophet snuck out of town with his father-in-law (and the future first Caliph), Abu Bakr. As soon as the Meccans discovered the ruse, they rushed into pursuit, but none of their trackers could stop Muhammad from arriving in Medina; once he did, he had thousands on his side. Had the Meccans only let Muhammad go in peace, everything that happened after could have been avoided. But they had free will, too, just like we do, and chose, time and again, the course of aggression. Those who live by the sword, as they say . . . Having lost their bid to assassinate him, they decided on a new course of action. They'd take the Muslims' belongings left behind in Mecca, load them on camel, and travel north to sell them.

IN MEDINA, God guided the Prophet Muhammad to build a community that reflected Islamic ideals, established and emerging. In Medina, tribal ties were suppressed in favor of the bonds of faith. An obligatory form of charity, called *zakat*, was institutionalized; meaning "purification," it was a kind of tax, a payment made on the wealth you possessed, to reflect the debt you have to God. Giving a little of it back, from all that you got. Some of this was outlined in a remarkable constitution Muhammad dictated; perhaps the most fascinating element of it concerns his conception of his community's relationships with its new city's Jewish tribes. We are one ummah, Muhammad promised, composed of two faiths! Defense would be a mutual responsibility, though each community agreed to be judged by its own laws. A fateful decision for the Banu Qurayza tribe, as it turns out.

But events had not reached that nadir yet. First, Muhammad had to deal with the Meccans, who were not happy with his new position. The Meccans marched a caravan full of the Muslims' abandoned belongings, to be sold off in perhaps Palestine or Syria, but suffice it to say sold all the same. Muhammad mustered a modest force of 313 men to confront the caravan and demand the return of their belongings. The men were lightly armed but had the element of surprise—except that the Meccans got wind of their plans, and dispatched a formidable force of 1,000 soldiers to accompany the caravan, intending to make short work of the Muslims, and perhaps putting an end to Muhammad once and for all. The Muslims only found out about this Meccan contingent when the two forces met up at the wells of Badr, not too far from Medina.

Most of the Muslims did not want to fight.

They were overruled.

They would have to stand and fight. Since this is the beginning of Muhammad's career as a general, it deserves to be meditated upon. Why would God command them to fight? Probably because, time and again, Muhammad had tried turning the other cheek. They had fled rather than retaliate. Run away, time and again, rather than stand their ground. At some point, you have to stop, at least if you want to survive. Giving in to the bully never actually stops the bully, it only emboldens him. The Battle of Badr did not go as the Meccans—or probably most of the Muslims, let alone the rest of the Arabian Peninsula—expected. The mighty Quraysh, with far better arms and far more mounts, were demolished in battle, with many of the greatest opponents of the Muslims killed that day.

When the Muslims returned to Medina, they must have had a glow about them; the Meccans, in turn, were convinced the Muslims had gotten lucky, that perhaps they hadn't taken them seriously enough. But next time . . . next time would be different. There were several more next times. The Meccans tried, again and again, to defeat the Muslims in battle. It is fair to ask what their ultimate intentions were. To simply overthrow Muhammad's rule? To imprison him? Or, as was likelier, to kill him and kill off his community? Islamicide. The only Muslims in the world were the Muslims who lived in Medina. Every battle was an existential conflict.

In 627, the Meccans managed to forge a confederacy of ten thousand men at arms.

They meant to crush Islam once and for all.

At a loss for how to prepare for such a massive army, Muhammad consulted his companions. One, a Persian called Salman, suggested digging a trench around the most vulnerable part of the city, on the northern side. The rest of the city was protected by thick date orchards, high hills, tough terrain, and at the southernmost end, the fortresses of the Banu Qurayza, a prominent Jewish tribe, who were obligated by the aforementioned constitution of Medina to fight alongside the Muslims against any common enemy. This meant the Banu Qurayza were inside Medina as the Quraysh marched to its peripheries; the choices the Banu Qurayza made in battle would very well decide the outcome of battle.

The trench, as it were, worked beyond expectations: the Meccans and their allies had never encountered such an obstacle. They could not cross it without sustaining terrible losses, and they had to settle in for a long siege, the ultimate outcome of which nobody could predict just then. Would a war of attrition be enough to starve Muhammad into submission? Prior to this, relations between Muhammad and the Muslims, on the one hand, and many other Jewish tribes of Medina had deteriorated significantly; this put the Banu Qurayza in an awkward position. But they had an alliance with the Muslims, you might object. They did—but they also faced an existential threat.

Previously, prominent Jewish tribes had violated some of their agreements with Muhammad; the resulting conflicts saw some exiled to their desert redoubts, leaving property and wealth behind. The Banu Qurayza must have been rattled by these events. All of them, they believed, were instigated by Muhammad, whose very presence in the city was the reason the Meccans were besieging them in the first place. What did they have to do with this new religion, this story of Islam, that audaciously claimed to be the rightful inheritor of their predecessors—was he really telling them their ancient religion was being superseded by his or, worse yet, he was practicing what their religion was originally?

All of these feelings must have been at a boil by the time the Siege of the Trench was underway. The Banu Qurayza were also well aware that it was quite possible, given the customs of the time, that the winners in battle would kill all the men on the losing side, and certainly sell the women and children into slavery. If the Meccans triumphed, and it looked like they would, then the Banu Qurayza would die alongside the Muslims—when they hadn't even wanted Islam in their town to begin with. From the Muslim point of view, though, while the Meccan confederates had a chance of wiping them out, should the Banu Qurayzah join the invaders, it'd certainly be all over. Exit stage left. Islam, 610–627. Rest in peace.

What happens next has fueled distrust between Jews and Muslims for too many centuries to count. I certainly don't believe the Israeli-Palestinian conflict is about "ancient hatreds"—it is a modern conflict about territory, sovereignty, and indigeneity—but nevertheless, that conflict draws on deeper historical traumas, which makes it that much harder to solve. For some Jews, the results of the Siege of the Trench confirm Muslims' inbuilt, violent anti-Semitism. For some Muslims, the results of the Siege of the Trench reveal the genocidal intent of (some) Jews toward Muslims. Which one of these views is right? How do we come to terms with such an episode?

For the Banu Qurayza did take the Meccans up on their offer.

Muhammad got word that the Jewish tribe, supposedly allied to him, had decided to switch sides. Did he wonder what motivated them—an eagerness to avoid Meccan wrath? A desire to be on the right side of the Siege? Greed for the spoils of war? A deep, lasting hatred of him and his religion? Already the Banu Qurayza's choices had proven troubling. Though the Meccans had arrived to lay siege to Medina many days before, the Banu Qurayza had not, contrary to their treaty obligations, lifted a finger to help the Muslims. Surely, they knew the threat Mecca posed. Mecca had already proven its desire to use violence to extinguish Islam, down to killing the Prophet. The Jews of Banu Qurayza did not make up all of Jewry; Muhammad's Medina, however, was all of Islam.

Treachery was a poor choice, morally as well as strategically. The Muslims had intercepted Qurayzan and Meccan communications, confronted the Jewish tribe, and under immense stress, the inbuilt tensions between the two allies of threadbare convenience exploded; the Qurayzah hadn't wanted to take sides, after all. The Siege then collapsed when key Arab tribes withdrew, unwilling to leave their home territories for so long, and the Quraysh recognized that they had lost their bid to smash Islam. It would be the last time they would be able to try. This left the Banu Qurayza all alone. As they failed to defend the Muslims, the Quraysh failed to defend them too. Once the Meccans and their confederates fully withdrew, Muhammad appointed one of his companions to look into the Torah and determine the punishment for treason.

I am no expert on Jewish scriptures, although I can imagine that the laws of war in the relevant part of the Old Testament period might be unyielding. On the surface, Muhammad's decision seems to follow from his founding of Medina: one ummah of two faiths. It would only be fair to do as the Jewish scripture instructed. That was the whole agreement between the Muslims and Jews in the first place. Except that, according to Muhammad's investigator, the punishment for treason was the death of all the males in the tribe. And Muhammad ordered it done. The Muslims killed every male from this prominent Jewish tribe. They went from the threat of wholesale elimination of their own community to the obliteration of the threatening tribe.

What do we do with this story? An answer, but an answer that may not ever satisfy many—and I'm not sure what to do except admit as much—is to look to the larger thrust of Muhammad's life and see where this episode fits. If it is any consolation—and it very well may not be—Muhammad once again reached for peace as soon as it was offered. He could not tolerate betrayal with potentially genocidal consequences. (Indeed, what leader of people ever would?) Still, even though the Meccans had tried to massacre him and his people too, he settled for a truce with them, known forever after as the Treaty of Hudaybiyyah. The terms of the agreement were entirely imbalanced in favor of the Meccans; Muhammad, nevertheless, took it. A Prophet of peace: when offered the chance to end a conflict, even to his disadvantage, he leapt at the opportunity.

Because his purpose, his intention, his mission, was never to fight. He was forced into that. Liberated from the cycle of violence by agreement with the Meccans, he was free to do what Islam was meant to all along, what formed the core and the kernel of the faith: preaching the Oneness of God and the equal access all women and men had to Him, through worship, supplication, and remembrance. Like Noah would have. The belief that through a life of prayerfulness and kindness, one could reach a deep inner calm, which would lead to everlasting peace in the life to come, where each and every blessed soul would be in the company of God and those beloved to God. That, and not statehood, ethnicity, identity, or politics, is the purpose of Islam.

DURING THE TWO YEARS that the Treaty of Hudaybiyyah held (628–630), most of Arabia offered its oaths of allegiance to the Prophet. That meant that when a Meccan ally attacked a Medinese, violating the treaty, Muhammad could respond from a position of remarkable advantage. Mecca made desperate attempts to salvage the peace, but Muhammad was doubtful. Some ten thousand men answered his call to arms and converged on the city a few dozen of their founding brothers and sisters had unceremoniously fled from, often under cover of darkness. Just eight years before. Eight.

Mecca's elite knew they were doomed and begged for mercy, even as they did not expect to receive it. Which made it all the more remarkable that, although Muhammad's troops poured into the city from all sides, in numbers that might've been greater than the entire municipal population of Mecca, they were ordered to sheathe their swords and lower their bows. Muhammad declared a general amnesty and forgave the majority of the Meccans their crimes, including the leader of the city, Abu Sufyan, of the Banu Umayyah. They had been enemies. Abu Sufyan had repeatedly tried to destroy Muhammad. But he converted, then and there, repeating the shahada. That there is absolutely no god but God, and Muhammad, his longtime nemesis, was the Messenger of God. And now they were brothers in Islam.

This was an unprecedented moment in Arabian history. Such magnanimity from a long-persecuted enemy, a precedent that overruled the Banu Qurayza, perhaps, and suggested a strong desire to finally heal the wounds that had torn their tribes to pieces. Muhammad was, however, less generous toward the idols in the Ka'ba.

One by one, each of the idols of the Ka'ba, 360 in all, were destroyed, cast down, smashed apart, or hacked to bits. It was a war on associationism, and it is sometimes taken as a template by Muslims past and present as a mandate to destroy idols wherever they are. Certainly, that was an opinion some Muslims held in the past and a handful hold even today; the Taliban, after all, in 2001 ruined the remarkable and ancient Buddhas of Bamiyan. But Afghanistan has been Muslim for incomparably longer than the Taliban have been around, and all that time, nobody seemed particularly bothered by the presence of Buddhist iconography.

What to make then of the forcible monotheization of the Ka'ba?

If you consider that the Ka'ba was founded as a House of the One, removing the idols therein restored the structure to its original condition. Moreover, by the time this happened, much of Mecca, and nearly all of Arabia, had become Muslim. Much more of it would soon convert, not by force of arms—though force of arms must have had an impact on them—but by the feeling that history had delivered its verdict on their faith, and that, had their gods been very useful, they would have certainly intervened by then.

But upon the successful liberation of Mecca, Muhammad made a remarkable decision.

He would not stay in Mecca. Even though he was from there.

The Muslim theme of dislocation and reinvention continued. The Prophet returned to the Medina that embraced him, but only briefly. He died in 632, two years after Mecca's conversion. Sunni and Shia Islam were born the day after his death, not in the form we recognize them in today, of course, but their antecedents were there, as the young community debated what to do now that their channel to the Divine had been terminated. The majority, who are the predecessors to the Sunni, coalesced around Abu Bakr, who became ruler. A new title was invented for him, but it should be familiar to you. He would be *Khalifa*. Caliph.

But not the Caliph of God, like Eve and Adam, and in fact all people. That title is meant to be universal, or universalizable. Abu Bakr was *Khalifat Rasul Allah*, the Caliph of the Messenger of God, though what that meant was unclear. It was never resolved. The period between Abu Bakr's reign and the assassination of Imam Ali, one of the other first Muslims, the Prophet's cousin, who reigned as Caliph from 656 to 661, was under thirty years. This short-lived period was followed by an oppressive monarchy that seized power and moved the capital to Damascus, ruling as earthly kings elsewhere did, handing power down through their descendants.

This period of three decades after Muhammad is sometimes viewed, especially by pious (Sunni) Muslims, as a golden age, a template for the ideal society, the brief extension of Muhammadan morality into secular politics—and I say "secular" because no one's actions could receive explicit or indubitable Divine assent—but this is a sometimes problematic claim. These twenty-nine years were marked by great achievements as well as unclear mechanisms of succession, infighting, the birth of religious extremism, and assassinations. Three of the four Caliphs who ruled died violently while in office, two of them killed by fellow Muslims.

Ultimately the demise of this Righteous Caliphate (and I don't mean that flippantly) was likely inevitable, even if it came at great pain and moral cost. But for now, let us return to Muhammad's life, which I have largely outlined from a military and political perspective. Ironically, that is the only way to cut the legs out from under excessively worldly interpretations of Islam, which lead to fanaticism and militarism, that have caused great harm across the planet, but most of all, perversely enough, to Muslims themselves.

8

WHAT'S PAST IS PROLOGUE

IN THE ACADEMIC CIRCLES I used to travel in, earnest Christians were often mocked for their pious enthusiasms. Some of my colleagues, for example, heaped high-handed scorn on bracelets that read *WWJD*—"What Would Jesus Do?" I found such sentiments upsetting, not least because Muslims often ask WWMD? If the Qur'an is God's revelation to humanity, Muhammad's life is the living embodiment of that revelation—it is its exegesis, its analysis, its commentary. It is how we humans live out a text. And since the Qur'an is meant for all times and places, so necessarily is the Prophet Muhammad. This raises some challenging questions.

What, for example, do we do with the times and places where Muhammad diverged, and even markedly, from the values we now hold foundational? For those of us who cherish our Prophet, any close and honest examination of his life demands answers to questions that wouldn't sit well with many Westerners, conservative or progressive. Why did the Prophet marry so many women—and at once? Why didn't he ban slavery outright? What was his position on homosexuality, or bisexuality, or really any orientation other than heterosexuality? What was his attitude to war? What were his relationships with the Jews of Medina really like? And, finally, in a question that should be of interest to Islamophobes and Islamists alike, were his politics incidental to his piety, or his piety incidental to his politics?

I want us to try to answer these questions because, if we don't, I believe there cannot be any sophisticated, compassionate, or relevant interpretation of Islam for us or the generations after us. Over the next few chapters, I will explore these questions and sometimes come to conclusions that may surprise, unsettle, and even unnerve you.

It may be helpful, therefore, before proceeding to keep in mind several considerations.

First, the Prophet Muhammad was one of those rare individuals who created a civilization—literally in his image—so we must respect the fact that he redefined religion as much, if not more than, he simply demonstrated religiosity. Sometimes the right question isn't, "Why would a religious leader do that?" It's, "What do we mean by 'religious'?"

What is a religion meant to do?

What kind of person is it meant to cultivate?

What does it assume a person is, anyhow?

Second, we must be honest about where the answers we discover take us. We might be tempted to make Muhammad conform to the early twenty-first-century West—and that is an understandable temptation—but Muhammad doesn't belong to any one period (or place). He can speak to us, but he can also say things that challenge us. It's up to us as Muslims in the West to figure out what to make of those differences.

And third? When we engage these questions, we Western Muslims do so as minorities within the political framework of our societies—secular democracies, nearly all of them. That doesn't mean secular democracy is exclusive to the West, but simply that most of the West is secular and democratic. Moreover, our answers might not be the same as the answers those Muslims who live as majorities choose for themselves, and that's okay. Circumstances differ, priorities diverge. The ummah is a religious value, the translation of which, for the modern age, I'll consider especially in chapter 12, "The Case for the Caliphate." Nevertheless, holding a religious value in common doesn't mean the translation of that value has to be shared. The ummah contains multitudes. Let it.

9

ADAM AND EVE AND
EVE AND EVE AND EVE

I DON'T KNOW that we could ever arrive at percentages of incidence, but polygyny was relatively common in pre-Islamic Arabia. The practice was generally unrestricted, the only apparent limitation being the number of spouses a man could afford. (There wasn't any expectation that spouses had to be provided for equally or at any minimum standard.) This left poorer men without partners, but it was rare for the rights of those poorer than oneself to be systematically considered. There was little concern for whether the women themselves wanted this arrangement either, nor could they themselves practice polyandry; or, rather, I should say, I have found no instances of the practice. Nor any inkling, so far as I have seen, that this was ever socially considered.

And while plantation slavery did not exist in pre-Islamic Arabia, there were few limits on slave ownership beyond what one could afford, with this system of slavery, as in the Americas, containing a racial component. (Though slavery was not, unlike in the United States, limited to people of a specific ancestry.) There were few restrictions on what one could do with and to one's slave, and little regard for the children of slaves or the maintenance of their families.

Many men raped their female slaves; though women appeared to own male slaves, it's not clear if they did the same. Pre-Islamic Arabia was thus a polygynous, patriarchal, slave-owning society, a hierarchical and classist context—and I should add, a heteronormative one too.

Sexual desire, of course, extended beyond the conventions of binary heteronormativity then as it does today, but pre-Islamic Arabs did not acknowledge same-sex relationships (or passions) the way we do today, never mind signing off on same-sex marriage. There are many reasons why, but one of them cannot be overestimated: this was a premodern, tribal society in which belonging, identity, and social possibility were constructed and maintained biologically. People married within tribes or to create alliances between tribes. Marriage was rarely, if ever, conceived of as a romantic union; it was a practical, procreative, or strategic union. That does not mean pre-Islamic Arabs did not have a rich tradition of love and romance. It just means it wasn't a quotidian concern.

The Arab world of that time was hardly different from most of the world, most of the time.

And what do we make of Muhammad's response to all of this?

An honest examination would find that Muhammad limited polygyny, but did not abolish it; that he restricted slavery, with the ambition to see it erased, albeit gradually, from the earth; that while he celebrated heterosexuality, within the bounds of marriage, contract, and convention, he showed little if any such openness toward acting on other sexualities. Not because he did not know about them, but because, as he preached, God did not approve of them. To conclude, I will ask if Western Muslims can reconcile these conclusions with the remarkable transformations our societies are undergoing.

ON POLYGYNY

Muslim men have traditionally been permitted to marry up to—but no more than—four women at a time. Their wives can be of the

Muslim, Christian, or Jewish faiths. (Islam apparently recognizes Zoroaster as a Prophet, but proscribes marriage with Zoroastrians.) While Muslim men are granted these freedoms, Muslim women can only have one husband, and they are usually also bound to marrying only Muslim men.* To many, that is essentially unfair. Hence the complication: like a fair number of men of his era, Muhammad was (for a time) polygynous. But he was not limited to four wives; he was married to nine women at once. One way to come to terms with this is cynically. Patriarchy. Prophecy. Privilege. Etc. But no Muslim would feel comfortable ascribing mendacious motivations to any of their Prophets.

What then do we do with these facts as they are read against our sense of fairness?

Some will simply say that if Muhammad was allowed more wives than the Qur'an permitted other men, then this is because God exempted him, and if men are allowed to have more than one spouse and women are not, then this is because God wishes it to be so.

That doesn't satisfy me, however.

I believe there are reasons behind Divine rulings. Even though we might never fully understand God's commands, individually or collectively as an ummah, we can certainly approach a fuller comprehension. For example, let's look at Muhammad's marital history. We find that he was only polygynous when he arrived in Medina and became the leader of a conglomeration of previously divided tribes. Part of his polygyny thus must have been Prophetic statecraft, a reflection of governance in an age of what we might call biopolitics: relationships, lineage, and kinship were the stuff out of which societies were made, not national histories, flags, civic education, and the like. Marriage was a political instrument.

---

* I should note that while it is reasonably common for Muslim men in the West to marry women who are not Muslim, the Islamic tradition itself limits Muslim men who choose not to marry fellow Muslims to marrying believing Christian and Jewish women—arguably, the tradition would not historically recognize the validity of a Muslim man's marrying a woman who is Christian or Jewish only by ancestry.

Unsurprisingly, the world—and marriage with it—has changed tremendously.

We would've been astonished had President Obama arranged marriages from the White House. Whereas, that's something Muhammad did and was expected to do. His authority merged spaces that we moderns separate, but statecraft alone doesn't explain why he had more than one wife at a time. (Or why he had more than four wives at a time.) Muhammad mediates the relationship between revelation and humankind. It may be that the Prophet modeled different types of relationships not so that we would feel compelled to reproduce these exact circumstances, but so that we would have templates for the remarkably different contexts we live in across times and spaces. So that we would know how to act in a relationship depending on the kinds of relationships extant in our own eras.

Muhammad's first wife, Khadija, had married twice before him. She was his only wife during the entire twenty-four years of their marriage together. She proposed to him. She was older than him. He was a virgin; she was not. He became a father with her. Of all Muhammad's relationships, arguably theirs is most analogous to how we in the mainstream West conceive of marriage today. It was what many South Asians call a "love marriage," as opposed to an arranged marriage. Some time after she died, he became a polygamist. He married previously unmarried women and previously married women. The (Christian) patriarch of Alexandria even sent him a concubine, Marya. Slavery was a fact of life during this time, and the decision of a Christian patriarch to send a Muslim Prophet a woman would not have raised their eyebrows, even if ours remain arched.

What would have raised ancient eyebrows is that Muhammad treated her as an equal partner, not property. Indeed, according to some historians, he only married her—with her consent—after she was freed.

Muhammad had a son with Marya and considered their child, Ibrahim (Abraham), to be the equal of his other offspring. This wasn't just reflective of how his morality, his compassion, and his consideration unfolded in the context of the time, but it conveys how

Muslims should comport themselves in sundry situations. What if you live in a society in which slavery exists? What if you can't abolish it—how then are slaves to be treated? What if you're married to an older woman, previously married, or a younger woman, never married? How should a husband comport himself? How should a wife comport herself? Muhammad's function in Muslim religious life is singular, different from that of every other Muslim; he tells us how to be Muslim. It could be that a reason Muhammad had so many wives was because each of these relationships is meant to be a template for a certain kind of relationship that may or may not apply to our social circumstances, but does apply to *some* circumstances somewhere—not because we need to be polygynous. And there are many different types of circumstances, some of which are shocking to the modern mind. This carries us to one of the more common criticisms of Muhammad, the vilest and, for Muslims, the most hurtful. It is the accusation that Muhammad was more than lascivious; rather, he was an outright pedophile, owing to his marriage to Aisha, the daughter of the first Caliph, his close friend Abu Bakr. They were betrothed when she was still a child, although she did not go to live with him until she was a teenager, and the relationship was not consummated until she had passed puberty.

Still, it stands out: What kind of Prophet is arranged-married to a woman almost forty-plus years his junior? There are two obvious concerns here. First, there's the question of when the marriage was consummated—when the marriage became physical, intimate, sexual. According to every reliable historian of Muhammad's life, while Aisha was betrothed to the Prophet Muhammad during her childhood, the marriage was not performed, let alone consummated, until she was physically mature. That, of course, still sounds distressing. Until we remember that in that era, teenagers were adults. A fourteen-year-old boy was a man, albeit a very young one. Our concept of maturity did not apply. (Theirs, however, does not have to apply to us now.) This was more common than we might imagine today—in my circles, many of my peers' grandparents and great-grandparents consummated their marriages during their teenage years. This was simply when those societies considered adulthood to have arrived, with all its attendant responsibilities and expectations. We, of course, can have our own standards of adulthood and propriety; what is relevant here is the intent behind the action.

But the action, too. Beyond the first concern, namely the age of consummation—what of the age of marriage itself, Aisha's betrothal to the Prophet when she was just a child?

It deserves to be noted that Muhammad did not actually marry Aisha when she was a child. Their future marriage was *arranged* when she was a child. Perhaps it is because I am the child of South Asian immigrants, but this practice is also not *unusual* to me. Exactly zero of the many Pakistani and Indian adults I knew growing up married out of choice. They were all arranged-married.

Although marriage and society were organized patriarchally, men hardly had any say in who they would marry either. Marriages were between families, not individuals; when we go back only a few generations, many of those same grandparents and great-grandparents I mentioned were not only arranged-married but promised to each other by their respective parents at a remarkably young age.* Sometimes it was known who they would marry from infancy. Does this mean they actually lived together before they reached adulthood? Of course not. Was this something I would be happy with? Of course not. But it is also how many people lived and had to live. Through Aisha, Muhammad modeled for Muslims how to behave in an arranged marriage, and with a much younger spouse, which was and still is the marital circumstance of many across the world even now. To impose our judgment on this

---

* It should also be noted that, in most premodern societies, marriages took place between families and even within families, which would increase the likelihood that the future spouses would be compatible, taken care of, and emotionally and even physically secure, as opposed to the presumed greater danger of letting one's children marry into networks of strangers. In Muhammad's case, Aisha was the daughter of Muhammad's closest friend, whose status in the Muslim community was so significant that he led prayers during the Prophet's terminal illness and succeeded him as leader of the ummah after his death.

custom is to expect our world to exist in another world, which, of course, is not possible. One might still come back and say: Well, if Muhammad's life is meant for all times and places, doesn't that legitimate the betrothal of older men to much younger women?

And that's a good question, to which I have an answer, albeit not an easy one. It's true that Muhammad's life is supposed to be valid for all times and places; it's true that Aisha's example doesn't seem relevant for the people most likely to read this.

But nothing about Muhammad says it has to be.

WHEN WE THINK of right and wrong, we tend to think in black-and-white. Either/or. We don't see shades of gray. Modern-day Islamists and jihadists are guilty of this sin. Even the use of the adjective "Islamic" is problematic—insofar as Muhammad never called anything, to the best of my knowledge, "Islamic" or "un-Islamic." His morality was far more nuanced, sophisticated, elastic, and generous. Subsequent Islamic (sic) scholars—and back then, they were just called "scholars"—elaborated on his teachings and discovered a schematic. Actions were judged on a gradient of at least five categories: actions that Muhammad reported that God (1) demanded, (2) recommended, (3) stayed neutral on, (4) discouraged, and (5) forbade. Moreover, Muhammad believed that the same action could have a different moral status for two different people. Because no two people are the same.

One could even argue that what is demanded for one society should be discouraged for another, or what is neutral in one world is recommended in another. Here is our way not out, but forward, the way in which Muhammadan morality speaks to modern circumstances—without losing either its primacy or its consistency. Muhammad's life shows us relationships of very different kinds. Some we may like to see, and others we may not want to see, but at no time did Muhammad ever compel any type of marriage. It's true that he offered models for how to behave in different kinds of relationships, but he strongly recommended *monogamous* marriage and never privileged one type of marriage (a romantic relationship, an arranged marriage, and so on) over another. Further, he did not encourage polygyny. The first marriage was Adam and Eve. Not Adam and Eve and Eve and Eve and Eve.

Muhammad left the door open for us to interpret his statements and his precedents for ourselves and our contexts. Instead of focusing in the here and now on Muhammad's marrying a much younger woman, we can focus on the monogamous marriage of Muhammad and Khadija, which speaks to our context more than the former does.* And when it comes to polygyny, it cannot ever be forgotten that in Muhammad's time, polygyny was widely practiced. Muhammad sought to set down strict restrictions on how to practice it, define it, and protect women in these relationships, given the rampant abuse and maltreatment at that time. Most schools of Islamic thought have, for example, held that a man cannot marry another wife without the permission of the current wife. Islam pushed for a more monogamous norm without legislating polygamy out of existence.

Islam just made polygamy that much harder to do.

Does that mean Muhammad's long-term intention was to see polygyny end? Or maybe another reason he was commanded by God to marry many different types of women was not just to model how one behaves in different kinds of monogamous relationships but also how to behave in polygynous relationships, as much as that obviously makes most of us uneasy. We should remember that the modern age isn't always going to be just what we in the West do. There are extant societies in which monogamy is not the only norm; I have colleagues from some Muslim countries whose family members are in polygynous relationships. To them, their answer for what Muhammad would do now.

In societies where polygyny is practiced, robust protections should, at the very least, be implemented, legally as much as cultur-

---

* Even if we look at the premodern forms of marriage Muhammad's life also spoke to, absolutely none of these ever overrode consent, involved the marriage of children, or sanctioned any abuse of one's spouse. Indeed, Muhammad even told his male followers that the best of them were those of them who were the best to their wives.

ally, to prevent abuse and oppression. If those societies determine that no such protections would be adequate, then those societies must act decisively to protect the vulnerable. Recall that polygyny is permitted, not encouraged; for overriding reasons, it can be discouraged or altogether restricted. (Rights exist in hierarchies: your right to get married doesn't override my right not to be harmed.) Marriage was conceived of as a contractual relationship to offer legal protections to both partners, mechanisms and channels through which to address harm.

To us, our own answer for what Muhammad would do now.

Had Muhammad been born in twenty-first-century America and received revelation in this context, would God have gone about *inserting* polygyny into a society that rejects it? One argument for the legalization of polygamy today is that it carries forward a certain liberalizing momentum; we have not only redefined who can get married, but perhaps we will go still further and rethink how many people can get married. Maybe some Muslims will support that argument because of a certain kind of progressiveness or because it allows them to sneak polygyny in through the back door. I don't think either of those is a good enough reason to so redefine marriage. Not least because polygyny can cause grave social harm—not in every single instance, of course, but in enough to cause concern. Conversely, such maltreatment may be the only argument for its legalization: sunlight is the best disinfectant.

While polygyny is not widespread in most Muslim societies and is extremely rare among Western Muslims, all Muslim thinkers and leaders should keep in mind that it still exists, and likewise keep in mind that many restrictions (once) govern(ed) this practice.* Those restrictions reveal important concerns, uppermost in the Prophetic mind. At no point did Muhammad countenance any relationship that involved coercion, misrepresentation, or abuse. I can make

---

*I have not seen any statistics on the prevalence of polygyny among Western Muslims—for reasons I think obvious.

the argument that his relationships were models for subsequent, variegated social contexts, but that doesn't mean they weren't relationships full of love, affection, even silliness and humor. That is the Muslim model for marriage. That is how husbands should be. Muhammad's life redefined masculinity. He was known as a doting husband and father; not only did he never lift a finger against anyone in his household, but he cherished his family.

He often behaved toward his wives in ways that sterner men in his society would've defined as too soft and too effeminate (and sometimes they did so explicitly).

He joked with his family, he teased them, made romantic gestures, and put the interests of others above and beyond his own.

And these gestures were reciprocated.

There is a reason the Night Journey and the Ascension to Jerusalem happened after Muhammad lost his wife, Khadija, and uncle, Abu Talib. It is because he needed and missed their presence, and especially hers. Her love for him strengthened him, and her loss gravely wounded him. That compassion—as God said of him, "We have not sent you except as a mercy to all the worlds"—is the value that guides all these conversations. When Muhammad received Marya, the slave sent by the patriarch of Alexandria as a gift to him, he treated her as an equal. Muhammad challenged Arabs to do better. He once expressed astonishment at meeting a man who did not kiss his children, judging such hard-heartedness to be not just emotionally worrying but spiritually revealing. You should love the ones you're with.

And you should show that love.

As before, then again: As we do on Earth, so with heaven. If you claim to love God but have nothing to show for it, what kind of love is that?

ON SLAVERY

When Muhammad received Marya, he was gifted a human being as a gesture of friendship from one ruler to another. In his life and during his rule over Medina, slavery, as a practice, was never formally abolished but continued.

For what possible reason(s)?

It is true there was no general and complete manumission, no edict comparable to the Emancipation Proclamation.* But a closer examination of his life strongly suggests that Muhammad intended for slavery to disappear through three strategies. First, he encouraged his followers to set slaves free, declaring manumission to be among the greatest works a person could do in her lifetime. Abu Bakr, who became the first Caliph because of his religious stature, earned that merit in part by spending greatly of his wealth to set slaves free. He purchased their freedom, it should be noted; he did not purchase them to simply find them a kinder master. The second strategy was to reform the institution itself. The master must treat and provide for the slave as if he were a member of his family, from the clothes he wore to the food he ate. Second, slaves had the right to consent to intimate relationships, and masters who engaged in intimate relationships with their slaves automatically created a legal relationship with that slave equal to matrimony, the consequences of which included any issue. Of course, by our standards, this is not the active consent we are looking for, and the imbalance of power suggests the impossibility of consent as we understand it. (But premodern Islam largely perceived consent to be the absence of no, not the presence of yes.) Third, the children of slaves could not be slaves. The institution was not heritable. I believe Muhammad relied on these three strategies to diminish, transform, and end slavery, gradually but irreversibly. Of course, after witnessing the horrors ISIS inflicted on the Middle East, or the long history of the Muslim slave trade in Africa, or the raiding expeditions of steppe horsemen eager to harvest humanity and press it into servility, one might ask: Why not full emancipation?

Perhaps the Islamic conception was that slavery could be piecemeal reformed out of existence or thereby altered beyond all

---

* "Manumission" means release from slavery.

recognition. Maybe it'd never work otherwise—not in that time and that place. Maybe there was no future for freed slaves in tribal societies that tended to sideline those who were not blood relations, which was especially dangerous in harsh climates like Arabia, where the margin for error was slim. Or maybe Islam did set slaves free, just in ways we don't immediately recognize. This is not to mention that the liberating mechanisms Muhammad did command were very often ignored after his passing—or subverted to terrible ends. For one thing, Islam's prescription of forced equality—of treating a slave as an employee, not a piece of property—was soon discarded. Even decisions the Prophet made to abolish slavery incrementally had perverse consequences. Take this example: the children of slaves could not be slaves. This can and should be read as a clear desire to destroy the cursed institution. But since slavery could not be maintained biologically, some Muslim dynasties responded by pursuing (raiding for) new slaves, replenishing their numbers.

Hence a number of Muslim dynasties practiced or encouraged many such deranged expeditions, each year trying to find new people to force into servility—given that their existing slaves' children would not be slaves. Fortunately, we in the modern world have almost completely done away with slavery. There are significant and unfortunate exceptions, of course, such as sex-trafficking and groups like the Islamic State, which is functionally a violent criminal gang of, among other things, sex traffickers calling itself a Caliphate. Muhammad would have cheered the progress made thus far toward emancipation, and vociferously resisted any attempt at reintroducing slavery. He would have preferred a world with more equality, not less; he would have fought for more compassion and decency. We know that because that's what he did. Thus, on polygyny and slavery, we have ample evidence of Prophetic tendencies—of circumspect permission under demanding circumstances, in the former case; and gradual but inevitable elimination, in the latter—demonstrating that he would altogether reject the renewal of slavery in any modern circumstance.

Consider, for example, the secular zenith of his life when his armies liberated Mecca. Eight years after fleeing as refugees, the persecuted returned to settle the score. Which they did, astonishingly, not by following tribal custom, which would have been to kill, or enslave and sell off the defeated, but by declaring a nearly universal amnesty. Up to and including times of war, slavery was no longer the operative norm, as the last pertinent instance of Muhammad's life reveals.

ON HETERONORMATIVITY

It might surprise some to know that the Prophet Muhammad recognized that desire and attraction were not narrowly heterosexual; what other reason, after all, could there be that he counseled men to dress modestly not only in front of unrelated (and therefore marriageable) women, but in front of other men, too? This helps to explain how Muslims dress, and specifically when addressing, petitioning, or engaging God.

But let us not stray from the point at hand.

After Muhammad, and especially but not only in the vast Indo-Persian, Muslim world, same-sex desire was often celebrated, although in most of these instances it was older men making young boys the objects of their physical and emotional affections. This would suggest that Islamic civilization had a complex attitude to sexuality. Works by scholars like Scott Kugle and Joseph Massad certainly complicate the narrative of Islam as homophobic or strictly heterosexual.

Those incredibly complex historical legacies mean there is room for Muslim progressives to argue for the moral legitimation of different understandings of intimacy and companionship, up to and including marriage. But, of course, in pointing that out, we are simultaneously admitting that, arguably in the view of the majority of Muslims today and the scholarly Islamic tradition, grounded in dominant readings of the Qur'an and Muhammad's life, sexual expression should be limited to certain kinds of relationships between certain categories of adult men and women. That is a fact that might be hard for many in the West—but not only the West—to accept, but it is an important one to acknowledge, for at least two reasons. The first is, how do these legacies affect how Muslims in the West relate to their religion and their societies?

The second asks us to look at the world more broadly. While many might be uncomfortable and even angered by conservative Muslim views on sexuality, it deserves mention that Muslims are almost one-quarter of the world's population, rapidly growing in number, and often skeptical of certain sexual freedoms we in the West take for granted. Which is what makes this conversation so charged. For some, Islamic attitudes are benighted, ignorant, oppressive—and even dangerous. Conversely, many Muslims experience those on the other side of these questions as domineering, sometimes processing Western sexual freedoms as continuations of aggressive colonialism in new forms. To the first of these concerns, I believe the only way forward lies in political secularism.

To the second of these, I confess I do not know how these conversations will or can unfold. But I do know that if we are not able to acknowledge the strength of convictions, and the powerful emotions, experiences, and fundamental human needs involved, we cannot make progress.

With that, let us humbly approach this fraught topic in greater detail.

IF WE BELIEVE the arc of Prophetic biography to be inclusive of all legitimate moral possibilities, what do we do with what's excluded? Muhammad instituted radical reforms in his time—freeing many slaves, giving them positions of authority, and demanding that those who entered into intimate relationships with them treat them as they would spouses of equal social standing, giving their offspring status no different than children whose mothers were free. These weren't just moral reforms, however: they were legal reforms. They had teeth. It wasn't enough to ask people to be better. There also had to be consequences if they were not. When he needed to be or wanted to be—or, rather, as a Muslim would see it, when God wanted him to be—Muhammad could be abrupt in his reforms. At other times he could be gradual.

But neither God nor Muhammad showed any openness toward sexuality, intimacy, and companionship beyond the heteronormative. Some Muslim progressive scholars have argued that the story of the Prophet Lot and Sodom and Gomorrah is not about (male) homosexuality, but about highway robbery and rape, among other crimes, for which reasons those people were Divinely punished. I am not sufficiently expert on the sacred history to decisively opine on that, but we should remember that the absence of Qur'anic condemnation does not mean the absence of Prophetic condemnation, nor should it mean Qur'anic or Prophetic endorsement. That is, God may not condemn homosexual *activity* in the Qur'an—although historically, most Muslims would argue He does—but neither does God or God's Prophet encourage the expression of such deeply felt desires.*

More than this, the Prophetic record features numerous instances in which Muhammad rejected, condemned, or prohibited expressions of sexuality if they were not between (mature) women and men; also, the Prophet was keen that maleness be constructed, acted on, and expressed in ways that demonstrated not only a heteronormative concept of sexuality but a strongly binary construction of gender (complicated, of course, by the fact that his masculinity challenged the masculinity of the times). By not just staying silent on the topic, which would give us some interpretive leeway, but by speaking out against it, Muhammad made God's position clear. The liberal and progressive Muslims who argue against heteronormativity are pushing against the weight of established tradition. That is certainly possible, but it creates a grievous complication: such reinterpretations undermine the status of the Prophet in Islam

---

* Qur'an 7:81 condemns the people of Sodom and Gomorrah thusly: "Indeed, you approach men with lust instead of women—you are a people who have exceeded all bounds."

and the place of revelation in religious life. Arguing that times have changed and that our sexual morality should change with them, which is a common sentiment today, requires that we demote Muhammad from Divinely guided and morally normative to a mere product of his times.

Which demotes God from omnipotent to merely generally competent.

Throwing the rest of the tradition into doubt, too. I'm not sure what to do with that, except point out that the entire edifice of Islam would come unmoored, and that is a heavy price to pay. It would not collapse immediately, and maybe not irrevocably, but the religious tradition would be profoundly destabilized and, most likely of all, some entirely new understanding of the faith would rise in its place. (In fact, such understandings are already under construction, which many Muslims who hew to conservative positions on this topic are loath to acknowledge.) If the Qur'an, after all, is just a product of the seventh century, and if it is not, as Muslims overwhelmingly believe, co-eternal with God, then on what basis do we argue it is relevant for all times and places? What beliefs are universal, and what are contingent, and on what basis do we make the distinction? If secular humanism should decide our course of action, why not relegate Islam to no more than an important part of our heritage? I'm not saying that one cannot make the argument against heteronormativity. What I'm saying instead is that if one argues against heteronormativity, one should be intellectually honest, and admit that one is making this argument contrary to Muhammad's statements and God's speech, and not that one has secretly divined what God and His Prophet intended all along, as if they didn't know what they believed.

To do otherwise would leave us in the intolerable position of arguing that God and the Prophet had, out of fear or timidity, condemned countless millions to a life of misery, loneliness, and hardship, only because they couldn't muster up the courage to say what they secretly knew was right. Other arguments trying to find an Islamic proof against heteronormativity often feel intellectually unsatisfying. This includes, for example, that Muhammad never knew sexual orientation was genetic, and since now we know that that's the case, we can override these specific rulings. But since we believe God instructed Muhammad, and God evolved human beings, does that mean God didn't know what is and isn't genetic? (Moreover, an action with a genetic basis can be forbidden; indeed, one could argue most acts, good or bad, have genetic bases.) The ummah, however, is on challenging ground here because, without Muhammad as its normative model, the popular understanding of Islam would crumble, but with Muhammad as a normative model, much of the ummah is at odds with the direction of most of the United States and most of the West (and, perhaps increasingly, much of the rest of the world, too).

How will Muslims navigate this tension?

How will the wider world respond to those moves?

At the very least, we can predict that some Muslims in the West will move politically to the right, while others may embrace many progressive causes but hesitate to embrace what has become increasingly a matter of mainstream moral consensus. (All the same, I predict we will see more and more Muslims line up with progressive ethics on these and related questions—and not just among Western Muslims, but among Muslims in majoritarian contexts, too. We would be naive if we failed to recognize how rapidly those societies have changed in just the last decade—a consequence of, among other things, failed, oppressive, rigid Islamisms and the rapid spread of social media.) Nevertheless, let us pause for a moment and consider the phenomenon of the Muslim who hews to what, for lack of a better term, we might call a conservative position on sexuality.

THIS KIND OF MUSLIM will not yield their ground because they have little reason to believe they should or even believe they can, morally and theologically speaking. As they see it, Muhammad's authority transcends secular reason because God was in communication with him. God intended for His message to apply to all times and places, and if God stayed silent on an issue, or spoke out against one, then that must be given its due weight. This is different from the topic of polygyny, where Muhammad never encouraged, let alone demanded the practice, but rather gingerly granted permission for it, and under very strict circumstances. From the perspective of the conservative Muslim, a more precise analogy would be a scenario in which Muhammad had not ever permitted polygamy, and, in fact, spoke out against it; and subsequently, someone attempted to argue that Muhammad had gotten it wrong or really meant to say it was okay.

The long and short of it is: in an Islamic context, it is far easier to make the case that polygyny should be restricted than it is (and will be) to say that heterosexual relationships are not the only permissible forms of sexual relationship, and even within the bounds of marriage. It could be noted that even conservative positions on this topic limit themselves to physical expressions of desire and attraction, and not the underlying emotions, sentiments, and needs. Of course, it is unclear what meaningful difference that makes to the person who desires intimacy and companionship with someone the tradition has historically proscribed they have any such relationship with. Which is to say, these are fraught, challenging, and difficult conversations, but let us keep two things in mind. The first is that these conversations are happening and will continue to happen and second, that we can look to (political) secularism to mediate between different perspectives.

Not everyone will agree, but, as time goes by, more and more Muslims will—at least in the West—concur with what has effectively become a mainstream consensus. There will be more and more progressive Muslims—or, perhaps I should say, Muslims who concur with progressive ethics on these topics—who welcome the expansion of normative sexuality and intimacy to include other kinds of relationships; for those who do so by arguing that they represent what Muhammad actually wanted, however, there will be robust resistance (grounded, of course, in the fact that the Qur'an and Muhammad are quite explicit about their position).

Regardless.

Why should Islam belong to only one type of people, or one school of thought? There will be disagreements. Any Islam we practice in the world must, however, be dominated by love, compassion, and kindness; the emphasis should be on welcoming people, and creating opportunities for spiritual community, especially between groups of people who don't agree with each other. There were differences in approach, and will continue to be.

We can, as I explained above, look to secularism to balance these.

Just as in the case of polygyny, secularism squares the circle, creating enough room to resolve the apparently irresolvable tension between, on the one hand, how some Muslims now and in the future will practice their faith, and the consequences for others, Muslim and otherwise. There's a significant difference between saying I believe God wants such-and-such an outcome and believing that outcome to be politically mandated, especially if that outcome is a religious position to which the secular, agnostic, or atheistic person cannot or will not subscribe. Policies should not be grounded in religious norms unless there are also other universalistic rubrics through which those policies can be arrived at. Religion can be a rich and autonomous moral enterprise within the boundaries of secular statehood; it can be smaller than the state, and should be. Religion can also be bigger than the state, and should be. It deals with our fates as individuals and speaks to us as a species, beyond the national, ethnic, linguistic, and racial borders we impose. But religion can never forget what happens when it is fused with political authority, when it *is* the state.

Whether you are a Muslim who approves of heteronormativity or rejects it, you have no business using the state to persecute those who do not share your belief systems or denying others rights you allow for yourself. After all, if a Muslim were to say that marriage equality was wrong and should be politically reversed, then what is to stop that Muslim from then saying that marriages between Muslim women and men of other faiths—which are, in most schools of thought, expressly forbidden—should also be banned? What if a Catholic were to say that any form of sex that is not procreative should be forbidden, or for any person of faith to argue that public schools should be used to advance one particular sexual morality? This is treacherous ground. If we think secular humanism can be coercive (and it can be), imagine how much greater harm would come from theocracy. Muhammad only established a community in Medina when he no longer had the option of living in Mecca. We are not forced to that outcome.

Fortunately, as we shall see, there isn't much room for theocracy in post-Prophetic Islam anyway.

By definition, Muhammad's authority cannot be replicated. He was a Prophet, which meant God spoke to him. He was the last Prophet, which means God will speak to no one else. The law, as it were, is now in our hands, and no one interpretation of the law should be *imposed* over others, because all attempts at understanding the law are necessarily contingent. I am well within my rights to argue that someone else's interpretation of Islam is wrong, misguided, or dangerous. But they are free to challenge my interpretation too. In a secular society, both interpretations (and more) should freely compete without governmental interference. Beyond the issues on which we have consensus, such as the Oneness of God, the sacredness of life, or the sacrosanctity of the Qur'an, we have many areas of dispute. Look at what happened to Islam after Muhammad.

We Muslims agree, down to today, on practically all the intimate details of life—how to pray, how to fast, how to perform pilgrimage—and the grander, cosmic components of Islam—what happens after you die, what heaven and hell are like—as well as the core beliefs, in angels and destiny, in prophecy, and sacred morality. That agreement transcends and binds even Sunni and Shia. But where we disagree—that's where the sectarianism started, and that's why politicizing Islam is so dangerous, because politics is the divide. Had God and Muhammad intended for Islam to be a political movement, a governing ideology, a state, you'd think you'd see a little more preparation for the inevitability of Muhammad's death and what came after. Early Muslims, after Muhammad, attempted this experiment all the same. They united faith and power, and the state they built didn't even last half a century. It was doomed to fail. It had to fail. If only because there was no other way for Islam to survive.

THE FABLE OF THE
STABLE THEOCRACY

TONY JUDT WAS one of my favorite public intellectuals, so when he collaborated with Yale historian Timothy Snyder on *Thinking the Twentieth Century*, Snyder became one of my favorite academics, too. I enjoyed the former book so much that when Snyder's next work, *Black Earth: The Holocaust as History and Warning*, was published, I quickly picked it up. (It'd be hard to recommend it too strongly.) I had a copy of another one of Snyder's monographs, *The Road to Unfreedom: Russia, Europe, America*, within days of its release. In it, Snyder argues that Russian president Vladimir Putin had made the destabilization and fragmentation of the West a foreign policy objective, and details the many routes Moscow had taken to achieve this end.

This in itself was not a surprise to those of us who had been tracking Islamophobia, especially in Europe, where connections between Russia and far-right, anti-Muslim (and anti-European, and often anti-Semitic) forces have been in evidence for years.

Snyder's monograph exposed just how depressingly far Moscow had gotten. Up to and including interference in the US elections themselves, which strangely never provoked the kind of widespread outrage one would expect such an action to elicit. What is the end point of this foreign interference? What will happen to the West from here on? Is Trump an aberration or a new normal? Are the great institutions of the mighty West truly in permanent decline? In *The Road to Unfreedom*, I found a particular passage I wish every Muslim teacher and preacher would read. Snyder tries to make sense of why European elites in nations like Britain took so long to wake up to the xenophobia and anti-Western sentiment in their midst. He is even more concerned with why small European nations would cave in to the same sentiment; one would think vulnerable nations would do whatever they could to preserve the European Union that had brought them peace.

They caved in, Snyder explains, because they misunderstand their histories. The citizens of these nations are taught an incomplete, shortsighted, and self-defeating national narrative, an erroneous explanation of who they *were*, which in turn mars their ability to accurately judge who they are or can be. Snyder calls it "the fable of the wise nation," the romantic conceit, held to as if rock-solid truth revealed on Mount Sinai itself, that there was a time when these small nation-states weren't just independent, but prosperous, all on their own, free of foreign influence, be that, as it is conceived, Ottomans or Austro-Hungarians or Russians or the EU. These nation-states were discrete, stable, and distinct. And, of course, if it was like this before, it can be like this again. To concretize what this means, apply the fable of the wise nation, this fantastical historical mythology, to Poland.

Led by their own historical self-conceptions, some Poles would believe that they didn't need the European Union to prosper, or even need the EU at all, because long ago, Poland flourished solo. Poland went it alone, so Poland can once again go it alone. The Nazis and the Communists were aberrations, interruptions of a historic destiny. Drawing from the fable of the wise nation, European radicals credibly argued against pan-European politics, while enough citizens credulously went along, believing that doing so would unlock keys to remarkable prosperity and meaningful independence. History, Synder warns, shows how untenable such a conceit is. Like the nonsensical promises Boris Johnson made to Britain, leading to the blunder of Brexit. In truth, Johnson, like Trump and others around them, were Putin's useful idiots.

Without America, the European Union is vulnerable; without the European Union, individual European nations are easy prey for Russia (and for China). These wise nations, small and powerless, will be picked off one by one. And indeed, we can predict this will happen because this is what has always happened. For European nations have two realistic options, Snyder argues. Either they can choose to affiliate—as they do among one another in the European Union—in partnership with an America-that-was, a democratic multinationalism, or they can be subject to some kind of more traditional and malicious empire. The latter is what happened during most of history: a few states lorded it over everyone else. There was hardly a time when, say, the Czechs were ever really on their own and doing well for it; mostly, they were under someone else's control. End European integration, Snyder is warning us, and you will not see a renaissance of national flourishing, but a redux of imperial history, with, say, Poland once again subjected to the whims of powerful despots.

Many Europeans, in other words, thought history was something different from what it was. And because they did, their future will play out predictably. The first time as tragic occupation and domination, the second time as farcical hegemony and interference. But isn't it insanity to try the same thing and expect different results? Something similar happens in Islamic history. Call it the fable of the stable theocracy. This arises first because some Muslims believe, or are taught and taught not to dispute, that Muhammad built a state in Medina not in circumstances specific to his time and place, but because statehood was a religious obligation divorced of context. And so, as he did, we must do. And second, they believe that the first four, or Righteous, Caliphs who succeeded him, reigning from 632 to 661, represent an Islamic golden age, the best translation of Muhammadan theocracy into post-Prophetic history, which we Muslims can—and should—return to.

But what if Muhammad's state-building occurred not because Muslims have to build a state, but because (a) God wanted to show Muslims how they could act *should* they be in position to build, or need, or inherit a state, or (b) the historical circumstances of Muhammad's time and place made state-building necessary, or perhaps both are true? And what if the stable theocracy, that twenty-nine-year golden age, that reign of the Righteous Caliphs, was not so uniformly golden? This might incidentally explain why Islamism, the move to turn Islam into a political ideology (usually to the detriment of Islam, politics, and anyone in close proximity), has thus far failed and failed so spectacularly. Usually, it provokes severe suppression and ends in defeat and still worse tyranny than it aimed to undermine, or if it succeeds—the rare instance is the Islamic Republic of Iran—it's hard to know what was gained.

Yes, Iran is a highly educated society with several meaningful social, political, and technological indicators. Did thousands have to be tortured and even killed to accomplish that? Was there no other way to accomplish these ends?

And when did people becomes means to an end—not ends in themselves?

If people otherwise refuse to go along, then violence becomes inevitable. And people refuse to go along because now is not then. The world is not, to borrow a Reza Aslanian formulation, a cosmic drama in which the same story endlessly repeats itself—where the smaller and larger details change, and a failure to accommodate these changes results, unsurprisingly, in catastrophic failure. Some Muslims have a strange habit of imagining that the formative era of Islam was exempt from history, that Muhammad, his family, his companions, and his opponents made decisions in an environment possessed of no memory, no context, or no basic human calculation, as if everything was manufactured somewhere far away, and only dropped down in western Arabia for reasons God only knows. But there had to be some reasons why the light of Muhammad, the soul of the final Prophet, was embodied in this man's form, place, time, and among those people. If I were to recommend that every Muslim leader be a reader of another book, it'd be G. W. Bowersock's *The Crucible of Islam*.

Bowersock's slim volume—you have no excuse now— examines the formative social, political, and cultural conditions under which Islam took shape. Some Muslims would recoil at this, seeing it as an exercise that robs Islam of its sacredness and divine origin. I disagree. I believe God evolved human beings through comprehensible laws; I believe history moves according to comprehensible principles, however much we might (rightly) argue over them. In other words, I can believe reasoned investigation and intelligent excavation yield pertinent historical knowledge, including about the period of formative Islamic history. We can learn from this knowledge and apply it to new or other circumstances, including for Muslims in the West, a small and sometimes very vulnerable minority, in its own way a wise nation that would do well not to believe in myths and legends.

FOR A LONG TIME before Muhammad, Christian Romans and their Ethiopian co-religionists had engaged in a tug of war with Zoroastrian Persia over the Arabian Peninsula. Many, if not most, of Arabia's tribes were affected by this contest. Building on research by other scholars alongside his own, Bowersock finds that Muhammad's early career was not exempt from this competition and that the Meccans, and Medina's Jews, believed him to be a fan of Rome and maybe a little more than that. They viewed, for example, his first exodus to Christian Ethiopia as evidence of sympathy for mighty imperial Christianity or, worse still, proof of some dastardly connection brewing between Constantinople and this Messenger who claimed connections with Christ. When Muhammad migrated to Medina, seizing control of a city on Mecca's trade routes, it was not surprising that the tribe of the Quraysh were alarmed, and those of Medina's Jews who were allied to Persia sniffed out evidence of some further, deeper Roman intrigue.

Bowersock even finds evidence that the Romans may have encouraged their associationist proxies in Medina to issue an invitation to Muhammad (although I remain skeptical of this—and, anyway, it seems Muhammad had no knowledge of it). Still, we might consider it for a moment, because it does offer us a potentially plausible secular explanation for sacred history, which is an exercise I want more Muslims to engage in. Observed through a human, locally focused lens, the second exodus is the desperate escape of the Prophet of a persecuted people. But through a macro, statist lens, it may be a ploy by the Roman empire to secure an alliance on its southern flank as it prepares for an imminent war with Persia. (The most powerful Medinese Jews were allied to Persia, as were Jews to the north, in their holy land, long suffering Christian hostility.) Why, these scholars ask, would a city far to the north of Mecca be so eager to welcome a modest merchant with a modest following *as its ruler*? But if the Romans had pushed some of their Medinese allies to do so, that'd make more sense, they contend. The Romans needed quiet on their vulnerable southern border as they pressed their advantage against the Persians; a unified Medina, sidelining the Jews of that city, who were sympathetic to Persia, might have been a prize for them.*

This early intertwining of Romanness and Muslimness was so complex and layered that it moved Professor Juan Cole to argue, in his book *Muhammad: Prophet of Peace amid the Clash of Empires*, that "Islam is, no less than Christianity, a Western religion that initially grew up in the Roman Empire. Moreover, Muhammad saw himself as an ally of the West."** These Romans could've had no idea that in a matter of decades, the Muslims would swallow

---

* I am skeptical of this particular part of the thesis because, one, it seems to exaggerate the importance of Yathrib/Medina to the Romans; and two, it downplays the Prophet's biological connections to Yathrib/Medina, with which many of his family members had direct or indirect associations. That is not to mention that it seems not to take into account the power of belief—and attraction to, and commitment to, a different religious tradition (namely, the Yathribites' attraction to Islam).

** This assertion is taken from page 3 of *Muhammad: Prophet of Peace amid the Clash of Empires* (New York: Bold Type Books, 2018).

half their empire. Or that, many centuries later, their Ottoman co-religionists would digest the rest. Historical overdetermination: there are multiple causes for the same event, and the more causes you can identify, the better are the lessons you take from it.

We can even make much more sense of ostensible Muslim anti-Semitism.

IF ONE WERE to pretend that Muhammad's Prophetic trajectory must be reproduced uncritically regardless of our circumstances— the reasoning being that because his life ended with him in a position of political power, so too should ours—then we would come to some uncomfortable conclusions about Islam and Judaism. Namely that Jews will always only stand in the way of Muslim power, and thus conflict, if not war, is inevitable. Better to prepare for it now than be blindsided by it later.

Or we can go back to the thesis of Roman statecraft Bowersock relies on.

Although Muhammad went out of his way to accommodate the Jewish tribes of Medina, these two factions eventually went to war, their alliance eventually undermined by open hostility. But here's the thing. Although it's possible to speak of "the Muslims" in this period since there was only one Muslim community and it had a single leader, it's not possible to speak of "the Jews." Therefore conflict between the Muslims and the Jews is a fiction, another fable. Even while tensions between some of the most prominent Medinese Jews and the Muslims spilled over into war, many other Jews coexisted peacefully with Muhammad. Many Muslims, as well as critics of Islam, have no idea of this and prefer to remember a history in which an infant Islam was almost strangled at birth by a domineering and dangerous Jewish big brother, or one in which Muhammad, given his first taste of power, turned into a genocidal, anti-Semitic conqueror. The actual truth is far different.

While Muhammad was looking for sanctuary for his community, it may well have been that the Romans, through local agents, offered him one in the form of an alliance in Medina. Or it could have been that his long-standing kinship with the city inspired its people to reach out to him. Or they were genuinely moved by Islam and deeply adored Muhammad and were ready to embrace him no matter the cost. Or all of these things.

All the same, once in Medina, Muhammad understood that this refuge needed to be protected at all costs—there was nowhere else for his people to go. Those Jews allied to Rome enjoyed fruitful relations with Muhammad up to and beyond the 630 conquest of Mecca (thus including the events of 627). The Jews allied to Persia saw things rather differently. This explains that, as unfortunate as the deterioration in relations between major Medinese Jewish tribes and the Muslims was, it was not evidence of any inbuilt anti-Semitism, any necessary hostility on Muhammad's part that modern Muslims should reproduce (or modern Islamophobes should ground their hatred of Islam in). Nor does it prove any endemic Jewish hostility to Islam. It's simply that some tribes that were Jewish fell in with Muhammad's enemies and so found themselves arrayed against Muhammad himself. The other Jewish tribes, having no inclination to ally with Islam's opponents, did not. These tribes lived in Arabia, apparently for many centuries after Muhammad died, though it appears they largely disappeared under the pressure of conversion and Wahhabi puritanism during the eighteenth and nineteenth centuries.

If Muhammad had been an anti-Semite, this bigotry would have been part of Muslim religiosity, which in the premodern age—and especially the centuries closer to Muhammad—was far more complicated. When Umayyad Muslims intervened in Spain and Portugal in 711, their closest allies were Jews. This alliance was so close that when the last independent Iberian Muslim state was overrun seven centuries later, the victorious Catholics so closely connected Jews with Muslims that they went ahead and expelled all the Jews too. Columbus sailed the ocean blue—in 1492. When the Jews of Spain were forced out, the Ottoman Caliph encouraged them to settle in his domains. This was never a history of the kind of coexistence that secular democracies aspire to, but neither was there the anti-Semitism endemic to so much of Western history; that is a rather more recent phenomenon, reverse-projected into Islamic history and, especially, its crucible.

This means that as we ask how we can prevent Islam from tilting into violence, or promote an Islam that can act as a check on the violent tendencies of many governments, or wonder about how to tackle anti-Semitism in Muslim spaces, we must first and honestly examine our history. If we decontextualize Islam, then decisions made in specific historical contexts become universal maxims, even as the actors themselves never held those decisions as such. Beware Muslims bearing uncritical sacred history. Politicized Islam imagines that Muhammad simply rocketed to power in Medina, that the transition from refugee to ruler was instantaneous, that there were no *secular reasons* for why he ended up in Medina, or how, or what motivations or influences shaped his decisions and those of the people around him. The fable of the stable theocracy proceeds from here: there is no worldly, discernible explanation for Muhammad's success except a nebulous Divine Will, and this success continued unchanged into the early post-Prophetic period, when four of Muhammad's close kin and companions superintended Islam for twenty-nine years.

While the Righteous Caliphs' system of government was far more egalitarian, honest, and in some instances remarkably more tolerant than their successors', it was also markedly more unstable, given that these Caliphs combined in themselves political and religious authority to a degree that was inevitably untenable. Rightly guided by God, they might have been, as Sunni Muslims describe them, but the world they lived in and ruled over existed alongside immense suffering for . . . Muslims themselves. It could not have been otherwise. The struggle to succeed Muhammad and create an Islamic polity resulted in civil war. In the present, the struggle to create an Islamic polity has accomplished the same. It doesn't work, and it won't work, because it never worked. Because it was never meant to work. There cannot be a stable theocracy because there is no theocratic source of authority that can be stable (hence the civil wars): Muhammad is gone, and he is not coming back. His position cannot, should not, and must not, be reproduced, except if the intention is to further fragment Islamdom.

That's why the project of the stable theocracy failed under the rule of Abu Bakr and Umar and Uthman and Ali. If they weren't up to the task, it's for the simple reason that none of them was Muhammad, and if they weren't then, we certainly aren't today. To be clear, I'm not blaming them. It would have been impossible for them to theologically theorize the office of the Caliphate such that it be rendered stable and sustainable, never mind that they were in the middle of ruling a burgeoning Islam, struggling to keep tribal pressures and ethnic tensions under control. And all of that came down to this: there is no way a single authority can command the will of the Muslim world unless that authority is Prophetic. These upstanding men did the best they could and performed incredibly under impossible circumstances. They are paragons of Islamic virtue, probity, and wisdom.

They are lights to be guided by.

But your piety does not guarantee secular success. Conversely, secular success does not translate into virtue. The command of Islamic fraternity and sorority is not thereby suspended; it just means we have to find another avenue for its expression.

THE EMPTY THRONE

"SHIA" IS SHORT for *Shi'at Ali*, "the partisans of Ali," who only became explicit about their partisanship when Ali's authority was bitterly contested. "Sunni" is short for *ahl as-Sunnah wa'l jama'ah*, "the people of the path (of Muhammad) and the community (of Muslims)," a term that nobody needed to use when the (small) Muslim ummah was united under the leadership of the Prophet Muhammad.* Whereas Protestants broke from Catholics some 1,500 years after Jesus, the divisions between Sunni and Shia began almost immediately after Muhammad's passing, even before his body was in the ground. (Muhammad's Islam hasn't even been around for 1,500 years.) One of the most remarkable facts about Sunni and Shia is that, for two sects that have sometimes suffered bitter enmity and outright violence with one another, they also share tremendous overlap in theology and practice.

For a person new to Islam, Sunni and Shia mosques are hardly different. Worship services, ritual law, rules of modesty, and diet are all surprisingly similar. What we differ on is minor in number,

---

* In a lecture at the Islamic Center of Greater Cincinnati on August 20, 2021, Mufti Hussain Kamani noted that "community" here referred not abstractly to the ummah at large but specifically and exclusively to the Companions of the Prophet Muhammad collectively.

but major in consequence: Politics. Authority. Sources of law and validity. We come to similar conclusions, time and again, according to similar readings of similar sources from different chains of authority. Sunnis trust Muhammad's youngest wife, Aisha, for many hadith about his life; given the bad blood between Aisha and Ali later in their lives, Shias are far more skeptical of her as a source and look to others of Muhammad's family and companions. Still, both still arrive at many of the same rulings. Except, of course, on the question of who should rule after Muhammad—suffice it to say, it's not surprising how terrible the feuding became.

Politics has a way of taking us all on a shortcut to bitterness and nastiness.

WHEN MUHAMMAD DIED in 632, two years after the conquest— Muslims call it the liberation—of Mecca, he was the undisputed leader of the entire Arabian Peninsula. Muslim armies were already skirmishing with Romans who, fresh from a remarkable turn-around in their war with the Persians, were troubled by a united Arabia emerging on their underbelly. With the news of his death, though, some Muslims were incredulous. How could the Messenger of God leave them? Was he to die like any other man? In that moment, his closest family, including the aforementioned Ali, were busy with funerary preparations. Abu Bakr, meanwhile, emerged as a rock for the remaining community. He was conscious that should the community remain rudderless even a day or two longer, great trouble would follow.

Someone had to rule.

That someone would be him. He gave a heartfelt speech about how Muhammad was a man, and all men are mortal, and therefore Muhammad could and would die, and had died, but God was Life and could not die, and Abu Bakr was acclaimed and applauded for seeing clearly what had come to pass. He saw better than that even: he saw that, in the absence of the Prophet, there would be chaos, and the community agreed with his concerns. Were the Arabs to go back to their tribal feuding and petty ethnocentrisms? To their harsh slavery and vicious infighting? A new office was created for him, *Khilafat Rasul Allah*, the Caliphate of the Messenger of God, which in the Adamic iteration had been applied to all humankind.* This office would be different. It would have a political mandate. It would be about ruling a religious community.

This Caliph was ideally the most pious and capable states-man. He was the best follower of the Prophet, however—not a Prophet himself. Abu Bakr, in the minds of most Muslims, eas-ily fit that standard. Though he did not want the office, he was forced by overwhelming consensus to take the position and helm the young ummah.

The first edition of this second, more specific type of Caliph-ate lasted from 632 to 661 and was a unique creature. This state expanded dramatically as it imploded internally, a volcanic erup-tion that destroyed itself in the process of remaking the world. Its government was run in the name of a person who had died, and it appealed to his legacy to justify its statecraft, even as it was dramatically unclear to its constituents, and even its leaders, what exactly his legacy meant for their politics. Take the simple question of Abu Bakr's Caliphate. Shia Islam grew out of those Muslims who believe that when Abu Bakr and his close companions devised the office of the Caliphate to fill the political vacuum left by Muham-mad's death, they were acting out of turn and stealing the right of Muhammad's own kin.

For Shia Muslims, Ali was not just meant to rule after Muham-mad, but he also inherited a religious authority that transcended what Sunnis believed the Caliphate could or should claim. For Sun-nis, the picture is rather more complicated. Sunnis descend from those who revere Ali as among the most spiritually significant of all of Muhammad's male companions (if not the most significant) and a primary progenitor of the spiritual practice of Islam known colloquially as Sufism. But Sunnis also believe that Abu Bakr was

---

* King David, who is also a Prophet in the Islamic tradition—and so, may God's peace and blessings be upon him—is also named in the Qur'an as a *Khalifa*.

not wrong to create or claim the Caliphate as an office devised to meet a need in a pressing moment. For them, the office was the outcome of human beings interpreting God's words using their own resources, in response to their own context.* This was how many very religious Muslims believed things should be, and Sunni Islam is the product of those who came to terms with, acceded to, or loudly approved that decision.

The two sects can at least agree on this much: in 656, twenty-four years after Muhammad died, Ali came to power—for five short years. He was the fourth Sunni Caliph but the first sovereign Shia Imam. After him, the two communities once more diverged, this time for good. Ali is thus a unifying and divisive figure all at once, a tragedy given his spiritual status in both sects. After Ali was assassinated in 661, the Umayyad governor of Syria, Muawiya, took over and transformed the Righteous Caliphate into a monarchic office. The people who (much later) came to call themselves Sunnis became disillusioned and increasingly focused their attention on the human relationship with God. For Shias, the experience was still more disastrous; what was seen as Abu Bakr's impolite elbowing aside of Ali became, by 661, the tyrannical usurpation of Muhammad's family's right to rule by a clan of Arabs who'd been at the vanguard of *violent* opposition to Muhammad during his lifetime. This trajectory reached its nadir in 680, when the third Shia Imam, Ali's son and Muhammad's grandson, Husayn, raised the banner of revolt against Muawiya's son and heir, the particularly dissolute Yazid. It was not a peaceful affair.

Husayn was abandoned by his allies at Karbala, in southern Iraq; Yazid massacred his camp. Under the baleful influence of Wahhabis, who were born in the eighteenth century opposition to traditional Sunni Islam, many modern-day Sunnis are identified with Yazid. No sincere Muslim of any sect, however, cannot but

---

* Indeed, for many Sunnis, Muhammad made clear that Abu Bakr was to lead the ummah after his death. As such, these interpret Abu Bakr's selection as the fulfillment of a Divine command.

be heartbroken by the murder of Muhammad's grandson, and it is hard to understand how any Muslim of any sect can find Yazid a remotely sympathetic figure. Sunnis may not believe that Ali was Muhammad's intended political heir, but he was among his spiritual heirs, and Sunnis likewise believe that, with the death of Ali, the Caliphate as an office had lost whatever religious legitimacy it had. Nevertheless, relations between these factions fast soured. Had the text of the Qur'an not been agreed upon before Muhammad's death, it is hard to imagine these two divergent proto-sects, who were at odds with each other from literally Day 1 of the rest of Islamic history, could have possibly come together on what the text said (let alone on what it means).

THE DIVERGENCE OVER WHO should rule suggests, however, that there was not only no agreement on the matter, but also—I know this is a Sunni position, and probably not a popular one at that—it suggests that Muhammad didn't prioritize politics the way some think he did. Considering just how much Sunnis and Shias have in common, it's unproblematic to note that Muhammad made clear where he stood on many such ritual matters, the right and wrong of religious and spiritual life. Meanwhile, considering how not just contentious but downright ugly post-Prophetic Muslim history immediately became—of the four Righteous Caliphs, three died violently (Umar, Uthman, and Ali), and two of them (Uthman and Ali) at the hands of fellow Muslims, and the whole period lasted barely longer than the length of Muhammad's prophethood. On many occasions, Muhammad warned about this very thing: that Muslim would soon turn on Muslim and that bloodshed between Muslims would not cease for many ages (if ever). I can still remember sitting in an NYU course on political Islam when our teacher, the very gentlemanly Peter Chelkowski, remarked offhandedly that many times more Muslims died fighting Muslims than fighting anyone else, and wanting to protest even as I realized he was possibly right.

Like many Muslims, I was sad that our history had begun to go south so soon after Muhammad's death. But over time, I began to see a silver lining to this dark cloud, that the warnings Muhammad issued—about violence between Muslims—hid within them the one and only consolation that can be gleaned from post-Prophetic violence.

It prevented Islam from being limited to an ethnonational tradition.

Imagine for a moment that things had turned out very differently. Imagine that, instead of reluctantly coming to terms with Abu Bakr's assumption of the Caliphate—as many Shias and some Sunnis believe he had done—Ali had wholeheartedly endorsed the new position and its occupant instead. What if the second Caliph, Umar, hadn't been assassinated? Or what if Ali had never been assassinated, and Muawiya and his Umayyad clan hadn't assumed power—what then? It might have been great for the new state, but it might've eventually turned terrible for Islam. Because the religion would've become identified with the state and may very well have been limited to the subjects of that state. Even if it had not, the two entities would've grown so in tandem that the collapse of the state would've struck a blow, and maybe a mortal one, to the prospects of the religion.

Paradoxically, this means that the failure of Islam as a political project opened the door for the success of Islam as a global religious project—not the property of any people, let alone any state. Arabs dominated early Islam, but they weren't meant to be the only recipients and adherents of the new faith. Failure liberated Muslimness to become independent of ethnic, linguistic, and political affiliation; converting to Islam did not (and should never) have to mean picking one part of yourself over another. One of the great misunderstandings of early Islamic history is that though the early, largely Arab Muslims conquered huge territories, by and large, they were more concerned with each other than those they ruled over. Christian and Jewish communities usually prospered under early Muslim rule, even while huge numbers of Muslims went to war with each other. It was almost worse to be in power than out of it. New churches sprung up in the Levant while the Prophet's closest companions and even family were bloodied.

By the time the Umayyad Caliphate collapsed, in 750, after some ninety years, its successor Caliphate tried futilely to hold on to the idea of a single Muslim state. Ironically, the first breakaway was a remnant Umayyad faction that declared an independent emirate in Andalus in 756, though at first, it was too timid to claim back the Caliphate. But the damage was done: the Caliph's authority was no longer hegemonic. It had been disputed since that Day 1, but now it was increasingly widely dismissed. But even as Muslims massacred each other, their religious prospects were absurdly converse. There's a lesson in that: Islam and politics means disaster. Islam and the human soul? Much good seems to have come from that combination.

By and large, the places we consider to be the Muslim world today didn't convert to Islam for many centuries. In some cases, it was only three or four hundred years after Arab Muslims entered as conquering forces that the territories in question even became barely majority Muslim. By then, the conquerors themselves had long since disappeared, melted away, or fused into the local population, but the patterns of conversion were very similar across a very different range of places.

In most cases, religious scholars who made it their business to study and apply (to themselves above all) their interpretation of revelation attracted students, acolytes, adherents, and even the simply curious, and entire communities formed around them. People of different faiths began to participate in Muslim rituals and were gradually Islamized. These religious scholars pursued shari'ah as the law governing their exoteric ritual life, but as a mystical path in their interior life, and they believed, with considerable evidence on their side, that the purpose of religion was purification, accomplished through "remembrance," or zikr, recalling God by invoking His names and attributes, the antidote to the primordial human forgetfulness that has marred us since Adam. These proto-Sufis described their connection to God through the language of love. Their interpretation of shari'ah, their brand of Islamic law, dominated most of Muslim life from not very long after Muhammad's death until the onset of colonialism and modernity.

If not for them, Islam might've never been more than an identity to me.

WHEN I WAS president of the Islamic Center at NYU, which serves as my alma mater's Muslim Students Association (MSA), I wanted very much to reconstruct our religious life on campus. I felt very strongly that we could reach many more people and become a model for other Muslim communities in the process. I watched with envy as there was (rightly) a Black History Month, as indeed there are many such months dedicated to the underrepresented, and wondered why we couldn't even have a designated block on the calendar, even just a week. The only template we had within Muslim spaces was the oddly named "Islam Awareness Week," which made Islam sound like a cancer that fellow students were being warned about, or the even weirder "Islamic Awareness Week," which seeks to raise your consciousness about an adjective. And anyway, who'd want to go to an Islam/ic Awareness Week except the very limited number of students who cared that much about being Muslim already?

I approached NYU's administration and asked how we could secure additional funding for our Islamic Center to put on our own week of celebration. Their answer initially dismayed me. In every rejection, though, is advancement. We were told that theme weeks only happened if you could find co-sponsoring organizations, and reasonably enough, there were few if any organizations who would co-sponsor Islam/ic Awareness Week. I didn't even want the Islamic Center to co-sponsor it, and it was my club's ostensible theme week. Why not, I wondered, instead have a theme week that celebrated the arts and culture, achievements and contributions, of Muslim societies and thinkers? We could join with the Pakistani Students Association to talk about *qawwali*, a South Asian art form deeply shaped by Sufism. We could do a walking tour of Muslim Harlem—there's a reason there's a Malcolm X Boulevard in Manhattan. And we'd get beyond a narrow obsession with pietism and view religion and culture more expansively and generously.

The event that emerged, "Shuruq"—sunrise—started off as five days of festivities and fundamentals, opening with an Iranian-Kurdish concert and closing with an event the theme of which I forgot—I'm getting old. Years later, it grew to a whole month. The reason I'm telling you this isn't just because I want to beg and plead with every MSA out there to stop wasting time and money on a week appealing to the narrowest constituency of Muslims possible—and, just in case you forgot, to also avoid associating Islam in the public imagination with disease and danger. What I want to say is, I'm proud of how far the Islamic Center at NYU has come and view it much as I imagine one would a child of theirs now off on her own. I helped to raise that person, but she is her own person now. But as much as I loved the work, I never felt quite spiritually at home at the Islamic Center at NYU. Maybe that's because any possibility of deep religious community was muddled by the leadership roles I had invariably taken on. It's hard to focus on God when you feel like the place you pray is your job.

In a city of nearly a million Muslims, indeed the largest Muslim city in the Western Hemisphere, and as someone who had made Muslimness his (poorly compensating) trade, it was surprising, dismaying, and revealing that I was Islamically homeless. Not that I didn't try. A Moroccan friend invited me to join a zikr circle, an intimate gathering where the like-minded convene to invoke God's name and deepen their attachment to their Beloved. The zikr was nice enough, but any positive vibes I'd experienced were more than amply canceled out by the speech the Shaykh gave afterward. He decided that a spiritual gathering was the appropriate venue for a substantively ridiculous monologue on presumed Islamic vigor. Somehow the subject got to secularism, by which I had hoped he meant the cultural form and not the political model. That is to say, I hoped he was concerned about a cultural indifference to faith and disconnect from belief, which I myself am often discomfited by, and not the separation of institutional faith and governance, which I support.

The Shaykh soon turned to Europe, the epitome, as he saw it, of whatever kind of secularization he was so concerned about, and then he claimed that Europe was on the verge of being overrun by Muslims. Europeans, he said, by which he meant white Europeans of Christian faith or ancestry, were disappearing, demographically speaking, while a younger, more conservative Muslim population was booming. Therefore, we were poised to take over that continent. Somehow this was a good thing, although given how many problems course through our Muslim communities here in the West, as minorities, I'm not sure majoritarianism is something we should eagerly pursue. Islam is a missionary faith, it's true, and I would love for more people to get acquainted with Islam, to learn from it and contribute to it, but my goal in life is not to see my faith run roughshod over anyone's else way of life, let alone continent. That is an idiotic prospect to celebrate, not just because it won't happen, but because pretending that it will empowers people who want to restrict, deport, or even eliminate our communities.

Can you imagine how any normal person not of the Muslim faith would react to this? It'd be understandable if that person was scared—or angry. Nobody responds well to being made to feel endangered; nobody wants to imagine his way of life is under siege—because that's what this Shaykh was describing with enthusiasm, and explicitly connecting political triumph to spiritual activity. Yes, Muslims are younger, on average, than their fellow Europeans of different faiths, but they will very quickly—that is, within a generation or two—converge with European demographics. Meaning that even if there is a modest spike in the growth of Muslims in many Western societies, that'll soon settle down. And don't forget: How many of these Muslims are religiously Muslim in a meaningful sense, or want to be? If you can't beat them, outbreed them: the desperate mantra of the one who confuses religion for identity, and wishes to transform Islam into a passport concerned with the recovery of power. The fable of the wise nation indeed.

We don't worship God, we worship our imagined community.

Think about how many Muslims in America actually want to be part of mosque communities. Ask yourself why that number is low. And then ask whether any of this would change were Muslims to become a majority. Wouldn't we just import and amplify our internal problems onto a countrywide scale? People in glass houses, after all, are warned not to throw stones.

IT'S BAD ENOUGH that people's concerns about globalization are exploited to instill fear and loathing of Muslims, translating into policy with very real and deleterious effects. We don't need to further empower those opposed to our flourishing. Had the Prophet Muhammad's mission been political, his legacy would have been mixed. Yes, there was a great Arab golden age and mighty Muslim dynasties and empires, but the years after him are also often painful to look at up close. Had his purpose been to reinvigorate monotheism, though, then his legacy is awesome. A marginal part of the world became the beating spiritual heart of a religion that, less than a century after his death, could be found from France to India; within several hundred years, Islam was part of cultures from the shores of the Arctic Ocean to Mozambique, Malaysia, and Morocco. A secular historian might argue that Jews invented monotheism. But we Muslims universalized it. We stitched together great and disparate civilizations, creating cultures so immersed in faith that their very languages evolved in the direction of Arabic, from script to vocabulary, from West Africa to Southeast Asia.

From all across the planet, people arrive on the hajj pilgrimage; they take what Hagar and Ishmael and Abraham did and carry it back to their villages, towns, cities, megalopolises. They've helped make fringe Semites into global icons, they've created an entire civilization oriented around God, and if it is the case that that civilization appears to be confronting an existential emergency, all the same that is not so bad for a faith that started with the exodus of a few dozen women and men in the year 622. Much will have to be done to reinvigorate our community, a challenge complicated by the vast number of Muslims today, and how differently we all see the world. With no Muhammad, the problem of a singular authority was always going to become more and more significant; by this point in history, the story of Islam as a political experiment, as fascinating as it was, has exhausted itself. Down that road is nothing but disappointment and darkness.

Now comes the moment when we pivot from Islam's beliefs and Islam's history to the place of Islam in the world today, first collectively, and then individually. Or rather, I should say, what if we collectively appealed to our individual authority? The age of the Caliphs of Muhammad has ended. The last of them was removed from office in 1924, almost exactly one hundred years ago. The next iteration, the ISIS Caliphate, was so brutal that one wishes it were never mentioned again. The office of the Caliphate, generally speaking, though, was for Sunni Muslims a worldly response to a religious need. The moment has passed. What, however, of the Caliphate of God, which commenced in the persons of Adam and Eve, but applies to all of us? Indeed—*is* all of us. That Caliphate lives and, so long as there are humans, cannot die. When we speak of ummah, the worldwide community of Muslims, can there be any connection between our individual stature and the fraternity and sorority we are meant to feel for each other in communities? The Caliphate of Muhammad has perished. The Caliphate of God, the Adamic and Eveian, endures.

Could we rethink it for today and, more importantly, for tomorrow? A democratic Caliphate of individuals and their democratic communities?

12

THE CASE
FOR THE CALIPHATE

THERE ARE FAR MORE people in the world today than there were during World War II, but it is still alarming that there are more refugees in the world today than at any time since then. Of these refugees, the majority appear to be Muslim. Most of the world's poorest countries are disproportionately Muslim. And many of the countries most vulnerable to climate change are mostly Muslim. One, in particular, the Maldives, threatens to disappear altogether. If we think the threat of terrorism and extremism is bad now, wait until the massive population dislocations of some of the world's younger and more desperate populations take hold.

The Muslim world is ill equipped to address this existential challenge; our numbers may be growing, as our overpoliticized, underinformed Sufi Shaykh might have bragged, but we lack the ability to address current problems, to say nothing of those around the bend. Muslims of all kinds widely lament the general weakness of the Muslim world, though there seems to be next to no consensus on what to do about it. If only Muslims were more united, I often hear. If only they worked together like they used to. (I'm not sure when this was.)

There is one thing that is hard to deny, however. A long time ago, Muslim societies were powerful, creative, sophisticated, generous, and pluralistic—for their time and their context. Today, the ummah is more riven by division than ever before; frequently dependent, neocolonized or occupied; and not a leader in many fields, if, sadly, any at all.

Whereas the future was once Western, now it sounds East Asian.

The Muslim world was entirely skipped over in the process.

Sometimes people say that Islam needs its own Reformation; usually, those who suggest this have no clear idea what the Reformation was, where or how it happened, or what it actually resulted in. This suggestion is therefore little more than condescending narcissism: your problems now are the problems we had a long time ago, since you are who we were a long time ago; and once you fix everything on your end, there won't be any more problems, because all of our problems with each other really are only of your making. To give just one example, you made us occupy Iraq to look for weapons of mass destruction that weren't there. Needless to say, the twenty-first-century Muslim world is not sixteenth-century Mitteleuropa. The latter was poor and backward by the standards of those times—and indeed our time—but it was not occupied by any foreign forces, and certainly did not exhibit the diversity that modern-day Islam does. Nor does modern Islam feature anything like the transnational Catholic Church, against which Martin Luther protested. If anything, the opposite is true. The Muslim world has too few transnational institutions and binding mechanisms, and appears to be suffering from ever greater degrees of atomization and dissolution.

Indeed, by the standards of the Protestant Reformation, Islam already had its Reformation—it was Wahhabism. The only reason there was not a Counter-Reformation is because, even as Wahhabism declared war on Sunni Islam and Shia Muslims, the Muslim world was on the precipice of colonization. Since then, indigenous authoritarianism, vapid religious extremism, and new forms of imperialism have choked off any promise of renewal, or at least repurposed it toward its own ends. (The notion of "moderate Arab states" is a good one.) But there is a solution that can be found in history and resurrected for modern conditions. With the selection of Abu Bakr as Caliph, in 632, until the assassination of Ali, in 661, there was a Righteous Caliphate; after that, a second dynasty, the Umayyad monarchy, claimed the office, until it was overthrown by the Abbasids in 750. The Baghdad-based Abbasids started off marvelously wealthy and remarkably powerful but soon lost their potency and prestige, gradually declining until, in 1258, they were finished off by the Mongols. A relative of the Caliph reportedly fled to Cairo, where he stayed under Mamluk suzerainty. The Mamluk dynasty preferred to have him, as he bolstered its legitimacy.

But he had no real power.

In 1517, when the Ottoman dynasty, based in Constantinople, swept across the Near East, picking up Jerusalem, Mecca, Medina, and Cairo from, of course, fellow Muslims, the Sultan in Thrace declared himself the Caliph, the fourth iteration of that office.

That lasted until the Great War, the First World War.

In 1923, the Turkish leader Mustafa Kemal, known to us as Atatürk, separated the temporal and spiritual authorities of the Caliphate; the former went to the Turkish Grand National Assembly, while spiritual authority remained with a descendant of the line of Osman (the Ottomans). In 1924, however, concerned that the office could be manipulated by foreign powers who ruled over far more Muslims than he did, Atatürk abolished the spiritual office altogether. After all, if the British ruled over India, which they did, and India had more Muslims than Turkey, which it did, then who was to say the Caliph was not more spiritually beholden to India than to the country he lived in? Either that was Atatürk's rationale, or he wanted to eliminate all rival claims of authority so he could accomplish his authoritarian march toward a crude and derivative cultural and political secularism.

The point is, the Muslim world was at a loss for how to respond.

First, there was no clear alternative to the Ottoman Caliph now deposed. Second, should there be, he would have had to rule over a large number of Muslims, or at least Mecca and Medina, and maybe Jerusalem too, to have some kind of religious authority. (No one seemed to be able to imagine a religious office without such qualifications.) Unfortunately, most of the Muslim world was colonized and more interested in liberating itself than submitting to another dynasty. The age of Abbasids and Ottomans running roughshod over huge portions of the world appeared to be at a firm end. And third, the world had moved on. New models revolved around capitalism and nascent communism. These were the ideologies to which young Muslims were attracted.

But there are some points of relevance in the Atatürkian moves. For one thing, separating religious and spiritual authority indicated a secularity that would have been laudable had it not been for the inferiority complex that powered Atatürk's despotic drive toward juvenile Westernization. Still, if we tease out the various strands we can find wisdom in some of them. For another thing, there was something democratic in the idea that authority could be moved into an ostensibly elected body, even if that was a branch of government. All this is to say, we have reached a new age—our own kind of Abu Bakr moment. The ummah is a religious concept with spiritual significance. God wants Islam to be a brotherhood and sisterhood. This has to mean something, or our religious lives are incomplete. I am asking us to complete our religious obligations in a way that does not set us pointlessly at odds with the world, or array ourselves against ourselves.

I am making a case for a Caliphate.

To replace the ones that were naturally selected against.

THERE'S A SAYING about church basement coffee: it is not very good. There can and will be such truisms about American Islam too, as our different racial and ethnic groups mix, mingle, and mediate a shared identity. My mother inadvertently did her part to install some holiday ritual in the American Muslim pantheon. A few days before Ramadan's end, she would go to the Big Y grocery store and buy Pepperidge Farm's three-layer fudge cake. That is: chocolate cake, a layer of chocolate frosting (I think that's the fudge part), another strip of cake, more frosting, a final horizontal bar of cake, and then the icing on the cake, which actually was not icing but frosting. (It now occurs to me that I don't actually know what fudge is, let alone the difference between icing and frosting.)

We took this cake to the mosque on Eid morning because we wanted to troll our stomachs.

After thirty days of denying our stomachs their daily bread and water, we feasted. Most people reacted by collapsing into food co-mas just hours after waking up, and so passes the holiday. And since it's, you know, a holiday, most of the items we gorge on are sugary, savory, chocolatey, or some other kind of wacky, which isn't the gentlest way to ease yourself back into digestive normality. But the actual parallel to church basement coffee is the mosque basement doughnut, far more ubiquitous than any maternal offering. Every Eid, someone would bring dozens of doughnuts, usually Dunkin' (Donuts), because we were proud New Englanders; many of them were munchkins (the doughnuts, not the Muslim New Englanders), and we snacked on those without caution, popping them like over-sized pills.

My time in New York divorced me from suburban Islam and its many evolutions and transformations, but when, years later, I went to the Islamic Society of Baltimore for Eid—the same mosque that America's first Muslim president visited for his only domestic visit to a Muslim house of worship—there was a Dunkin' food truck outside the front doors. Food truck. Once we brought the dough-nuts to the basement. Now the doughnuts brought themselves to the mosque. World domination, I was sure, couldn't be far behind. And world domination is probably what you think of when I say Caliphate. But what I mean this time is something different. When Abu Bakr stepped forward and was widely acclaimed the Caliph, some Muslims disagreed. If only that didn't have to end violently. If only there were mechanisms to channel debate before it turned into vicious and persistent division.

Suffice it to say, the Caliphate is the first secular institution in Islamic history; it is arguably the first decision of any significance to have been made without the Prophet Muhammad directly participating, and as such, without direct Divine input. This explains, incidentally, why it was the origin point of Islamic infighting—with no Prophet to announce his heavenly approbation of Abu Bakr's inauguration, room opened up for difference, diversity, and, of course, discord. The one depends upon the other. Given that history and legacy, you may well ask, why a Caliphate *now*? Because the ummah needs to make another worldly decision of historic importance. The ummah is beset by huge problems, and requires some mechanisms to bring it together, to allow it to translate its potentials into possibilities, its possibilities into actualities, not least because of the aforementioned crises—climate change, terrorism, neo-imperialism, foreign occupation, new technologies, burgeoning cities, misogyny and racism, to name but a few. You may argue that a Caliphate has been tried before. But I am making a case for another kind of Caliphate.

IF THE MUSLIM WORLD needs anything right now, it's a sense of genuine, positive, and humanistic transnationalism. A Counter-Reformation, I say, that would pursue a new Caliphate, utterly unlike any Caliphate that preceded it: it could be global, which means it should not be governmental. Rather, it should come about through the development of ever more robust and sophisticated institutions, dedicated to educational, cultural, spiritual, ecological, economic, and human renewal, growing outward as it scales upward, a collection of like-minded individuals, agencies, organizations, and institutions. This new Caliphate, this fifth iteration of the office, must furthermore develop organically. It must insist on independence from politics and politicization. It must advocate for a vigorous civil society, free of the agendas of authoritarians, whether secularist, Islamist, or nationalist. It must promote the basic rights of individuals to choose the societies they wish to live in. It should have no set form, either: it would change shape, for it must endlessly evolve.

It would be characterized by qualities of flexibility, resilience, and consensus. Attempts to unify the Muslim world by force create greater disunity and cause Muslims more harm. In so diverse and global an ummah, it would be nearly impossible to accomplish any such end. What I have in mind would move slowly and deliberately, inviting Muslims to participate in the upliftment of their communities through their own points of entry, be they religious education, charitable service, environmental activism, travel and tourism, commerce and trade, or science and technology. Of course, there would be one very obvious and significant source of opposition to this Caliphate, which we can already and easily anticipate, and which suggests my area of focus could be more limited (and there are other good reasons for that too). The idea of a large conglomerate of bodies working to achieve ever greater levels of cooperation among themselves, while eschewing politics, undoubtedly terrifies dictators, some of whom are these days the very source of strife in the politics of Islam.

It may make more sense to begin this process in the West, to make it of the West and for the West—a process comprising autonomous, secular, civil institutions that serve Muslim communities whose members have far more in common with each other than they do with Muslims in other parts of the world. That is not because I wish to dissociate Muslims from each other, but because the West has a more distinct identity than many parts of the world, and Muslims cannot help but take on the colors and contours of the countries they're so deeply a part of. (Imagine that.) And also because, given our greater relative wealth, political stability, and institutional sophistication, I fear the prospect of building networks of institutions that are imbalanced in favor of the same part of the world that has, for so long, dictated to the Muslim world, or even gone so far as to install, support, or encourage dictators in the Muslim world. It would be unseemly at best (and far worse at worst) if Western Muslims took on the mantle of neo-colonialism deliberately or otherwise and proceeded to tell their co-religionists how to address their most pressing problems in their very different contexts.

The idea I have for a networked, apolitical, organic Caliphate, with no single figurehead and no single geographic center, would be far more relevant to Islam in the West, and while it could build outward, and I hope it does build outwards to reach other Muslim communities, it shouldn't (anyway) worry too much about that right away. The destiny of Muslims in the West will diverge from Muslims in other parts of the world. So long as neither imposes upon the other, so long as we share common beliefs and practices, we can differ in matters of social organization, cultural activity, and moral priority—because our contexts are that different. This argument becomes especially interesting if you think it through to its logical conclusion. Should Muslims in the West make more effort to work together to improve their communities, they would necessarily partner with the majority of their fellow citizens, nearly all of whom are not Muslim. We should. We will. In the process of so doing, we will strengthen the West, as principal advocates for the idea of the West at a time when it is under unprecedented attack.

I am fully conscious that the majority of Western Muslims are people of color and that they are often either the descendants of immigrants from countries colonized by the West or they are the descendants of people forcibly transported by and to the West. But we are here, now, from here and of here, and despite the grave shortcomings that afflict Western societies, there is far more promise with the West than without the West, far more hope for change in the West than against the West. We owe it to our fellow Westerners to defend this amazing thing we all have constructed, which some of us might not see the value of. That's one of the advantages of being a member of a minority or the offspring of immigrants. You get to look at things very differently. Of all the powerful countries in the world—Russia, say, or China—none has what the United States enjoys. Not just alliances or partnerships, but deep friendships with fraternal countries, bonded not just by shared values or a common outlook, but also by blood and sacrifice.

Australians and New Zealanders, Americans and Canadians, the French and the British all fought and died together and still fight for each other. At a policy conference I attended in New York, one talking head pointed out that Western countries conduct foreign policy the same way they handle domestic politics. You bicker, and you disagree, but with civility and decency. What is remarkable is not just that the United States and Canada share such a peaceable border or have so much in common, but that they pool intelligence, that they see each other not as different countries but as neighbors— and how many of us, when we think of neighbors, think of them as foreign? Much of the rest of the world envies what we have but cannot enjoy it for itself. There's so much talk of Islamic brotherhood, yet not one part of the Muslim world has accomplished the kind of trust, openness, and mutual cooperativeness that the West has built up over the decades. Sometimes people say the Muslim world is collectivist, either in praise or condemnation, and the West is too individualistic, but I think that's backward.

It's the Muslim world that is full of egos that cannot restrain themselves, individuals who judge themselves more important than institutions. Muhammad once warned that a time would come when Muslims would be great in number but as ineffective as the foam on the sea; when asked why, he blamed love of life and fear of death. He might have perfectly described the undemocratic politics of the Muslim world. Leaders who are afraid to die, or unwilling to die, will not acknowledge that politics must continue without them, and so they make no preparations—they appoint no successors, they create no autonomous institutions—for what will happen after them. Even talking about their mortality can get you into trouble. They hoard wealth and power as if they're meant to live here forever. Whereas Western leaders are far more accepting of death, understanding that while individual lives end, institutions and governments can and must transcend these limitations—and are empowered to do so by their autonomy. We don't go to war with each other when we lose elections.*

We know how to wait our turn.

We accept defeat with good grace, or at least most of us used to. The outcome is remarkable. Can you imagine visa-free travel across vast chunks of the Muslim world? Partnerships in science and education, culture, and religion? Some of these things exist there, but they are mediocre in most of their instantiations, and hardly the achievement that is the modern West. Let us never, ever forget that. Let us vow never, ever to allow that to go to waste. It's not easy to know what to do in a crisis because it's not easy to know if one's question is even the right one—forget about the answer. But even as part of us should prepare for a West in which Islamophobia is ever more normalized, we should also push back with something positive—a vision, not just a reaction. It is in our interest for a secular, pluralistic, and fraternal West to survive the storm that is cracking it apart. We need the West, and the West needs us. Minorities, including Muslims, are the canaries in the coal mine. The defense and renewal of the West requires the defense and renewal of Western Muslim communities and cuts across partisan boundaries.

There will be cooperation with Muslim civil society in other parts of the world, but we in the West will have to decide how to prioritize our resources, and it's hard to understand how to justify spending many of them in places that religionize politics. Note that I do not mean forswearing charitable aid and assistance, or advocacy for more just and intelligent foreign policies. Rather I mean to ask: What is it we would like to construct? Where do we want to be in ten, twenty, or fifty years' time? What will it take for us to get there? Imagine that we begin to think bigger. Beyond just mosques

---

* Of course, we have been known to go to war with Muslim countries that dare demonstrate an interest in democratization. Thus the paradox: friendly to democracy where it concerns us (literally), we are opposed to it where it challenges our interests. This enormous contradiction in foreign policies should be challenged by ever more diverse electorates: human rights at home and abroad. We should want for others what we want for ourselves.

and Islamic schools and toward federations, cooperatives, and alliances that work with people of all faiths, strengthening Muslim communities even as they strengthen the places those communities live in, a way of realizing ummah that enriches modernity. An ummah that would advocate for religious values in a public square afflicted by cultural secularism. That would advocate for compassion and decency in the face of sometimes unyielding and bitter capitalism. That would advocate for strengthening our intergovernmental bonds, not only because closer ties between the US, Australia, and Albania would be good for those countries' Muslims, but also for everyone else in them.

I know it'll be hard to get there, but I know that we will—because we are already on the road to it. American and Canadian Muslims, for example, are already operating with ever greater degrees of institutional sophistication. We know what it is we need to rise to the next level in our communal development. We have the healthy differences and positive divisions that come about as a result of the diversities of our societies. We will ask ourselves, like other minority communities often do, if we should be more particularistic or more universal. We will wonder whether our often progressive politics and often conservative morals are evidence of a political distortion at the current moment or a reflection of a unique Islamic synthesis, which has something of value to aid a West ailing from hyperpartisanship. We will not just ask for foreign policies that do more for Palestinians, or Rohingya, or refugees, but how we can build partnerships with Muslims who ask for the same things in other fraternal countries, improving and enriching the political and social landscape of the West—because we are already headed toward it. The fifth Caliphate isn't a theory I am hoping to put into practice. It is a nascent practice for which I am ex post facto providing the theory.

An outline for the new Caliphate, an evolution of the individualized Caliphate of God into a Caliphate of communities of autonomous individuals—grounded in and advancing collaboration, cooperation, and mutual engagement—means greater solidarity within and across Muslim communities. Rather than wait for a Caliph of Muhammad to monarchically establish itself, an anachronism at best, we are already working together at ever more sophisticated scales, building a Caliphate of Caliphs of God, which will expand and transform, which can accept that its constituent parts may mutate, die, or resurrect themselves, an agglomeration of democratic individuals organizing for democratic societies. We can and must free Islam from the grip of religionized politics and politicized religion, returning it to what it was always meant to be. How to talk to God. How to turn back to God. How to instill life with everlasting meaning. Hence this consensual and compassionate Caliphal collectivism will coexist alongside a rich practice of individual spirituality and religiosity; Islam as bigger than the state, as it were, but smaller too. After all, the point of Adam and Eve's exile was to become Caliphs, but this is a temporary condition. We all go home again. How we make that journey depends on who we have to guide us along the way.

13

THE END

IN 2010, a prominent American Muslim activist and her husband, an Imam, announced plans for a Muslim community center and mosque in lower Manhattan, inadvertently located in relative proximity to the site of the September 11 attacks. With many other New York Muslims, I quickly entered into conversation with them. We had to. Not only because we were intrigued by what the project could accomplish, but because we were scared by what it might become. There was too much room for error, and our worst fears, and then some, were soon realized. From a shadowy structure known as the "Cordoba House" it became "the Ground Zero Mosque," about the cleverest rebranding of a project I have ever seen.

Needless to say, it was not a nickname of approbation.

Most news stories, at least until Donald Trump entered our national political conversation, had very short shelf lives. That particular controversy, however, was the check that kept on bouncing. Day after day, week after week, misrepresentations of the so-called Ground Zero Mosque project emboldened anti-Muslim bigots. At the same time, several of the key organizers made one misstep after another, eventually dooming the project. I pleaded with them to change course, but while I had allies within the project, we were outnumbered. Few causes have left such a terrible taste in my mouth, but this was one of them. After several increasingly frustrating months, I walked away, dejected and defeated.

One morning, seven years later, I learned an appointment of mine meant for Morningside Heights had been moved all the way downtown, to Tribeca. Naturally. My plans for Friday Prayer at the Columbia University campus had to be rebooted. The move to build a monumental Muslim center near the old World Trade Center had failed, but the congregants it'd served still gathered nearby. I had no choice but to text an old contact from the days of Park 5 1, the actual name of the doomed project—combining a reference to the Islamic tradition of green space (very valued in New York, of course) with a numeric naming scheme all Gothamites would be familiar with.

"What time," I asked, "is your jumuah?"

He responded quickly. "Do you want to give the sermon?"

Which was not what I asked.

I answered this outrageous imposition by agreeing.

I'm glad I did.

THIS COLLEAGUE AND I met for lunch afterward, and we said many things I wished we had all those years ago but were too traumatized to. What had ended almost a decade before in acrimony was reborn with shared affection. He ended the meal by telling me there'd be a zikr at one of his downtown properties that very evening. Thinking he'd be there, I reported on time. It was in the basement of a condominium sales office, a very smart and sexy space with black walls and beechwood floors, over which several white sheets had been spread; someone had lit expensive incense, filling the space with surprisingly intense recollections of my year in Dubai.

When the next guest came downstairs, the first thing he said was that he recognized me from TV. My heart sank. I wanted to go somewhere where I wouldn't be that guy on TV, but just some guy. I only learned he was actually the Sufi teacher, the Shaykh for the evening—and for this small community, when everyone seated themselves in a crescent, and he became the star. My friend from Park 51 never showed up, incidentally, but I was nonetheless grateful I attended, for three reasons, in ascending order of importance:

1. *There wasn't a rigid hierarchy in the room.*

   The Shaykh left a short while after we all sat down, and returned a short while after that, when more people had gathered. But no one stood to greet him. This put me immediately at ease. My greatest fear of Sufism, the reason I had been so skeptical of it, was the uncritical obedience shown the Shaykh, who could quickly and easily abuse his power. It certainly doesn't help when the lodestar claims that, to reach God, you must pass through him. (On this one I'm with the Salafis, who look askance at such unsubtle associationism.)

2. *We emphasized modesty. We didn't enshrine misogyny.*

   Most mosques place women literally below men, in the basement, or sometimes, in a modest improvement, behind men, sometimes sans partition. I'm uncomfortable with both arrangements. But I also don't believe women and men should pray in the same rows or next to each other; it's immodest. We don't worship in pews, after all. Our prayer is a physical one, involving bending, bowing, prostrating. But modesty is a bidirectional boulevard, which is why I loved this Sufi order. When we prayed, women weren't behind us but beside us, separated by some distance for considerations of decency and privacy.

3. *Something genuinely sacred was happening.*

   I felt God in the room. In that simple, modest room, in a semicircle of a dozen people, not even all of them Muslim: God was there, with us.

Sufism is widely misunderstood. The word is derived from the Arabic term *tasawwuf*, which in turn probably derives from the infinitive "to clean." Sufism is a kind of *tazkiyat al-nafs*, or purification of the self. It's not a different denomination of Islam, nor an alternative form of Islam. It's a higher discipline of Islam, which begins where the letter of the law leaves off. For instance, Muhammad described backbiting as eating the flesh of your dead brother. So, goes the literal interpretation, don't backbite. It's very, very bad. Whereas the Sufi teacher would argue that refraining from backbiting is the barest minimum, sufficient for a decent moral life but hardly the aspiration of someone who desires to be genuinely close to God. For that, you must eradicate backbiting not just from your tongue but from your heart and mind. If it's wrong to say it, it's wrong to think it. Our inside should be as clean as our outside.

Sufism intends to get us closer to God, in the belief that a cleaner inside and outside accomplishes that end. I used to speak publicly about Islam and center on the mechanical, the external, the factual: there are this many Muslims in the world, these are the five pillars, here is when Muhammad was born, and this is when he died. While these things are important, I believe they are secondary to Islam's primary focus. The Unitary. But when you make God the center of your discussions about Islam, it should not be unexpected that this leads to a lot of questions about God. Once a student asked me whether God's demand that we worship Him was not, in fact, supremely egotistical, evidence that the Divine was a narcissist and, therefore, like all narcissists, endlessly insecure. I fell back on language that had been supplied to me at a very young age: God as Master and humankind as servant.

The servant does as the Master asks.

One cannot compare God to a human because, well, it's an apples and oranges kind of thing. There is nothing like the like of God. Though maybe that answer doesn't suffice you, either. If God is so great, why does God want me to worship Him? Over and over, God says He doesn't need our worship—but He also holds us accountable if we do not worship Him. There is another way to answer, a Sufi way, not stopping with the letter of the law but going into the language of the heart. The Muslim on the inner path of Islam would think not of God as an abstract, distant, and harsh Master to be feared, but as a Mighty Beloved to be awed by and enamored of. Beauty and amazement: these are the two principles around which worship revolves; His beauty compels our adoration, but not in the crude sense of obligation—rather, in the helplessness evoked by awe, and the amazement provoked by a different kind of obligation.

I once took a bus tour of Australia's Great Ocean Road, along the coastline of Victoria, and found myself in a deep spiritual reverie, beginning with the fact that the ocean I was dipping my toes into touched, on its other end, Antarctica. The tour ended at Loch Ard Gorge, where the ocean has cut a cove into the cliffs, creating a little lagoon that, properly speaking, is a sneak peek into paradise. The water that comes in through the gap in the rock face is seriously blue and looks intimidatingly cold. But as it pushes toward the beach and scrapes against the sides of the cliffs, it turns progressively chocolatier until it becomes, if it is not ridiculous to say, so delicious as to demand one takes off their shoes and run into the froth. Or as this author did: run in, in shoes. I was muted the first time I saw the Gorge and my mind was that much more blown the second time I did, half a dozen years and a lifetime subsequent. A true moment of reflection on the world around us—part of Islam's dying tradition of curiosity about the natural world—should deepen one's faith, not undermine it.

It was beautiful, but one of the names of God is also the Beautiful. What, then, if beauty had to exist? What kind of beautifulness would that be, and how would we respond to it? Sometimes I even imagine, for lack of a better term (and pardon me the potential blasphemy), that God is awed by God. By the fact of the necessity of His existence. He knows the reasons for His necessity, but that doesn't make it any less amazing. That Something—Someone—*has* to exist, and as such, always has. There *has* to be a God, and therefore there was, is, and will be a God. Of course, He must be for existence to exist, insofar as existence is not a property that matter, or energy, can independently possess or project. Still, He existed prior to and without us and everything in the universe(s) as well.

("Prior" is, of course, the only way language can attempt to arrive at His relationship to creation.) A Being so mighty, so unique, so otherworldly—isn't that amazing? Muslims frequently translate a word in our tradition, *taqwa*, as "fear"—"have taqwa," as many a Muslim would put it, just means "fear God." Like the analogy of the servant and the Master, this is onerous and off-putting. Worship God because He terrorizes you?

It will help to know this is also an appallingly bad translation. Taqwa rather means something like "awe," and awe involves feelings very different from fear. The title of Anne Lamott's *Help, Thanks, Wow* summarizes the three reasons she says we pray: When we need help. When we need to/want to/should thank God. And when we're overcome by something in existence, or even just existence itself.

Maybe there's another way to answer this question. Another way to think about why we need to worship God.

The answer, appropriately, lies in the past as much as the present.

HOW MANY BOOKS about religion skim over, if they consider at all, the faiths of one-quarter of humanity? (I mean Islam—at some point, we had to return to demographics.) Consider cognitive behavioral therapy, which is commonly considered a recent Western invention. The late, great Sudanese psychologist, Malik Badri, discovered a ninth-century text written by a Central Asian polymath, Abu Zayd al-Balkhi. In *Sustenance for Bodies and Souls*, Balkhi describes the ailments that afflict humans physically *and* mentally, and suggests spiritual, practical, and conceptual tools for their alleviation, including what we'd call cognitive behavioral therapy.

Balkhi even distinguishes between exogenous and endogenous depression. And he analyzes mental illness still more exhaustively. When discussing anxiety, for example, Balkhi argues that those prone to fearful thoughts and consumed by exaggerated and uncontrollable worry should avoid loneliness—for loneliness amplifies negative thinking and is, anyway, contrary to human nature. (He makes exceptions for research and writing, for spiritual practice—

although if you're with God you're also not alone—and strategic planning). He warns against idleness and recommends hard work and physical and mental exertion as a salve. Consume your mind with tasks, lest it consume itself with fretfulness. But what happens next is most interesting, and reveals—in a widely forgotten text, no less—how traditional Muslims, how classical Islam, viewed the world without, in ways that contemporary Muslims and modern Islam would have next to no idea what to do with.

To my Muslim readers: imagine covering this text in your Sunday school.

Eventually, Balkhi concedes, the anxious person pursuing his initial remedies would become "bored (after long hours of concentrated work)," for which reason the medieval therapist suggests the patient tired from work "can refresh himself with enjoyable pleasures such as food and drink, sexual relations, listening to moving songs and music, and looking at a delightful landscape and beautiful objects." I could not have imagined coming across this kind of writing in my early Muslim education, but the more I studied the tradition as it had been articulated, or just lived my life and grew up, the more I saw that these things were part of the fullness of human experience: writing and research, worship and prayer, a healthy intimacy, music and art, poetry and good company, and even simply meditation on beauty. A cure for exhaustion, and as a ward against the ill effect of negative internal thoughts.* If you have died inside, beauty can Jesus on Lazarus you. Early Islam developed a robust chivalric tradition, associating love for a woman with love for God, whether to make it easier to understand what it meant to obey God—to fall at the feet of your beloved—or because that's the language they had available to describe what it was that was happening to them.

---

* See Malik Badri, *Abu Zayd al-Balkhi's Sustenance of the Soul: The Cognitive Behavior Therapy of a Ninth Century Physician* (London: International Institute of Islamic Thought, 2013), 59–62.

Or put it more personally and bluntly: You're in New York City, meeting a friend at a café. You've met her a few times before. But, suddenly, on this occasion, some kind of veil is lifted. You didn't acknowledge how beautiful she is. You love the sound of her voice, the way she holds her coffee cup by the tips of her fingers, her crazy-curly hair, the way she makes silly and irreverent observations that cut to the core of what you always think but never have the confidence to admit. You're falling for her, and you need to tell her. You want to and need to praise her. But not because of self-centeredness on her part, or obsequiousness on your part, but because this is simply what must be. That is that man's answer. God wants us to worship Him because if we did not, we would lose not just our awareness of who we are but our sense of awe at and in the world. To pray is to be alive. Worship is not the sign of the docile, domesticated self, but the inevitable and necessary outcome of that self that is still curious, open to the world, in love with love and beauty, warmed by the world, even in the face of all the pain that comes with it. "God is Beautiful," Muhammad said. "And loves beauty." We worship God for the same reason we are awed by gorgeousness. Which is why we once produced its most refined forms.

MONUMENTAL ARCHITECTURE in Islam emerged only after the Righteous Caliphate disappeared. Large mosques were part of a culture of monarchy, and while they were evidence of tremendous wealth and sophistication—not necessarily bad things—they came at the expense of the more important things. Part of the problem is the waste of resources—and the forced labor required to build them. Part of the problem is an error of theology. We have this belief that to honor God, we must create humongous structures, confusing not just our egos for the Divine, but our spatiotemporal limitations for His illimitedness. We exist in four dimensions, whereas God created and is not bound to them. (It is critical to point out, however, that Islam historically and textually rejects pantheism. Just because God is not in any specific place does not mean that He is everywhere, let alone a far more heretical corollary: if God is in everything, then everything is God.)

One of my favorite mosques in the world is Gazi Husrev Beg, in Sarajevo. It exists in the heart of the Bosnian capital's modest old town, an Ottoman island left behind when that Caliphate receded. Some places tug at our heartstrings long after we leave. Some before we even go. It is a depressing truth, but the truth all the same: every generation of Muslims has a catalog of conflicts to identify with and be overwhelmed by. Wherever you look, there is some tragedy: whether it is Syria in the midst of a vicious civil war, or Kashmir, facing an occupation more brutal and violent than most in the world and yet rarely in the news—despite the conflict involving nuclear powers bordering each other—or East Turkestan (Xinjiang), where today China practices a form of settler colonialism that has escalated to outright genocide. Also, concentration camps. Many of these human rights tragedies have been active for decades, dating back to my youth.

But the one that seemed to have the most effect on me was Bosnia. Maybe it's because the violence happened so suddenly. Maybe it's because it was in Europe and happened to Europeans: If white, European Muslims can suddenly be confronted with genocidal violence, is Europe, and by association the West, closed to Islam altogether? In recent decades, far more European Muslims— overwhelmingly civilians—have been killed by Europeans of other faiths than the reverse, a point that goes unmentioned in heated debates about who *belongs* in Europe. It was many more years before I could go to Bosnia, but the trip's impact on me was far greater than I could have imagined; the Husrev Beg mosque was more beautiful than expected, too, because it paralleled, in miniature, the miniature-ness of Bosnia. A tiny, landlocked nation, where Muslims are a significant plurality, if not a slim majority, a reminder of when there were far larger populations of European Muslims, from Hungary to Greece to Romania to Poland to Ukraine, who converted at the hands of Sufi Shaykhs once present throughout the region.

To call the Bosniaks, the indigenous Muslims of Bosnia, an anachronism would be offensive and wrong. But there is something remarkable about their resilience, their survival in the face of adversities that eliminated far larger populations. All of these thoughts were probably swirling around in my head when I first entered Gazi Husrev Beg, which is tiny, as mosques can go, delicate, almost ethereal. If God is not limited to dimensions that we are limited to, why does bigness convey Divinity? God doesn't need a large mosque, because God isn't large. Of course, I'm not condemning practicality. You need skyscrapers in Manhattan because there's nowhere to go but up, and limiting building heights could inflate prices, keeping out those without ample means. You need large mosques where you have lots of Muslims, because where else would they gather to pray? If a society has tremendous wealth, as many Gulf countries can rightfully claim, then it would be untoward at best if its cities, and the palaces, houses, and hotels within, were spectacular, but the mosques were pathetic, ramshackle affairs. All of that is true.

But all of that can be true and you can still miss the point. The most meaningful spaces are the ones that have feelings attached to them, that convey something greater than architectural ambition, that embody spiritual truths, especially now. Now they must whisper secrets too softly for a materialistic world, consumed with noise and genuflecting at the altar of distraction, to hear. Where the dimensions we live in and judge by are not confused for the dimensions God lives in and esteems. The places where He's to be found. The reasons, in the end, we are who we are.

BACK IN NEW YORK CITY, I began to join the zikr every Friday night I wasn't traveling. The Shaykh led us in chanting God's names and in divinely sanctioned invocations, invariably beginning with the Muslim creed, *la ilaha illa Allah*, that there is absolutely no god except God, and then contracting from there. *Illa Allah*, except God. *Allah*. God. Then *hu*. Which is meant to evoke the Divine breath, the special whisper God blew into Adam and His progeny, that spark of the otherworldly in each of us, the souls we have, the promise we swore to, the possibility of Caliphates, of individual agency in the world God descended us to. When I first started going to the zikr circle, I had no idea how to do zikr, what effect it was supposed to have on me, and usually, about ten minutes in, I found my frenetic mind struggling very hard to not think about what emails I was behind on. By about half an hour in, I was busy composing the emails themselves.

The Shaykh would tell me to focus my breath on my spiritual heart, to say God's name there, but my overanalytical brain just wondered what that means. What is a spiritual heart, anyway? Where is my spiritual heart? How do I know if I've focused on the heart? Has anyone messaged me anything important? Did I charge my phone? Alhamdulillah. Just as I hesitate to use the word "religious," but even more so, I'd not call myself a "Sufi"—it's presumptuous in the extreme, and anyway, it is a loaded term too. People get more hung up on the appellation than on the intention. But I can speak to what doesn't work. I went into the zikr with the expectation that this was mindfulness meditation, which is a very good thing, a practice I unfortunately but in typically lazy fashion left behind, except that the Muslim zikr is not always meditative. My Shaykh did encourage me in breathing and other exercises to calm my late-capitalist mind, but here, in this circle, what I felt, more and more, was desperation. I'm not sure if that was supposed to happen, but it did happen.

There was not really centeredness, calmness, coolness. There was apoplexy. I was sucked in by a kind of theophanic gravity, not absorbed into God—I am more egotistical than that, speaking honestly about my faults (I'm self-centered) and my aspirations (I like Iqbal, who liked robust individuality within an Islamic framework)—but at least I was spiraling tightly around Him. By crying out God's names, *Rahman, Rahim, Salam*, I was learning how to rend the veils of worldliness, self-consciousness, forgetfulness, obstinacy, arrogance, that keep me apart from the Beloved. Each repetition of His name would come to feel more furiously immediate. Crying out in unison helps us to shed any lingering inhibitions, petitioning Him by His titles directly, focusing on His various qualities, not in the abstract, intellectual exercise I would be most prone to otherwise, but as humble beggars, prostrate before the Divine. That, incidentally, may be the most helpful definition of Sufism I can find for you. Ritual law teaches you how to prostrate in prayer.

Where your body has to be, how it has to be arranged, and how often your forehead should touch the floor—this is all valuable, which is why authentic Sufism doesn't forgo the practice. Rather, Sufism teaches you that external prostration is the first step toward internal prostration, the lowering of the body of the self until it touches the ground in humble joy—and stays there, preferably for the rest of our lives. As I said: I'm just at the threshold. Of what, sometimes I can't even tell. But I call out to Him, not because I want to be at peace inside myself and with myself alone, although that is a welcome if infrequent byproduct. Rather, I call out to Him because He is real, and more real than I am, more perduring than anything else I have relied upon. Being. The source of being. I am calling out to Him because I am lonely. He hears because He hears all. He responds too, in His own way, sometimes—very few times— loud enough for me to feel in my bones or hear with my ears.

Paradoxically, the collective form of the zikr smooths the way toward the individual relationship with Him: we lose ourselves, our outer and baser selves, and try to form a direct connection with God. How this plays out for me depends on the week. Most of those weeks I spend struggling against a busy travel schedule, or inertia even to make it downtown to the zikr circle, conscious that each and every single time, I am letting down a Shaykh who I am enamored of. But sometimes I get there, and some of those times, during the zikr, something happens. Something miraculous. Maybe I take the wrong lesson away from it, but at least I take out more than I put in. Later, in zikrs, we would start to spend a lot of time chanting *Hayy*, or "the Alive"; God is God. The Alive is God. God is the Alive. The ninety-nine names of God don't just describe Him. They are His proper names. What does it mean to really be alive? What is life itself?

When we look for life on Mars, we expect it to be water-based. We assume it might have DNA. We suspect, at times, that life here began there, or was carried here from somewhere else. But on this same planet of ours are jinn, who are alive, but who I presume do not have DNA, and do not contain water, and aren't even sensorily accessible to us under ordinary circumstances—even as they can and do act on the world, a unidirectionality that inspires many a campfire horror story. If another mortal life can be so different from ours, how different is God, the Alive? But how are my life and His life even remotely comparable? What does it mean to give life to a thing, to breathe Your spirit into a thing? These are the thoughts that sometimes consume my mind instead of me doing whatever it is I am supposed to be doing during a zikr, or which take off from the ninety-nine names and rocket outward and away.

Another one of His names is *Qayyum*, the Self-Subsistent. Else He wouldn't be God. I beg Him to find subsistence for me.

On and on, these names go. My mind wanders. It returns. It stumbles.

One evening, I was struck by strangeness.

His.

Before I existed, before the world existed, before there was even time or space, somehow there was this Being, which moreover had to be. And because He is *Aleem*, too, the Omniscient, and because He is not bound by time, He has always known why He has to be, which is such a wondrous and overwhelming thought not just to meditate on, but to pray through and petition via, that I was overcome in that moment. No wonder we praise Him and worship Him and come to Him on our hands and knees. When the zikr was over, we usually sat and talked over cups of tea, coming back down to earth after a brief ascent toward heaven. We've become friends, or at least a kind of community. It's a small group, and better for that. I went and sat next to the Shaykh and described to him the thoughts that rolled around my head, crowding out my heart. He assigned me a book, as if I needed more to read; this one was Shaykh Abd al-Qadir Jilani's *Secret of Secrets*. He then shared with me a *hadith qudsi*, part of a collection of sayings that are the direct speech of God, albeit not recorded in the Qur'an but otherwise passed through the Prophet Muhammad. I found that hadith in Jilani's book too: "Man is My secret," Muhammad said that God said, "and I am His secret."

I contemplated this Prophetic teaching for the length of the late-night subway ride home. My fault for then living in the Bronx. "Nothing in the universe can contain God," a Muslim tradition says, "except the heart of a believer." He is looking to come to rest inside you. And you, and you, and you. Because when we speak of the heart here, we do not speak of the organ, but of a spiritual counterpart to it, an otherworldly body attached to our own, which survives the decline and fall of our physical self. (Until that self is resurrected in the world-to-come.) "He is closer to you than your jugular vein." That which gave you life, which sustains your very being, sustains each and every molecule that makes you you. So to look for God elsewhere is to look too far in the wrong direction. Your focus should be on yourself.

It presents an interesting contrast to how we presume to think about the alleged incompatibility of science and religion. Once a man said to me, "Look at how big the universe is, and you're telling me God cares how I hold my hands when I pray?" He confused bigness and smallness, presumed that creating the whole universe was harder for God than creating a single person, that anything for Him is hard at all, or that size matters in the way we perceive it to matter. "And there can be none like Him." It's said that the Copernican and Galilean revolutions had the same effect the Darwinian did, that these three knocked us off our pedestals sequentially. By making an anthropocentric worldview less plausible, they somehow made a theocentric worldview less believable. I am still not sure why the latter follows the former, but there you have it. Instead of Earth being the center of the universe, the sun is the center of the solar system, and the solar system isn't even the center of the universe either. A satellite circles Earth, but Jupiter has dozens too. We are tucked away into a corner of the cosmos, a physically unremarkable species on a minuscule planet in a nonspecial corner of a vast galaxy that is a speck in a gargantuan universe, which might be a mote in the span of the multiverse, all of which, though, was created by God; He buried us, as it were, in a little footnote to an endless realm.

We seem inconsequential.

And yet? "Man is My secret." It is on this little bluish marble, mottled by green and brown, streaked with cloudy white, that no less than God's own Caliphs are found. No wonder the angels were dismissive of the creation of this second, third, umpteenth Caliphate of God. Maybe the Caliphate was meant to be an iterative process. That's evolution, after all, with a telos. Maybe that's a part of the story we missed. "Your representative," the angels seemed to scoff, innocently, angelically, disbelievingly, "will be a relative of life down there, on *that* world?" Perhaps they judged life thus far on that world quite unspectacular, especially compared to themselves. What they knew. What they saw. What they experienced. Spatially, too, God hid Himself from us, inventing dimensions that create an unbridgeable distance between us. "Except the heart of a believer." "And I am His secret." Because the believer prostrates to nothing but God, hollowing herself out so that she can receive the Divine. And only we can receive Him the way that we do. Not angels, not the great heavens, not the mighty galaxies.

Temporally, too, we are a secret. Look at the vast stretch of deep time. Consider just how long the world has been around. Dinosaurs dominated the planet for tens of millions of years. Their reign was unfathomable to us; modern humans appear to have been around for just some tens of thousands of years, and most of that history is not ordinarily recoverable. Even the split between our ancestors and Neanderthals happened in under the last million years. This doesn't even get us started on how long the universe has been around; how long the planet has been spherical, life has been struggling, surviving, reproducing. We're spliced in at the very end. Maybe He was lonely, and so He created us—"I was a hidden treasure and wished, desired, loved to be known, so I created creation." There's that *hiding* again. There is pleasure in looking. We are curious creatures. Adam wanted to know what that tree was all about. It means more to connect with Someone you have to search for. Absence makes the heart grow more pious. That is why we were made to love the mysterious. So we could fall flat on our faces and ask for His help in standing up again.

Not just because He made us want to, but because He breathed something of Him into us. We can't help but be mirrors. Ours is not a static God, not a dull Prime Mover, but a ceaselessly creative Progenitor. What does my zikr tell me? Language is imperfect. It was made by imperfect beings. (Own it.) It comes down to individuals. "I am making a Caliph on the Earth." Adam and Eve. Not nations and tribes. We are resurrected singularly. Judged atomically. I feel more faith from the atheist who scours the heavens for signs and explanations, who is unsatisfied with what is known, and inspects the world as if it were a sacred object, the pursuit of whose mysteries is the ultimate act of fidelity. How much more invigorating and satisfying is she than the believer whose entire life consists of mindless repetition, ritual for the sake of ritual, never going beyond the form, never bothering to let awe lead where it will. Thus Islam is impoverished. "An hour of contemplation is worth seventy years of prayer." Think of how small you are in the universe. Then realize that God doesn't have size. That your dimensions don't capture just how important you are.

IN THE THIRD and final act of Lisa Halliday's novel, *Asymmetry*, there is a conversation between a journalist and a famous author in his golden years. The elderly Ezra Blazer reflects on the work he's done, the books he's written, the women he's loved—including Samantha Bargeman. Blazer tells his much younger interviewer that to be old is to "go about your business reminding yourself to look at everything as though you're looking at it for the last time. Probably you are."

She asks, in response, "Do you worry about the end?"

Blazer's answer moved me, which is why I reproduce it. "I am cognizant of the end," he said. "Maybe I have three, five, seven years, at most nine or ten years." But. "What do I think about the end?" he echoed her. "I don't think about the end. I think about the totality, my whole life."*

The Sufis call the death of a *wali*, a friend of God—in effect, a saint, although as a decentralized religion, we have no standard for canonization—his "wedding," where the human becomes the bride, and God the husband, which isn't an inversion of anything unless you commit an error of theology. God has ninety-nine names, some of which are associated with traditionally masculine qualities of forcefulness, conquest, and wrath. In contrast, other names are associated with stereotypically feminine virtues, such as compassion, kindness, and clemency. The universe was created to reflect these wholes, and men and women made partners to each other because in their unity, each makes the other more fully human. In their unity, each begins to understand God beyond their gendered imbalances. But what is God's most important name? *Rahman*, Loving to all, from which word we also have the Arabic for "womb." God asks us to invoke Him at the outset of any task, however seemingly slight or significant, especially through this specific name and a related one, "*Rahim*."

The masculine names aren't nearly as ubiquitous. Though this does not even begin to capture the difference, which is also the reason more Muslims should learn Arabic. If I begin every action not with "in His name," or some other such reference that might definitively suggest, especially to an English ear, masculinity—but with "in the name of God, Loving to all," this sounds pleasant at best.** But, if I say it in Arabic, *Rahman* and *Rahim*, then what we are saying is practically maternal. What does it mean to say God has feminine qualities? Muhammad is described as the *rahmah* to all the worlds, another associated word. It is important to keep

---

* Lisa Halliday, *Asymmetry* (New York: Simon & Schuster, 2018), 266.
** In Arabic, like Spanish, all nouns are gendered, which means there is no neutral "it."

this in mind, to remember that we impose upon God, even when we don't mean to, boundaries and limits that do not apply to Him.

We go to school to prepare ourselves for adulthood. We live our lives for the chance to live a better one forever, but either way, there's no actual death, just a transition, where we escape the sensory limitations of this life—which is why no one can see us go. You live as long as you do to have as much time as you need, maybe. Or as much time as He wants to give you. I went back and back again, reading and re-reading Ezra Blazer and Samantha Bargeman's adventure, trying to find the sinews of the thing, sure that I'd missed something, and I was right every time. You'll go back through your life in that same manner. In this life and the next. That's what I'd love to see Muslims do. Not bang each other over the head, metaphorically and otherwise, with rote expressions of faith, but the far more real, far subtler, far more sophisticated expression of our faith through our art, the way one feels the love and the loss at the Dome of the Rock, the way a little hint of something—"I think about the totality"—means one can in five words express an entire worldview.

Halliday assigns to another one of her characters, Amar Jaafari, a description of faith that few Muslims could provide and, so far as I know, the author is not a Muslim:

> If God has a definite power over the whole of existence, one can imagine this power extending to His ability, whenever He wills, to replace any given destiny with another destiny. In other words, destiny is not definite but indefinite, mutable by the deliberate actions of man himself; Allah will not change the condition of a people until they change what is in themselves. God has not predetermined the course of human history but rather is aware of all its possible courses and may alter the one we're on in accordance with our will and the bounds of His universe.*

---

* Halliday, *Asymmetry*, 189.

Did Halliday know she was channeling Iqbal? There's Amar, across her novel, drinking, loving, detained, restrained, punished, crushed, but alive. Believing. With more faith with his beer in his hand than half the mosques I've been to.* Because it means something. Sometimes, when I think about leaving New York City—because it feels like life might take me away—the thing that hurts most is losing a sacred space it took me thirty-six years to find. But even while I had it, I traveled so much and was so often laid low by illness and exhaustion that I missed most of the zikrs anyway. All the same, I got a language, litany, and life from it that is so much richer than what of these I had. The capacity to love God, which, I admitted in my first zikr session, felt impossible to me.

Love finds a way.

Your destiny can replace itself with another. God can do that, because He is awesome, and who would not praise that?

IT IS TRUE that the attempt to build a dynamic Muslim institution, Park51, that happened to be near Ground Zero, was blocked by a motley crew, many of whom were nasty anti-Muslim bigots and continue to spew hate, ignorance, and anger. They are the precursors whose counterparts spawned, in the Muslim world, the kind of extremism with which we are more familiar. But radicals all have a beginning. The same kind of origin point. It was ironic, all the same. You couldn't even see Ground Zero from the site chosen for Park51, smears aside. But it was still too close for the haters. Today Park51's exiled congregation can meet only on Friday afternoons, not at its original location but in a rented hotel conference room near it, entirely too puny for its purpose, its narrowness barely relieved by two windows on the western wall. Each window, though, looks out onto the Freedom Tower and the Oculus, that rib cage of a giant dinosaur bleached white by the passage of deep time, where trains come and go from a site that was commercial, and then sacred, and now both of those things. All its possible courses indeed.

---

* Dear Safa, Marya, and Reza: Drinking is still very much *haram*.

14

SERMON ON THE MOUNT

THE HARAM, or Temple Mount, rests atop the highest and thus the most exposed portion of Jerusalem's Old City, resembling an ancient, limestone plateau. There's nothing between you and the sun, beating down; it is a perfect place to develop heatstroke, which is exactly what happened to one of our students, Neil (and I think me as well, but I realized that later). Neil told me at the beginning of our disappointing tour (see first chapters), right when we'd entered the Temple Mount, that he was feeling unwell. Probably, he guessed, it was the temperature. March, yeah, but we were in Jerusalem. I slipped him some challah I'd picked up the day before, but it was not enough. By the time our group had exited the Dome of the Rock—we didn't get permission for our class to go into the Aqsa Mosque—Neil was clearly in bad shape.

The students made to return to the rest of Jerusalem, but Ruth (Ari's teaching assistant), two of our students, Emily and Sonia, and I stayed behind to give Neil company and courage, loitering until he was ready to get going again. At first, though, he was reclined against the white-and-blue outer walls of the Dome of the Rock, exhausted. One of the minders from our tour told us we had to leave, but I appealed to a guard sitting nearby, at an entrance to the

Dome of the Rock; he was far friendlier and told us we could stay as long as we needed to. Security guard > tour guide. Sonia and I pulled the Muslim card and went to Aqsa. By the time we'd gotten back, Neil said he was ready to walk. Ruth and Emily flanked him, and off we went, back to the Old City.

We exited on the southwest side and walked uphill, all of our stomachs grumbling. Neil especially needed nourishment, but all of us were famished. We stopped at Friends Restaurant, the first establishment on our path. We ordered too much. It was good. Like last time.

Friends was the first restaurant in Palestine I'd ever eaten at, all of seventeen years before.

THAT DOESN'T SOUND like a long time if you think about it abstractly. But really, actually, so much of life had accumulated, a pile of experiences to be proud of or to be pushed under by. By the time we were done with our late lunch, blood and color had returned to Neil's face, and he was eager to get on with the day. I had to decide what to do with mine. I could go back to the Haram, or I could go back to the hotel. The former was tempting: by that point we'd had two days in Jerusalem, that day included. On each, I had come to the Haram, and on each, I had not had the chance to do me, spiritually speaking. One day was the awful Friday Prayer experience that I lamented earlier. The other was this day, with the students.

True, I had gone to Aqsa, but I hadn't gotten to sit, salat, du'a, zikr. The whole point to being in Jerusalem. I wanted to be alone there, with myself and for myself, to talk to God. But I had also managed to exhaust myself in the course of the morning's tour around the Haram, and might have been suffering heatstroke too. So the hotel won out. I walked all the way back and fell face-first onto the bed in my very large room and passed out. I don't remember falling asleep, but I woke up feeling like I was drowning. It took me a few minutes to get my wits about me, and once they were abouted, I had to decide what to do. My spiritual heart told me to go. My dusty body told me to stay. I compromised: I decided to shower.

And then, all of a sudden, I was clean, shiny, myself, itching to go. It was late in the afternoon by the time I got there, and I'd missed 'asr prayer. The upshot was that Aqsa was mostly empty, and I could have the entire frontmost, most Meccan row to myself, where I busied myself with the list of supplications I had obsessively-compulsively typed into my phone's notes feature.

When I was finally done, I turned as I stood, ready to leave, all prayed out, only to find that the hall was much darker than I remembered it, and there was only one person left inside.

Me.

But Aqsa wasn't just emptied. The massive wooden doors that constituted the entryway were all closed save one. I rushed as best as I could toward that door, conscious I could be on camera, wanting to appear innocent or, at worst, indubitably touristic and cheerfully benign. But before I was out, having nearly escaped without any apparent witnesses, a very lanky man with a thin and wiry black beard appeared before me, as if summoned by a magical force. He was wearing black pants and a black polo tucked into them. He looked, if not official, then important. He looked at me as if I were neither of these things.

"Salam," he announced. His tone suggested I would be wise to stop and speak with him.

"Wa 'alaykum as-salam," I replied, doing my best to gutturalize my Arabic.

"What's your name?" he asked—in Arabic.

"Haroon," I said, as in "Aaron," the brother of Moses from whose descendants servants of the Temple were drawn. This explains why Mary could've been on the very same Haram when Gabriel arrived with news that she had been chosen to mother the Messiah. I volunteered my last name; I am not sure why. "Haroon Moghul," I said, flinching as I said it. The last name means "Mongol." Considering the region, this is not the best mental connection one would want to make, speaking historically. And how else, adverbially at least, does one speak in this region?

"You are Muslim," he judged conclusively.

I wanted to say, "Inshallah," but caught myself. This was not the time to introduce someone to my special brand of humor. "Alhamdulillah," I said.

"You are visiting?" At this point, we were more than just chatting face-to-face: the encounter was becoming uncomfortable. The exit from Aqsa was only a dozen feet away. It might as well have been a metric mile.

"I am from Pakistan," I said, "but I live in New York. I came to make pilgrimage." Truth, if not the whole truth.

"Come with me," he said and motioned toward the door I'd been trying to egress from.

I followed dutifully behind him, out of the mosque and to the security booth right outside it. Now, I should be clear as to why this interaction was so discomfiting. This was some of the most contested territory on Earth. I had been alone in the mosque while it had been closed. (I did not know it would be closed, of course, but did that matter?) I am a tall human being. He made me feel short. His beard looked fundamentalist. He was of a peculiarly stern demeanor. And he wanted me to wait by a security desk? I was already afraid of Israeli police. Now I was on the wrong side of Palestinian authorities. I probably gulped for good measure.

When he reemerged, his hand was in his back pocket, and he removed it swiftly, as if he were producing . . .

A brochure.

A map, to be specific. He handed me a well-folded map.

"Now you can know what all the buildings are!" he exclaimed, beaming the hugest smile I'd seen the whole trip. It was a map of the Haram. He clasped me in a hug and disappeared right after, leaving me with a printed guide to the various structures on the Mount, one which I could've used years back, when I was first there, and also on every subsequent visit. Where had these touristic aids been hiding all this time? I wandered counterclockwise around the Haram, finally understanding what the individual structures were, and then, as it was getting late in the day and my legs turned wobbly, sat down on one of the platforms that get used as benches and called Samar.

There is the Beloved, and then the beloved. She couldn't travel with me to Jerusalem, so I reserved an hour of every evening to hear from her how her day had gone and to tell her how mine had gone. The wonders of WhatsApp: it was surreal to speak to someone in Chicago from a perch where the great Sufi Imam Ghazali may have sat and studied and instructed. And so: "I don't want to leave," I admitted to her.

I would not be able to.

JUST A FEW MOMENTS LATER, when our call had ended, Israeli police stormed onto the Temple Mount. The Haram was on lockdown, and no one was allowed in or out, which unsettled me, but did not appear to faze the Palestinians around me in the least. I checked my phone, and our journalism class's WhatsApp group was blowing up with news of what had just transpired. Two of our students weren't far from the Via Dolorosa when a Palestinian man just in front of them pulled out a knife and stabbed a Jew. These students had to jump back against the old walls of the narrow street to get out of the way of the bullets that followed right after; a few pops, and the Palestinian was dead, killed by Israeli police. We checked in with one another to make sure everyone in the Old City was safe and made plans to meet by Jaffa Gate once the lockdown was lifted. In the meanwhile, I befriended a Malaysian tour group, all of them trapped too, and a group of local kids asked me to join their soccer game. I raised my rosary as if to say I had other, more sacred business, when in fact, I did not want to embarrass myself trying to kick a ball.

An hour later, those of us from the class, such as myself, who'd been trapped in various parts of the Old City had at last rendez-voused. We walked back to our hotel together, overwhelmed by what had happened and yet conscious that for most of us—the two students in the middle of it excluded—this was a minor inconvenience at most. We didn't live here. We didn't face this. And as for the people who did? In Bethlehem, which we had visited earlier, we met a Palestinian activist who, inspired by his Christianity, somehow kept faith in impossible circumstances. In the repeatedly pulverized village of Susiya, an inconvenient fact on the ground, I could barely hold back tears as barefoot children, several of them far too small for their age, offered *us* snacks. The emotional weight of it was too much for me, so I asked Ruth—who'd lived in the West Bank for a year, and got where I was coming from—if we could go to Ramallah.

During the trip, I wanted to spend money however and whenever I could in Palestinian places; my secondary reason: I needed to see more of Palestine and more of how Palestinians lived, to be with them, to be surrounded by their remarkableness, their warmth, their hospitality, their energy, and against what stunning odds. I needed to remember who I was and what I was doing there. I make it a point to shop in the West Bank, or East Jerusalem, whenever I go to Israel and Palestine, because I believe that the best way a Western Muslim can work toward a just and decent solution to this terrible conflict is by insisting on going, by making it known that there are people in the West, increasing numbers of us, who live in countries Israel depends on, discontented with the status quo, organizing, voting, and getting voted into office, who want to see change, who have money and resources, who will not fall for talking points.

Who have transcended the angry man at the microphone. Who want, who have, who can be, who will be so much more than that. The questions facing American Muslims are not of powerlessness alone but its opposite as well: what American Muslims, and Western Muslims, do with our strength, which we have more of than we realize. Because we can vote. We can organize. We can be in positions of influence. We already are. As I write this, the US House of Representatives includes two Muslim women in its chambers (making for three Muslims in total); soon, we will have Muslim senators (preferably plural) and more and more Muslims in positions of prominence. We can decide what that means. We can have a confident Islam, which builds upon and cultivates a culture of the responsible individual, which has as its foundation the relationship between a God who is always present and a human nature created to be His representative in the world.

THAT IS NOT to say that Islamophobia is unreal or unimportant.

But why is it so often so central to our identities?

I don't underestimate the danger of Islamophobia, nor the possibility that it may get much worse—see, for example, East Turkestan (Xinjiang). Anti-Muslim sentiment is prevalent on the far right, which itself is much more prominent now than it was in my youth. Certain administrations of certain Middle Eastern governments have a vested interest in seeing American Islam fail, too, and so actively contribute—even though some of these are Muslim too!—to anti-Muslim sentiments. But what if the opposite were also true? What if there were, alongside the potential for great danger, also the potential to flourish? How would we act then? Not to mention that the obsessive focus on Islamophobia is the flipside of Islamism; it may not seek to Islamize politics, but it does politicize Islam to the detriment of Islam. I mean, what kind of identity is that? If the focus of your community is on bigotry against your community, then you are in danger of existing only because other people don't want you to exist. You lose the time, ability, and imagination to contribute actively to the world around you. What would it mean, in that kind of institutional environment, to raise a child?

"What does it mean to be a Muslim?" the child asks. And the answer is, "To be hated on by some of our society"?

Then there is the phenomenon of Islam by heritage. This, too, is part of the landscape of Western Muslimness, but it is unlikely that it will endure more than a generation or two. Heritage cannot be passed on without commitment, and commitment requires belief in the thing, not just an acknowledgment of its past existence.

These are challenges, but let's not miss the grand opportunities, too. We inhabit a unique moment, ambivalent in its very marrow—pessimistic and optimistic, full of external causes of worry and internal sources of promise. Mosques are still full, if even that fullness doesn't represent a majority of Muslims in most places.

What potential then! Sufficient numbers of people still want faith enough that we have a critical mass. How long will we give our faith the benefit of the doubt, though? For us, the Qur'an is still unquestioned as the word of God. How long will that last while extremists, radicals, misogynists, and nihilists cherry-pick verses and manipulate interpretations? We cannot give them the chance to own our narrative, to tell our story, to control our sources of faith, to pollute our sacred well, to deny us the right each of us has to a relationship with God. This means finding something in our story that fills our future generations with pride, a story to tell about us that isn't a story of hopes extinguished, of Arab Springs followed by authoritarian winters. What could that story possibly be?

Because many Muslims I know think we inhabit the end times.

I fear that too, sometimes. With climate change alone looming, it is hard not to be terrified. But terror causes paralysis. It is the last thing we need.

IT TOOK EDWIN Hubble to prove that the universe was expanding; this meant the world as we knew it had an origin point; at a so-called Big Bang, in one awesome and overheated moment the building blocks of all that was, is, and will be exploded outward in every direction. Inventing direction as it went. Some say that the inflation of all-that-is will continue until gravity itself loses its attractive power, at which point galaxies will unwind and stars will be snuffed out, and all will be dark and cold. Others believe that the accelerative force of the universe is insufficient to overwhelm the force that pulls matter back onto itself. Eventually, in rather the manner of a supernova, all-that-is will collapse in on itself, to a point of infinite density, being as it is past Chandrasekhar's limit.*

---

* Discovered by the early twentieth-century astrophysicist Subrahmanyam Chandrasekhar, himself of South Asian origin, in essence this delimits the mass above which a certain type of star transforms—as I make reference to here—into a black hole. Basically, the star is so massive that it is unable to prevent itself from collapsing in on itself. I first read about Chandrasekhar's limit in Kip Thorne's *Black Holes and Time Warps*. I was in high school, at a bookstore with my mother, and when I spotted the title, she was excited for me to read it and so purchased it for me.

At that position there is neither space nor time, but a quantum landscape almost impossible to describe. The Big Crunch. That which begins, ends. And from that end, another beginning?

Maybe the very detonation that started this whole thing in motion was itself the other side, in more than one sense, of another universe's (and another Caliphate's?) conclusion, and the cycle repeats itself. Maybe that is an image it might do us well to reflect on. Because it speaks to us in this difficult present and promises us something better than this. In the early seventh century, in an unremarkable corner of the planet, far from the great civilizations of the time, among a desert people mostly unknown, God's beloved was born, a secret mercy unto the worlds. He gathered around him a small band of followers, extraordinary for their apparent ordinariness, yet within them burned a fire so brightly, a faith so furious, that they singlehandedly spawned an entire civilization. Out of a few simple truths, they altered the destiny of the world, in a beginning unrivaled by any history before or since. When else does the world change, forever, in a handful of years?

A whole civilization emerged, art and architecture, aesthetics and astronomy, habits and mannerisms, and poetics and semantics, which stitched together peoples that had once been enemies, enabling globalization the world had never conceived possible. I visited a coffeehouse in Bosnia that had Hafiz's Persian verse on the wall. My advisor at Columbia was a French Senegalese of Sufi lineage, whose father learned Persian meter from the South Asian Iqbal. I prayed at a mosque in Anchorage, full of Eastern Europeans and West Africans. In the eighth century, Muslims traded with Vikings in what became the heart of Russia. Several hundred years later, a new people erected a khanate whose northernmost boundary was the Arctic Ocean. Ottomans in Iceland. Ottomans in Indonesia. Mozambique, named for a Muslim merchant named Moses. Be proud of that history, Muslims. Be proud of who you were, who you are, and who you can be.

Be proud, above all else, of the most important thing you have accomplished, and make sure that this accomplishment does not disappear in the generations to come, if only for lack of commitment and compassion. I don't mean science or medicine or art, but something far more profound, something, if not for us, the world would have never had. We may have fought brutally and nastily with each other and still let ourselves down. There is so much work to be done. There are so many bridges to build. So many wrongs to right. But we held onto faith. We never changed it, altered it, diluted it, compromised it, and I want to see that stubborn fidelity last deep into however many decades or centuries remain for us. There is so little dissonance, if any at all, between the way we worship and the way peoples before us worshiped and the way our shared founder worshiped. We read the same Qur'an in the same Arabic.

We perform the same pilgrimage in the same city.

We venerate the same rock Muhammad rose from, shielded by a shrine almost as old as the occasion it was meant to mark.

We have changed so much, and yet, we have hardly changed at all.

Isn't that remarkable? No matter how down you are about the present, how much despair you feel, take heart and courage from this, and remember: if we could survive our past, we can survive our present. We are more than just the hatred directed toward us. Maybe this moment in time isn't the fraying of faith to the point of frozenness, sterility, and death, but its purposeful compression. A big crunch. Then the one becomes the other, exiting the universe to become a universe.

That which began with strangers, a secret on a planet that is itself a secret, can end, but it can begin again, and faster than you might imagine possible. The future of Islam is in your hands. Existential accordions. Just a couple of months after our trip to Jerusalem and the students had graduated (at Columbia the master's degree program in journalism is just two semesters long), I was waiting impatiently for another email from Ari, expecting to be called back as an adjunct assistant professor, with the chance to return to Palestine and Israel again. I had loved the experience the experience, but I needed it, too. Writing for me is like teaching. Both of them are like breathing. And I missed Jerusalem.

The email never came.

But other emails came.

Surprising forms of evidence accumulated.

The world will end for all of us. One day. But it ends for each of us too.

15

WHY I AM NOT A SUFI

I HAVE NO DOUBT thus far presented Sufism as it is often advanced: kind, tolerant, loving. The kind of Islam we can live with—if even it is associated with Islam. Sometimes Sufism is advertised as "syncretic," as if the only instance of Islam that could hold any attraction to any reasonable person is one that has been mingled with other faiths. On its own, this necessarily means Islam is toxic. But Sufism grew organically out of Islam, and for centuries Sufism was simply how Muslims approached, practiced, and conceived of their faith. The twin shocks of eighteenth-century Wahhabi reformism and nineteenth-century Western colonialism drove Sufism into violent retreat, but it feels to me like that vision of Islam made a remarkable comeback in the last few decades.

My journey, in other words, was not so unique. As I became more involved in my Sufi circle, I experienced a heightened exposure to its culture in the collective sense—I became friendlier to Sufism, and therefore to Sufis, and therefore to its leading lights. I even began to have dreams about Sufi divines. In one instance, I saw myself sitting next to a man we'll call Sufi Shaykh 2. (I reserve the first spot for the leader of my circle.) No. 2 was not, I must say, the leader of a Sufi circle, but he was a very prominent Sufi, one whose name would be quickly recognized by many Muslims invested in religious communities. In another instance, a man we'll call Sufi Shaykh 3 put his hand on my knee. I was honored. It meant someone who had a direct line to the tradition, to the Prophet Muhammad, to God Himself, cared about me.

While Shaykh 2 lived in a part of the Middle East I was never able to visit, Shaykh 3 lived in a country I briefly passed through during my itinerant existence. The first time he met me, he told me that his Sufi lodge was "a hospital more than anything else." People whose hearts were broken came there for healing, for convalescence, for restoration. My heart had been broken, I told him. Stay, he said. I could not, but the meaningfulness of that moment remained with me. I fell in love with the Shaykhs, I adored the weekly circles of remembrance—chanting God's names collectively, almost hypnotically—and I felt finally supercharged by Islamic piety. I was becoming the kind of Muslim I had long thought I should be.

There were two other Shaykhs who entered my newfound religious life, who I will call Shaykhs 4 and 5. Nos. 4 and 5 taught courses I attended, providing instruction in—dare I say indoctrination in—the specifics of their brand of Islam, which often advertises itself as "traditional." I knew of many other Shaykhs, of course, but these four were, after Shaykh 1, the most relevant to my spiritual life. They supplemented what I learned and, more importantly, reinforced my worldview.

This was all very good, until, the deeper I went into that world, the more I began to receive messages from fellow travelers, alarmed at certain practices they had encountered, frustrated by certain conversations they tried to have, damaged by encounters they innocently pursued. It started as a trickle but, over many months, turned into a flood. Too many people told me too many stories for me to dismiss them as coincidence. The Shaykh I dreamt of often put his hand on his wife, leaving her black and blue. The Shaykh who called his lodge a hospital serially married young women, and thereafter left them high and dry. Some of them needed psychiatric hospitals. The men they'd most trusted had done them the worst harm.

Certainly, this story sounds and feels familiar. The abuse by men of religion of their followers. But how can it happen in the name of Sufism, which is allegedly the good kind of Islam? Shaykh 4 was involved in financial fraud. Shaykh 5 sexually abused at least one student for seven years. I was convinced, and I was devastated. Nor was I alone. Whole organizations have emerged to address the abuse—of which there was much—and to serve the survivors of it. While these rumors never pointed to or even hinted at the leader of my Sufi circle, still the house in which I had sought spiritual shelter turned out to suffer great rot.

How was this possible?

The Shaykhs had all seemed kind, sage, generous, and compassionate to me. Then again, I am sure that is what many Catholics thought of some of their priests. Abusers can be charmers. Maybe they have to be. That's how they get you to lower your guard. And while traditional Islam is not a centralized institution, it is an interlocking set of networks and organizations and circles. Similar, I began to realize, to the new form of Caliphate I was advocating for in communal, cultural, and collective life, the sacred counterpart to the secular and identitarian component of Muslimness. If the Sufism complex, as we might call it, could be so corrupt, what was to say that my case for a new Caliphate would be any different? There is, as it turns out, a grave problem in apolitical Islam, too.

As I argued earlier, theocratic Islam is dangerous because it arrogates to human institutions the unique authority of the Prophet Muhammad. The politics that results is unavoidably manipulative, coercive, and eventually violent. It is also inevitably factional and unstable. But just because you eschew politics doesn't mean you've rid yourself of the fundamental error. Authority in Sufism is located in the person of the Shaykh. The Shaykh's authority is granted by his Shaykh, whose authority is granted by *his* Shaykh, and the chain continues ostensibly back to the source: the Prophet Muhammad. Like a Prophet, the Shaykh enjoys a special, interiorized form of knowledge, an inhabitation of deep spiritual states. The Shaykh can see things you cannot.

In other words, like political Islam, Sufism assigns Prophetic authority to the post-Prophetic, with potentially catastrophic consequences. Not just in a moral sense, but in practical and physical, and even sexual ones. The hierarchy of honored Shaykh and humble(d) student discourages rigorous questioning, hinders accountability, and encourages abuse and excess. About the only way you can mount a sustained critique—however well intentioned—of the Shaykh is to become a Shaykh, but your ability to become a Shaykh depends on the approval of a Shaykh. The strength of the Sufism complex—its historical depth, antiquity, and formidability—become its weakness. There is too much power concentrated in a web of many like-minded men.

Because this model mitigates against depersonalized institutions, it contains almost no mechanism to patrol itself. Because this model privileges secret knowledge, which can only be attained by strict obedience to the Shaykh, it contains almost no processes to avoid the abuse of authority. The Shaykhs oversee the students, but nobody—except other Shaykhs—oversees the Shaykhs. The same kind of problem, I suppose, (theoretically) manifests itself in other types of spaces, although these correct themselves (and ergo have realized they need to police themselves) through various inbuilt features, such as institutional safeguards and supervisory bodies that are independent or at least autonomous and capable of intervening to combat excesses. We must voluntarily cede some power to others to keep all of us in check.

That is the same spirit through which America's Founding Fathers diffused power between three ideally equal branches of government. We much more recently learned, through the presidency of Donald Trump, that even this principle of coequality was not enough, because much of our system depended on a voluntary moral restraint on the part of presidents, who supposedly would not do certain authoritarian things because it was unbecoming, undemocratic, and irresponsible of them to. But no *instrument* existed to prevent that abuse of the office, a weakness a vulgar man like Trump was eager and simultaneously helpless to avoid.

Am I saying that all Sufi Shaykhs are Donald Trumps?

Of course not.

I am saying, instead, that the system contains no apparatus by which it can constrain Donald Trumps. Many Shaykhs are good people. Many of them have caused and meant no harm. But too many of them closed their eyes to abuse if they did not practice it themselves, dismissed it or belittled it, and many of their followers excused them. Better to let a thousand vulnerable souls be shattered than your idols chopped down. (An ironic attitude for a Muslim, whose religion is supposed to be based on uncompromising, iconoclastic unitarianism.) This excessive reverence for the hierarchy also overlaps with authoritarianism. As a religious institution, the Sufi order does not sit well with a democratic orientation. The evidence lies in the number of Shaykhs who gravitate to authoritarian states, physically or philosophically, and excuse, if not celebrate, the dictatorial.

None of this should be surprising.

What is surprising is that a middle-aged man allowed himself to be taken in. I am troubled by the ease with which someone of my skeptical constitution fell prey to a naive romanticism; how easily I idolized and idealized human beings, making my relationship with God dependent on their authority. Perhaps, when you finally find yourself a spiritual home, a place to come to rest, finding the Islam you have so long looked for, it is easy to be credulous.

It is perversely and paradoxically too easy to trust.

OF COURSE, my disillusionment with Sufism threatened to overwhelm my attraction to Islam altogether. If Sufism today shelters abusers, and given its historical role in Islamdom, does that mean the history of Islam is the history of abuse?

Does a Catholic of conscience ask herself the same question?

I know many students who are decent, upstanding people, who refuse to believe the stories of abuse, intimidation, and aggression because they cannot imagine their moral paragons are so basically and grievously flawed. To do so would be to threaten the very foundations of the buildings they have made into their homes.

To them, I say that, inevitably, over time, institutions decay. I think I give myself the same answer. Arguably, Sufism as a set of practices was at its most vibrant centuries ago, and many of its iterations—I cannot say all of them, of course—degenerated, devolved, degraded, or simply fell out of step with the times (hence, I would argue, the attraction to the despotic instead of the democratic). The complex needs a Counter-Reformation, too. I still believe in Islam and hew to mainstream Sunni orthodoxy.

I just believe that the forms through which that is realized must reflect what we have learned in the ways of flaws and failures on the road here.

In effect, we must realize ceding too much authority to one individual is a step too far. Perhaps the goal should be for us to experiment with creating new models of communal worship, practice, and belonging that do not dismiss hierarchy. All stable and good societies need forms of hierarchy, but, in the manner of a robust and healthy democracy, they must also contain checks against that hierarchy becoming absolutized and immune from question or challenge.

We must also change our own mindsets, so that we give equal moral weight to a student as we do to a Shaykh, such that if the Shaykh violates the moral rights and sacred dignity of the student, we do not reflexively seek to protect the complex over the harmed soul. I believe we can do that and still benefit from what Sufism has given Islam. There's a difference between throwing out the baby and throwing out the bathwater. There still is significant beauty in the Sufi complex, an attractiveness to their worshipfulness that remains compelling and can be beneficial. The practice of transubstantiating the relationship between God and His servants into one of Beloved and Her lovers. That is much more endearing than the command-and-compulsion model that afflicts many interpretations of Islam.

There is much more beside.

For example, the generosity of a tradition that birthed so much art, poetry, music, and literature. The emphasis on the vastness of God's mercy. That a Shaykh can compare a spiritual place to a hospital for the soul. That great numbers of people can be drawn into Islam, sustained and nourished on Islam, and find welcome in it regardless of their personal strengths or weaknesses. That was and is much more compelling than the Islam I experienced in earlier times of my life. I should think it still is. But I cannot stay within the confines of traditional Islam. I am too troubled by its underlying construction and cannot live in a residence whose foundations are not just damaged but which I so thoroughly disapprove of, to say nothing of its political orientation or political predilections.

Of course, this means that as we patiently and diligently rebuild our ummah, as we conceive of and construct a Caliphate of Caliphs, which may well be a generational project, we are resigned to a kind of religious purgatory. I suppose this is apt. Purgatory is a spiritual waystation. An existential condition. If in its secular, worldly iteration it contains anything, it would have to be modesty. Limited epistemic claims. That doesn't mean you can't think on a global scale. After all, a planet full of robust democracies would be no less democratic for its universality. But none of these democracies could claim for itself what too many interpretations of Islam do, whether the literalist or the Sufist.

The twentieth-century South Asian philosopher Muhammad Iqbal borrowed the language of Sufism to preach a radical message of self-reliance and self-absorption; a rich, mature egoism; strong communities composed of robust individualities. Iqbal never allowed himself to become a Shaykh—he took no disciples in the sense that Sufism suggests—because it would leave him subject to the greatest charge of hypocrisy. In one of his most famous poems he wrote: "Once more our caravan measures the road." The world of Islam, he argued, had faltered. Fell behind. Needed to get up and get going. And never cease moving again.

Maybe that was the key. Maybe, I say, because I didn't know and still don't yet know. I had fallen out of Islamic practice before, but this time around it felt less existentially and ontologically disastrous. Indeed, I knew that, this time, my falling out of love with the Sufism complex was not a rejection of religion, but emerged out of the need to protect and preserve religion—understanding that this one interpretation of Islam's sources that I inhabited for a time contained great strengths but fatal flaws. It would be on me to search, with other like-minded refugees, for new ways forward. Maybe, then, that is what Iqbal meant.

You cannot have ossified hierarchy if you never stop moving.

Change is terrifying, even as it's necessary. A person plans, and God plans. Not so long ago, the shock of that spiritual blow would have cast me into grave distress, leaving me questioning not just the particulars of my life, but the value of that life entirely. The upshot of having fallen apart before? It's easier to watch things come undone a second time. A different sameness. You are readier to go where the road takes you, if only because you know that no matter how dark and gloomy the days ahead, there will be insights. Experiences. Spiritual moments of grace and blessing. You don't see that the first time around, it's true.

You can hardly see five feet ahead of you.

But God is closer to you than your jugular vein.

Start looking and He'll find you.

Fail once and try again.

Fail a thousand times and try once more.

The destination is always the same.

AFTER MY DIVORCE ten years before, I became so despondent and downcast that family and friends insisted I take time away from the world that had hurt me. A friend helped me move to Dubai, where I could be with my only sibling, his wife, and their two sons, and also drive a different Toyota Camry every month. Same difference. No difference? Weeks passed in the United Arab Emirates but I hardly recovered. I was no longer existentially paralyzed, it's true. I appreciated the palm trees and all the things I could never afford. But I didn't thrive either. Loved ones insisted that I should keep living until one day I'd love to—again. There was light.

The tunnel was just very long.

So, every forty days, I'd drive to the nearest international border to get a new tourist visa. I'd drive south, out of Dubai and to the border with Oman. I'd perfunctorily enter that Sultanate, receive an entry visa, and promptly make a U-turn, returning to Dubai. This legal maneuver enabled the issuance of a new tourist visa under whose diplomatic shade I was allowed to remain in the country forty more days, a process that could theoretically be repeated ad infinitum. And since I had forty days longer in Dubai, I had forty more days to find a direction to live in. These journeys, though, always made me nervous. In the years since my passport picture had been taken, I had lost sixty pounds. In those six years of my life, I had become increasingly sick. It was hard to imagine that a major part of it wasn't anger at my circumstances turned inward.

One of the many downsides to losing so much weight, so fast, was that every time I approached any border, I feared for my chances of entrance or exit and sometimes worried worse might happen to me. What if, as in Istanbul that one time, the authorities didn't believe the passport picture was mine? For someone as preternaturally anxious as I am, this made every excursion to Oman a terrifying adventure. I suppose all adventures are meant to be terrifying. Otherwise they would not be very memorable. Or, at least, they can have a little danger, leavened by some humor. On just one such trip, I had left Dubai, cleanly, entered Oman, smoothly, and made my way back to the border of the UAE, cocksure. I had this. I pulled up to a police officer sitting on what looked like a lawn chair, outside what looked like a tollbooth, bleached white either by paint and/or the sun.

He wore an olive uniform and gold-rimmed Ray-Bans.

He appeared not to have a care in the world.

I decided his name was Ahmad.

When I handed over my passport, Ahmad flipped to the photograph page and burst out laughing, looking down at the picture, back at me, down at the picture, back at me. That seemed to be it, though. He stamped my passport while still chuckling to himself and waved me on. But I was not fifteen minutes into my drive back to Arabian Ranches, the neighborhood where my brother lived (and I with him) when the car behind me—license plates from Oman—flashed its headlights. The driver gestured for me to pull over. Maybe in the desert wild, he intended to kidnap, kill, and/or eat me. Or maybe he just needed help. Car trouble in the deepest, emptiest desert could mean death. We both pulled into the breakdown lane and exited our cars. But as I walked toward him, hoping he just needed help, he started backing up.

Keeping distance between us, as if *he* was afraid of *me*, he yelled: "You go back!"

"Go back?" I asked. I put on my most American accent, conveying, in equal measure, total cluelessness and overwhelming, nuclear invincibleness.

"Police say you go back," he explained. Then he dove into his car and rocketed away, leaving me alone on the side of the road under a painful sun. I wondered if this was some kind of gambit to steal my car and leave me stranded, though I thought it strange he would invoke the police and race away.

Fearing I might be arrested otherwise, I hesitantly drove back to the same tollbooth, where Ahmad regarded me with great confusion. "What are you doing here one more time?" The answer to his own question then dawned on him. He turned to his left and screamed, "Muhammad!"

All this time, I had thought Ahmad was all by himself, though of course that would have made zero sense for an armed agent of the state, least of all one manning a border post.

Another officer, presumably Muhammad and evidently of superior rank, rushed out from a modest trailer, where apparently the more important officer(s) escaped solar radiation. Pointing to me and then Muhammad, but without getting out of his seat, Ahmad of the tollbooth commanded: "Show him your passport."

My jaw all but fell to the footwell. Ahmad here had deputized the citizen of *another* country . . . just to show his border-police friend my fat picture? No wonder the Omani driver had been terrified: he figured I was so dangerous that not even the police—the police force of another country, mind you—wanted to try to apprehend me.

Before I could say anything, though, Ahmad snatched my passport and opened the picture page for Muhammad, the contrast between big me then and skinny me now almost impossible not to comment upon. "You were so fat!" Ahmad cried. Ahmad laughed and Muhammad laughed. They laughed a good deal, in fact, but then both of them turned deadly serious, almost at the same time. A grave silence fell over the dunes. I realized how alone we were. I shivered in the way you do late on a spring day, before the cold of winter is entirely gone, when the warmth of the sun disappears and the evening turns brisk.

"How," Muhammad asked, "did you lose so much weight?" He asked this question in a way that suggested that, if he could only ask God one question, ever, it might be this one.

I was incensed by this point, exhausted, overheated, tired, and motion sick from driving too much and too fast. But I also knew he asked with genuine curiosity, with an almost childlike innocence and touching openness. Plus, he was armed and controlled my ability to reenter the country I was living in. What was I going to say, though? That the doctors' best guess was that I had an autoimmune disorder? That it was just that—a guess? That I lost my job, my savings, my apartment, my marriage? That I hardly cared how I looked or if I ate? Instead I did the Muslim equivalent of throwing my hands in the air. "Alhamdulillah," I said.

But weirdly I'd whispered it, lending the moment a sacred aura I'd not intended.

In Dubai they might suffer first-world problems. But they process them with seventh-century spirituality. In all times and all places. "Alhamdulillah," the officers repeated, transformed.

We might have come from different ends of the earth, but in that brief moment we became one. Today the ummah is many hundreds of millions. But once it was just Hagar, who contained in herself all the potential of this religion, all the stories of the religious, all its possible courses, as she ran from Safa to Marwa and back again.

There, at that border post, the product of postcolonial politics, our identities fell away and we were humans, naked before God. Not American or Emirati, but believers. Islam was, is, and will be the religion of intimacy. Three men whispering God's praise to one another.

We formed a modest community.

And then the encounter was over. Satisfied with my answer, Ahmad and Muhammad waved me onward, and I drove forward for the second time, this time sure I could rush back to Dubai at speeds that indicate an outsize trust in God and a general disinterest in physics, even though, oddly, the latter's not true. On the return journey, against my iPod filling the sedan with the raucuous rage of alternative rock, I burst out laughing. I hadn't laughed that hard since my divorce. I didn't think I ever would again. But the whole thing was so ridiculous. I'd been stopped so that two men trapped in a go-nowhere assignment could laugh at my fat picture, which might've been the most fun they'd had in weeks—months even. I knew then that I'd tell everyone I could what had happened. I'd have to. I'd pass my passport around too, for dramatic effect.

INCONSTANCY IS THE one consistency in life. Things will fall apart. There will be wrenching transitions. Sometimes, as a colleague once said to me, God gives us what we want, but not in a nice way. When we don't belong somewhere, He needs to move us, but because we don't go willingly—we can't read the tea leaves—He has to yank us out of place. But He's that invested in every single moment of (y)our lives. That doesn't mean it isn't bittersweet, though, to leave one house with the knowledge that there might be a better one around the corner. Or that there'll be a corner at all. Sometimes, when I'm really frustrated, I go back to this Dubaian story. I like it, yes. But I need it as well. When my life was closing in on itself, I now see that it was preparing to burst forth anew. When I lost faith in one kind of Islam, I see now that it was never the religion that was under threat, but just the failure of some answers to vibrant, necessary, vital questions.

It is time for new answers. The end is the beginning of the beginning. A moment of contemplation, Muhammad said—peace be upon him—is worth seventy years in prayer. The more you think about how the world works—or, rather, that it is at all—the closer you should get. God is the goal. Not Islam. I wonder about Ahmad in his Ray-Bans and Muhammad in his trailer, stereotypically sipping Arabian coffee. I wonder where they are now. I wonder if they retell this story, too. I wonder if they wonder about the unlikelihood of it, too. I wonder what parts they find funny, or melancholy, or odd. I wonder if the three of us would agree on the details, let alone the essentials. I can't even say how or where they'd start their stories. But I know this much.

All three stories end the same way.

ACKNOWLEDGMENTS

AT BEACON

Imam M told me to stop writing for a few months. "But I'm a writer," I protested. Still I did as he asked. The words built up and built up in me until I discovered, no less than a month later, that I had an idea for a book. This book. I reached out to Amy Caldwell, my editor at Beacon, to share the concept, and she enthusiastically welcomed it.

If this book does any good, it is because of the great work she has again done for me.

AT COLUMBIA UNIVERSITY (I)

I defended my dissertation prospectus, and even finished a chapter, but that was the ne plus ultra. In the years I was a student at Columbia, though, I learned a great deal, with my ways of thinking, analyzing, reading, and writing fully transformed—and for the better. I'd like to thank Gil Anidjar, Souleymane Diagne, Sudipta Kaviraj, Sheldon Pollock, Frances Pritchett, Anupama Rao, and the many other scholars and numerous students whose brilliance I so benefited from.

AT COLUMBIA UNIVERSITY (II)

One of the reasons I went to graduate school in the first place was because I loved teaching, and wanted to do so professionally; the spring 2018 semester I spent at Columbia's Graduate School of

Journalism was, for someone who never got the chance to pursue an academic career, an unexpected and beautiful blessing.

I must thank Ari Goldman for trusting me to work with and for him, Yogi for opening the door, Ellen for encouraging me, Thea for holding me up, Ophir for exceeding our expectations, and our students: Steph, Sarah, Liz, Augusta, Kanishk, Kat, Matt, Dan, Patrick, Colin, Courtenay, Vildana, Isobel, Fergus, Galie, and Hannah. You were all great.

The course and our travel to Israel and Palestine was made possible with the support of the Scripps Howard Foundation.

SOMERS, PITTSBURGH, BLUE ASH

When I was in middle school, my late mother signed me up for a writing course, the whole of which was conducted by postal correspondence. (This was before the age of the internet.) My teacher was Fred Bortz. Over twenty years after I last heard from him, we made contact—I was on my way to Pittsburgh, for a book reading, and would he like to have dinner? I was nervous we'd have next to nothing to talk about, but the hour we had together passed by in minutes.

Thank you, Fred.

Also.

My teachers, from long ago: Mr. Stoddard, Ms. Robbins, Mr. Riola, and especially Mr. Malone, who brought such passion and grace to the study of English.

More recently.

For his time and expertise, David Ligon, in the Faculty of Latin at Ursuline Academy.

IN DIALOGUE

A special thanks to Rabbi Sarah Mulhern, a thought partner. I aspire to Yehuda Kurtzer's remarkable model of public scholarship.

Maital Friedman always challenged me to do better. Elana Stein Hain pushed me to improve my ideas time and again.

And, of course, my dear friend Yossi Klein Halevi. Sometimes it feels a more surprising bond could not be imagined, but I am so much richer for it.

AT LIFE

A special thank you to Muddassar Ahmed, Murtaza Hussain, Imran Siddiqui, and Adnan Zulfiqar, who contributed tremendously to the conception and articulation of this book.

"The more rigid the belief system," James Pearl said, "the less room there is for faith."

AT HOME AND HEART

My late mother was the most spiritual person I have known. My father, the strongest person I have known. I am who I am and what I am thanks to their immense sacrifices and endless patience. Ami II and Abu II: I am humbled by your trust, kindness, piety, and love.

My big brother, Umar, and my big sister, Saema, did so much for me, above and beyond what anyone can expect. I am touched beyond words, and only hope, God forbid, that if ever they are in need in the ways I was in need, that I can help as they helped.

To my wonderful nephews, Zahid and Hafiz, and my remarkable niece, Aliyah, whose passion, enthusiasm, joy, kindness, and piety has inspired me. May you be blessed with rich, meaningful, awesome lives, full of God and good.

My Apa Khala.

My Rashda Khala.

May the Creator of all greet us all in His Garden.

The insights on Hagar and Ishmael come from Samar Kaukab's voracious reading and ceaseless curiosity. She was unsatisfied by the stories we told, a shared disappointment that provoked me to begin looking at my own beliefs and ideas more closely. I am overwhelmed by her hardiness, bowled over by her diligence, awed by her thoroughness, jealous of her remarkable memory, and supremely impressed by her ability to balance so many different ways of looking at the world. But those things only begin to approach what I want to say.

You are the most gorgeous woman in the world. The kindest, most generous, and easily the funnest. And the smartest. You work harder for your family than anyone I have ever known.

I am honored to be part of that family now.

So, my dear beloved: We didn't have a beginning. So let's not have an end. (Plein Air). Put your seatbelt. (Somewhere in Inwood.) Thank you for supporting me, nourishing me, improving me, challenging me, and always looking out for me—I hope I have eternity to reciprocate. I love who you are, I love my life with you, and I am so grateful for how you have helped me to grow.

I am a different, better, and more contented person, only because of your compassion and wisdom. And my world is much bigger and grander now.

To my brilliant, beautiful daughters, Safa and Marya, and my charming, sagacious son, Reza, thank you for being you. For bringing so much purpose, meaning, and direction to my life. I pray our Lord gives you only the best of this life and the best of the next.

Safa, you owe me a (good) retirement home—but maybe not in Chicago. Marya, you owe me two cats and a telescope. Reza, you owe me the theory of everything.

Everywhere and anywhere, the five of us. Let's go! No matter what it is we do, or where life takes us, or how life finds us, I am enriched beyond words.

I miss you all even when you're not gone.

P.S. Gary, not that that's his name.

AT LAST

Prayers and peace upon all the Prophets and upon the last of them, our master and teacher, Muhammad. May we honor him in all things and, through him, approach our Creator, in Whose name we begin, and in Whose shade I hope we endure, knowing neither fear nor grief, but only light, laughter, and endless love.

Amen.